SUPERFORTRESS

SUPER

The Story of the B-29

McGraw-Hill Book Company

FORTRESS

and American Air Power

BY GENERAL CURTIS E. LEMAY
AND BILL YENNE

New York   St. Louis   San Francisco   Auckland   Bogotá   Hamburg
London   Madrid   Mexico   Milan   Montreal   New Delhi   Panama   Paris
São Paulo   Singapore   Sydney   Tokyo   Toronto

1 2 3 4 5 6 7 8 9 DOC DOC 8 9 2 1 0 9 8

ISBN 0-07-037164-4

Library of Congress Cataloging-in-Publication Data

LeMay, Curtis E.
  Superfortress: the story of the B-29 and American
air power in World War II.

  Bibliography: p.
  Includes index.
  1. World War, 1939–1945—Aerial operations, American.
2. B-29 bomber.   I. Yenne, Bill, 1949–   II. Title.
D790.L46   1988   940.54′4973   87-36208
ISBN 0-07-037164-4

Book design by Kathryn Parise

Other books by Bill Yenne

The History of the U.S. Air Force

Northwest Orient

The Astronauts:
The First 25 Years of Manned Space Flight

Strategic Air Command:
A Primer of Modern Strategic Air Power
(*Preface by General Russell Dougherty,
U.S. Air Force, retired*)

Boeing:
Planemaker to the World
(*with Robert Redding*)

McDonnell Douglas:
A Tale of Two Giants

Lockheed:
Reaching for the Stars

*This book is dedicated to all the men and women
who helped to design, build, and test the Superfortress,
as well as to all the brave airmen who took
the product of that effort into combat
in World War II and Korea.*

CONTENTS

Contents

AUTHOR'S NOTE

To clarify the use of terms, U.S. Army military aviation was part of the Army's Signal Corps from August 1, 1907, to May 24, 1918, when the U.S. Army Air Service (USAAS) was established. The Air Service became the U.S. Army Air Corps (USAAC) on July 2, 1926. On June 20, 1941, the Air Corps became the semi-autonomous U.S. Army Air Forces (USAAF), which in turn became the fully independent U.S. Air Force (USAF) on September 18, 1947.

PREFACE

The Boeing B-29 Superfortress emerged from World War II as one of history's dozen or so truly great airplanes, and even the passage of four decades has not diminished its memory or its reputation. By 1945, it stood as having been the largest combat aircraft ever to have gone into full production. The Superfortress alone had the range to strike at the heart of the Japanese Empire and to bring about the defeat of that enemy without the need for American invasion forces to set foot in Japan.

Quite simply, the B-29 was the right tool at the right time. Its development did not, however, come about by accident. The massive accelerated effort that pushed the Superfortress off the drawing boards and through the factory gates in record time was well planned and well implemented. This book is the story of those who made it possible.

That story begins with General Billy Mitchell, who, having witnessed the carnage of World War I trench warfare, first theorized that air power could be used to defeat an enemy in wartime without the need for costly land battles. Mitchell's ideas, unpopular with the horse soldiers who dominated the U.S. Army's ranks in the 1920s, were kept alive by the young pilots who became leaders in the generation which emerged in the late 1930s. Among them were men like General Henry H. "Hap" Arnold, who rose through the ranks of the Army's Air Corps to become its chief of staff on the eve of World War II. Arnold, more than anyone else in the Air Corps, took the chances on the enormously expensive and speculative project—similar in secrecy and urgency to the Manhattan Project—that gave birth to the B-29.

Arnold found an able and willing partner in the Boeing Airplane Company of Seattle, Washington. Located in a distant corner of the United States, far from the (then) centers of American aviation, Boeing was presided over by Clairmont Egtvedt, who was determined to see Boeing Field become the "World Center of Four-Engine Airplane Development." The B-29 project would become a dream come true for Egtvedt and his able engineering staff as they set up the largest production operation ever created for a single airplane.

Boeing designed and helped produce the most sophisticated aircraft prototype in history in half the time it would normally have taken—and in about a quarter of the time that it would take for today's equivalent. The B-29 began with a Data Request dated 1940 and became operational in 1944, while today's B-1 program was begun with a 1969 Data Request and did not enter service until 1986.

Arnold knew that the speed with which he rushed the design and production of the Superfortress was a calculated risk. Had it not been for the designers and engineers in whom he invested his faith and confidence, the B-29 program could well have been a tremendous disaster, rather than one of the era's most fantastic success stories.

Having received an aircraft as technologically advanced as the B-29 on an incredibly tight schedule, Arnold dared further to create an unprecedented command structure to manage it. When the B-29 was put into service in April 1944, it was under the auspices of the Twentieth U.S. Army Air Force, an institution unique in being the only USAAF "numbered air force" in World War II not under the control of a theater commander. The Twentieth Air Force, instead, remained under Hap Arnold's direct control. While he ran the operation from his seat on the Joint Chiefs of Staff in Washington, he needed a field commander who could lead the B-29s into combat, someone who would be the last link in a chain that had begun with Billy Mitchell a quarter of a century before. The man was Curtis LeMay.

Curtis LeMay had been given command of the 305th Bombardment Group of the Eighth Air Force to England in 1942 at a time when America's inexperienced Army Air Forces were untried and unseasoned. He had quickly developed the 305th into one of the most efficient and successful combat units in the USAAF and had earned the reputation for leadership and determination that caused Arnold to tap him in the summer of 1944 for command of the B-29 strategic bombing offensive against Japan.

Upon arriving in the Far East, LeMay found a B-29 force based in India and flying its combat missions from crude airstrips located in China at the end of a long and rugged aerial supply route across the Himalayas. Despite the heroic efforts of the B-29 crews in China, the raids against Japan from these never-completed fields had not been a resounding success. Only when the Mariana Islands—Guam, Saipan, and Tinian—were retaken from Japan in August 1944, did the mighty B-29s have the bases from which they would at last be able to fulfill their mission to defeat Japan before a land invasion became necessary.

Between January 1945, when General LeMay arrived in Guam, and early August, when nuclear weapons were dropped, the B-29s broke the back of Japanese industrial production and rendered Japan's home-defense forces virtually incapable of any counter-operations save those by kamikazes. When it came time for the coup de grace against Hiroshima and Nagasaki, the B-29s transported those unspeakable weapons into the heartland of the Japanese Empire. By so doing, they helped to prevent an estimated 1 million American casualties.

This book is based on conversations between myself and General LeMay that took place at his home in Newport Beach, California, between May and October 1986. The historical data were compiled from official U.S. Army Air Forces archives, official U.S. Air Force records, and official Boeing Airplane Company archives. Many valuable firsthand observations have also been quoted from *Global Mission*, the 1949 memoir of General Arnold, the chief of staff of the U.S. Army Air Forces throughout World War II, whom I've cited as the man singly most responsible for inspiring and directing the effective development and deployment of the Superfortress. We are also most deeply in the debt of Marilyn Phipps of Boeing Historical Services for the materials she supplied and for the help she gave us.

The contributions of General Haywood S. Hansell (U.S. Air

Force, retired) are from conversations that he had with General LeMay in October 1986 and on material supplied to me directly by General Hansell. We are deeply indebted to General Hansell for his contributions to the book. As a member of the Air War Plans Division of the U.S. Army Air Forces Air Staff in the summer of 1941, then-Major Hansell played a vital role in formulating the blueprint for the application of Allied air power in World War II.

In 1942 General Hansell went on to serve as a member of the Joint Strategic Committee of the Joint Chiefs of Staff and then as deputy theater air officer for the European theater. Promoted to general, he commanded both the Third and First Bombardment Divisions of the Eighth Air Force before being named deputy commander in chief of the Allied Expeditionary Air Forces in Europe in 1943. The following year, he returned to Washington as a member of the Joint Chiefs of Staff Plans Committee and later as deputy chief of the USAAF Air Staff. During this tenure he devoted himself almost entirely to the planning of the B-29 offensive against Japan. In August 1944 he was named to command the Twenty-First Bomber Command of the Twentieth Air Force, the umbrella organization for all B-29 operations in the Pacific. In October 1944, he arrived in the Marianas as the first combat commander of the Twenty-First Bomber Command. He served in this role until General LeMay arrived in January 1945. His vivid insights are an integral part of the story, not only of the Superfortress, but of the entire strategic direction of American air power in World War II.

Bill Yenne
San Francisco, California
March 15, 1987

PROLOGUE

This is the story of the B-29 from start to finish, the whole story, not just the story of an airplane in combat. It is really about an accomplishment of the American people and about their allocation of resources to do a job. It is a tribute to the people who designed and built the B-29, and who then won a war with it. All this was accomplished in just four years, when today it takes seven to nine years just to design and produce an airplane. We paid a high price for the B-29, but American men and women answered the call. In fact, women did more to build the airplane than men, as they performed practically all the hands-on manufacturing work.

During World War II we had a unity of purpose: we were determined to win the war. Everyone was working like hell. Because the B-29 was rushed into production in such a short time, people were working long hours, particularly those involved in the design and modification work. Everyone got paid, and paid well, but I don't think anyone worried too much about salaries then. The American people got the job done.

Some men were truly visionary concerning the war-winning potential of air power. Even before he became Air Corps chief in 1938, General Arnold had been one of the most outspoken proponents of air power and the need for bombers. His boss, Army Chief of Staff George Marshall, was skeptical about the value of long-range bombers, but he and Arnold were old friends and Marshall had confidence in him. During World War II Arnold became chief of the U.S. Air Army Forces (USAAF), which was still a part of the Army under Marshall.

Despite this, Marshall treated Arnold practically as an equal and gave him a seat on the Joint Chiefs of Staff—a platform that he never would have had under another chief of staff. When the B-29 came along in 1944, Marshall let Arnold set up the Twentieth U.S. Army Air Force as the operational unit for the new bomber. The Twentieth was established under the Joint Chiefs and was directly managed by Arnold, rather than being placed under a theater commander, as was the case with the other fifteen U.S. Army Air Forces. This, along with Arnold's persistence and Marshall's willingness to listen, was the catalyst that finally got the B-29 program rolling. We were able to get the B-29s produced, and when we got to the Pacific in 1944 we had the Twentieth Air Force, which gave us an adequate command structure with which to use the bombers properly.

Because of the determination of men like Hap Arnold, the USAAF had gotten the B-29 program started in 1940 before anything was ever proved about strategic air power with the B-17 in Europe. By 1944, when the B-29 was finally deployed, we had still to prove a clear-cut case for strategic air power, although the postwar Strategic Bombing Survey later showed that, in Europe, air power had been a decisive factor in our victory. Overall, however, the defeat of Germany was considered at the time to have been a cooperative effort, with the Army as the lead partner, although the Army never admitted that there would have been no successful invasion of Europe were it not for the USAAF. We had done such a good job of suppressing the German air force that only a tiny handful of German aircraft managed to show up over the landing beaches at Normandy.

When air power came under the command of the theater commander, as it did in Europe, we expended a lot of effort on ground support targets—strictly *tactical* targets, which gave immediate support to troops in the field, but didn't let heavy bombers live up to their full potential. Those of us in the Eighth Air Force thought that we should be using our B-17s against *strategic* targets—targets deep within Germany itself, whose elimination would have a direct effect on the enemy's *ability to wage war*. This would still have left the Ninth Air Force and others to handle the tactical targets for which their type of aircraft were better suited.

Of course, the USAAF—and the whole American military establishment itself—had started with almost nothing in 1942, and we didn't have enough aircraft then to do any strategic bombing. Even after we got a sufficient number of B-17s to start the strategic mission, we were still bombing U-boat pens, railroad yards, and other tactical targets under the doctrine of "isolating the battlefield." By the spring of 1944, with the invasion imminent, we were expanding our resources, isolating all the *potential* battlefields in order to keep the Germans from knowing where the real invasion was going to be. By June of 1944, we had "isolated" practically all western Europe for the invasion, knocking out all of the railroads, train yards, bridges, and other lines of communication.

At the same time, however, we didn't get to spend the effort on the strategic targets that we wanted to. After the second quarter of 1944, we did attack oil facilities and the German air force, but most missions were still tied more into the notion of defeating the German land army than accomplishing strategic missions.

We believed that if strategic air power were properly applied to the war-making capacity of an enemy country, and if that country were deprived of the resources to wage war, it could be defeated without our having to expend as many American lives as would be necessary to defeat their armies on the battlefields. This is what is meant by strategic air power. We believed that this would be a cheaper way of waging war in terms of both lives *and* money, but this was the part of the struggle for air power that we hadn't won. In England we were under the command of General Dwight D. Eisenhower, who was a ground commander. He was interested in defeating the German armies in the field. His conception of air power was using a lot of airplanes to support his ground forces.

Had the B-29s been available three years earlier and been earmarked for use against Germany, the job could have been accomplished much more quickly because of the additional weight that could be carried by the individual bombers. We wouldn't have needed all the range capability of the B-29, and so we could have flown missions with heavier bombloads. We could have reached any target in Germany without the trouble that resulted from the limited range of the B-17, and the air war in Europe would have been a lot easier.

In the Pacific, General Arnold was able to get the Joint Chiefs to agree to a unified Twentieth Air Force under them directly, even though the B-29s would be flying over theaters under the command of Douglas MacArthur, Joe Stillwell, and Chester Nimitz. This worked for operational control, but for supply and logistics we would still be dependent on the theater commanders for the resources we needed to do our job. Ultimately, we succeeded with the B-29 because of the Joint Chiefs' unity of purpose regarding the Twentieth Air Force and the application of strategic air power. This was to be the only case in history where air power had done what all its early pioneers said could be done.

We succeeded in World War II both with air power and with the total scope of the war because of the American people's unity of purpose to win. Today we're having trouble, not only in regard to air power, but also in the larger arena of our economy and our relations with the world marketplaces because we've lost that unity of purpose. The very people who could not beat us on the battlefield during the war are now beating us in the world marketplace.

The full story of the B-29 is something to which historians haven't paid enough attention, even though it was a tremendous achievement. I think that we need to retell this story now because Americans today are not unified enough to produce competitively in the world market. Maybe it will remind us of what we did in the past, and that it's time we roll up our sleeves and do it again.

I

Getting the Idea
1918–1938

The concept of strategic air power did not begin with the B-29, but the B-29 proved its validity. The B-29 was one of the first aircraft that really pushed both the technical, and the operational limits of flying. Since the Wright brothers, pilots have known that aviation in its broadest sense had something wonderful to offer to the world, not only in the context of military air power, but also in commercial air transportation. But ever since the beginning, air power has had its detractors, those who were always quick to criticize any shortcomings.

At first, Americans even ridiculed Orville and Wilbur Wright. The way the Wrights' ideas and accomplishments were initially received in the United States so alienated them that Orville (Wilbur died in 1912) wouldn't even give their first airplane to the Smithsonian, but sent it to the Science Museum in London in 1928 instead. It wasn't until 1948 that the United States got it back. This negative thinking about air power prevailed in many circles during the first few decades of American aviation history, particularly in the Army, and particularly before World War II.

Though the idea had occurred to American airmen before him,

General William Lendrum "Billy" Mitchell (1879–1936) is recognized as the father and patron saint of American strategic air power because he did so much to promote it. In the end, his advocacy of strategic air power was to cost Billy Mitchell his career. The patron saint of air power became its martyr.

To say that the U.S. Army was dominated by ground warfare theoreticians was as much an understatement in 1918 as it was in the nineteenth century. The Army even had a hell of a time getting rid of the cavalry. Not until we were on the verge of World War II did the last horse leave the Army. However, by 1926, the Army did contain the U.S. Army Air Corps, which would eventually evolve into the U.S. Air Force. And it contained airmen like Billy Mitchell who were not afraid to speak their minds.

Billy Mitchell believed in *strategic air power,* the idea that air power could be used to strike an enemy's heartland and destroy his means and willingness to wage war. The net effect would be costly in civilian casualties, but theoretically it would, in the long run, prevent even more casualties by ending a war without the carnage of the indecisive land battles of the First World War.

Billy Mitchell was the grandson of Alexander Mitchell, a poor Scotsman who emigrated to Milwaukee, Wisconsin, in 1839 at the age of 21, and went about a commercial career with the same fervor that his grandson would display in the promotion of air power nearly a century later. First becoming a respected banker, then a railroad baron at the helm of the Chicago, Milwaukee & St. Paul Railroad, Alexander eventually became a millionaire, and by the 1870s he had earned the nickname "Rothschild of Milwaukee."

Alexander's only son, John Lendrum Mitchell, was a bookish boy more interested in philosophy and natural history than in business and commerce. Thanks to his father's money, John was afforded a chance to spend his adulthood going abroad to study at European universities, which is how it happened that Billy Mitchell was born in Nice, France, in 1879. Billy Mitchell spent his first three years in the country of his birth, learning to speak French before he learned English, a skill that would prove useful when he returned to France in 1917 with the airplanes of the American Expeditionary Force.

In 1890, several years after the family returned to a comfortable life as members of Milwaukee's social aristocracy, John

Lendrum Mitchell was elected to the U.S. House of Representatives and then, in 1892, to the U.S. Senate. The war with Spain in 1898 found Mitchell decrying American "imperialism" from his Senate pulpit, while young William Lendrum Mitchell quit college to enlist as a private with the First Wisconsin Volunteers. Before Billy could be shipped to Cuba, however, his father intervened and influenced a promotion to second lieutenant in a Signal detachment.

After seeing service with the Cuban occupation force immediately after the Spanish-American War, Lieutenant Mitchell served under General Arthur MacArthur in the Philippines and later spent two years establishing a telegraph line across Alaska. He returned from America's northern territory in 1903 as the Army's youngest captain, and in 1912 he became the youngest captain ever assigned to the Army's General Staff. Already a strong advocate of American military aviation, Mitchell now had a vantage point from which to observe the application of air power in the Balkan Wars of 1912–1913 and the opening volleys of the First World War in 1914. Sent to Europe as an observer in April 1917 before the United States entered the conflict, Mitchell—now a lieutenant colonel—arrived in France just after the United States declared war.

Mitchell immediately went to the front to observe the situation and became the first U.S. Army officer to fly over enemy lines, for which he was soon awarded the French Croix de Guerre. When his cables to the War Department calling for the establishment of an aviation branch of the American Military Mission to France were ignored, Mitchell convinced the *French* general staff to make such an appeal to Washington. When President Woodrow Wilson received a telegram from the French premier, Alexandre Ribot, the War Department's Airplane Division—whose staff included the young Hap Arnold—went to work on an appropriations bill to be submitted to Congress.

When General John J. "Black Jack" Pershing arrived in Paris in June 1917 with the advanced echelons of the American Expeditionary Force (AEF), he picked Mitchell—then the senior U.S. Army air officer in France—to put together an aviation program for the AEF. By September Mitchell had been promoted to full colonel and in October, Pershing made him AEF air boss for the

7

zone of advance. But despite Mitchell's efforts and Pershing's interest, American air power in the war was off to a pitiful start. When the first American division arrived in France on the Fourth of July, three months after the declaration of war, Mitchell's AEF "air section" consisted of a single Nieuport pursuit plane with himself as pilot. At the same time Secretary of War Newton Diehl Baker was confidently announcing that the United States, as part of its massive mobilization, was already building 20,000 warplanes. The War Department press release added that this might be a "slight exaggeration." In fact it was a gross and dangerous exaggeration. While there may have been that many airplanes on the most optimistic paperwork, actual production from July 1917 through July 1918 averaged only 144 service aircraft per month!

As the American ace Eddie Rickenbacker testified before a congressional committee after the war: "The Germans got busy immediately and enlarged their industry and manufacturing facilities, and when April 1918 came around, we did not have a plane on the front and they had twice as many as they would have had we not given them advance warning."

In fact, no American-built *combat* aircraft ever reached the front. Mitchell's AEF airmen were finally able to get into action in early 1918, but only in British, French, and Italian machines. Members of the first American combat squadron—Rickenbacker's Ninety-Fourth "Hat-in-the-Ring" Pursuit Squadron—didn't see service until April 1918, a year after the United States entered the war, and they were flying French SPADs.

By this time Colonel Billy Mitchell was the de facto commander of all American air power in France, which now included 1800 flying officers. Mitchell, however, was about to fall victim to the snarl of bureaucracy that would entangle the next generation of American airmen. He had stepped into his leadership role because he simply happened to be in the right place at the right time, but the job of overall air commander for the AEF did not exist until Secretary Baker got around to creating it in May 1918. The man he picked, however, was not Billy Mitchell, but Brigadier General Benjamin D. Foulois, one of the Army's first pilots who had been given his flying lessons by the Wright brothers.

In the meantime, Black Jack Pershing had developed his own ideas about how the AEF Air Service should be run. Shuffling

Benny Foulois off to the Loire Valley city of Tours to manage Air Service training and supply, Pershing picked Brigadier General Mason M. Patrick of the Corp of Engineers, an old West Point classmate, to oversee his air power. Patrick was, in today's vernacular, a systems analyst, the type of officer who could keep things running smoothly while field commanders commanded in the field. There were a lot of good men in the AEF Air Service, but, in Pershing's words, "They are running around in circles. Someone has got to make them go straight."

Both Patrick and Foulois (in 1921–1927 and 1931–1935 respectively), went on to serve as chief of the postwar U.S. Army Air Corps, a position Mitchell deserved but was never given. However, in 1918, Patrick's arrival on the scene did give Mitchell the opportunity to become an excellent field commander, which is how we remember him today.

On July 15, 1918, Mitchell himself flew the reconnaissance mission that gave Pershing the critical information he needed to launch the attack that defeated the Germans on the Marne. In September, Mitchell organized an aerial strike force of unprecedented size (1500 aircraft) and masterminded the largest massed air strike of the war as a key part of the American offensive in the Meuse-Argonne. Both Pershing and Patrick were so impressed with the success of Mitchell's performance that the latter recommended his promotion to brigadier general.

By this time Mitchell had evolved his theory of strategic warfare as an alternative to the carnage of trench warfare. One such strategic offensive, "deep into Germany," was under study when the war ended on November 11, 1918.

During the war, the British Army's Royal Flying Corps (RFC) had become the totally independent Royal Air Force (RAF) under a newly created Air Ministry, and Mitchell's friend and colleague General Hugh Trenchard had been placed in command. Many people—including Mitchell himself—supported such an idea for the United States. Senator Harry S. New of Indiana proposed a Department of Aeronautics to parallel the British Air Ministry, and it seemed only fitting that the Army's celebrated airman, the dashing General Billy Mitchell, would be named to head it.

In December 1918 the Army Air Service was officially emancipated from the Army Signal Corps, but it was still very much a

9

part of the Army. Billy Mitchell returned from Europe in March 1919 to find that the top job in the new Army Air Service had already been assigned—two days before Christmas—to an infantry officer!

This infantry officer, Major General Charles C. Menoher, respected Mitchell's technical and tactical ability, but, like most of his colleagues in Washington, he was developing a mistrust for the outspoken and flamboyant flyer with the disrespectful habit of cutting right through elaborate webs of red tape. The American armed services were all undergoing a rapid demobilization (one might say demoralization). For the Air Service alone this meant a reduction in personnel strength from 195,023 in 1918 to 9050 in 1920, the year that Warren G. Harding was elected to the American presidency on a platform of returning to "normalcy." In the face of this, there were few officers in positions of influence within the Army willing to rock the boat and get behind Mitchell's ideas about the use of air power in warfare—much less his heretical call for an independent U.S. Air Force. Even the men who should have known better—such as Black Jack Pershing and Mason Patrick—did not support him. This was, however, the point at which young captains like Hap Arnold began their pro-air power crusade from within the ranks of the Air Service.

Mitchell may have been something of an embarrassment to the war department, but this made him all the more popular with the press and the public. General Menoher finally went so far as to decry Mitchell's "persistent publicity" and to beg Secretary of War John W. Weeks for the authorization necessary to fire him.

The more controversial Mitchell became, the more his quotes appeared in the headlines. When he suggested that aerial bombardment could be used to destroy battleships, the *New York Times* queried whether America's overdependence on such vessels left the nation vulnerable to attack. Under this pressure, the Navy finally agreed to permit a test of Mitchell's theory. It is probable that the Navy actually believed that Mitchell couldn't sink a battleship, but much to their chagrin on July 22, 1921, his Martin bombers sent the captured German battleship *Ostfriesland* to the floor of Chesapeake Bay. The Navy Department was mortified and called Mitchell's success a fluke.

Even more than a decade after Mitchell's successful attack,

the Navy remained skittish about aircraft. In the 1930s, when I was out on a navigation tour in a Boeing B-17 several hundred miles south of Bermuda, we flew over a U.S. Navy task force. Embarrassed that we had located them so far out at sea, the Navy must have gotten in touch with the War Department, because within a matter of days we received a wire ordering us to fly no farther than 100 miles out to sea. In August 1937, during an exercise off the California coast, we located the battleship *USS Utah* and scored several direct hits on it with water bombs. The Navy was so embarrassed that it got the War Department to agree to a cover-up. No publicity got out on this until years later, and the Navy continued to deprecate the use of aircraft until Pearl Harbor taught it a costly lesson.

Although the successful results of Mitchell's bombing of the *Ostfriesland* demonstrated the capabilities of air power, Mitchell's outspoken stance continued to alienate many of those around him. Menoher finally went to Secretary of War Weeks with an ultimatum, but found himself, rather than Mitchell, out of a job. Weeks, however, did not promote Mitchell into the top airman's job, but rather pulled in Mitchell's old AEF boss, General Mason Patrick.

Patrick managed his vociferous assistant by keeping him as far away as possible. Mitchell traveled to Europe to consult with his colleagues in the Old-World air forces who either had flown with him during the war or knew him well by reputation, particularly in the wake of the *Ostfriesland* affair. Between December 1923 and July 1924, Mitchell conducted an extensive tour of the Pacific and the Far East. His voluminous report described America's Hawaiian Island defenses as being dangerously vulnerable to attack by Japan. This claim helped to set the stage for the final round of controversy that would destroy Mitchell's military career.

In February 1925, Secretary Weeks warned Mitchell that his public complaints about the sorry state of American defenses could get him fired, and Weeks returned Mitchell to his permanent rank of colonel and exiled him to Fort Sam Houston in Texas as a corps aviation officer. It was from this post that Mitchell delivered what was his own coup de grace. When the Navy airship *Shenandoah* crashed in a storm in September, Mitchell attacked "the incompetency, criminal negligence, and almost treasonable administration of the national defense by the Navy and War Departments

...as a patriotic American citizen, I can stand by no longer and see the disgusting performances...at the expense of the lives of our people, and the delusion of the American people."

Those were strong words to be issued by a soldier about his superiors, and were certainly ample grounds for him to be brought up on charges—which he was.

By coincidence, President Calvin Coolidge had just convened a special presidential commission, under his old friend and law partner Dwight Whitney Morrow (later Charles Lindbergh's father-in-law), to investigate the future of American aviation. The Morrow Board was taking testimony across town in Washington at the same time that Mitchell arrived to prepare for his court-martial. Mitchell was invited to appear before the Morrow Board, and he did so. However, he missed a tremendous opportunity to make his case by insisting on simply reading long passages of his book *Winged Defense* into the record, rather than answering the board's queries.

Major Hap Arnold, at Mitchell's side throughout his preparations for the Morrow Board appearance, later wrote:

> We of the Air Service practically squirmed, wanting to yell: "Come on, Billy, put down that damned book! Answer their questions and step down, that'll show them!" But he read on and on like a schoolmaster until Hiram Bingham [of the Senate Military Affairs Committee], a friend of air power and former air officer though he was, became so restless that he said: "Colonel, in view of the fact that each of the members of this Committee has a copy of your book and has read it..."

Mitchell interrupted Bingham and continued reading from his book. In the end the Morrow Board would reject the idea of establishing a separate independent air force—on budgetary grounds—although it did support the creation of an Air Corps to replace the Air Service.

Mitchell's court-martial was in turn covered in the press as a landmark trial. In fact, General Frank R. McCoy, one of the panel members, remarked to Mrs. Leonard Wood, wife of the former Army chief of staff and would-be presidential candidate, that it was probably the public's perception that "the War Department is on trial instead of the festive Bill." Many other people, too, would see the court-martial more as a forum in which Mitchell crucified the American military establishment, rather than vice versa.

The trial ended on December 17, 1925, the twenty-second anniversary of the Wright brothers' first flight at Kitty Hawk, but that coincidence did not bode well for Billy Mitchell. As Hap Arnold would later observe, there was little question of the outcome: "The thing for which Mitchell was really being tried, he was guilty of, and except for Billy, everybody knew it, and knew what it meant."

The decision was not unanimous—General Douglas MacArthur (who would become the Army's chief of staff in 1930), for one, voted in his favor—but it was the irrevocable end of Mitchell's colorful quarter century in uniform. The sentence was five years' suspension from duty without pay. Bowing perhaps to a groundswell of public support for Mitchell, President Coolidge restored him to half pay, but this tended only to underscore Mitchell's humiliation, and his pride gave him little choice but to resign, which he did on February 1, 1926, thus forfeiting his well-earned pension.

Air power as it evolved in the United States can trace its origins to a comment that Billy Mitchell made when he was invited to appear before Congress later in 1926. He described quite clearly how he conceived *strategic* air power should be employed. For centuries, he explained, wars had been fought by armies each trying to get at the inner, interior, sensitive areas of the other side's sources of support for war operations: the will of the people, the manufacture of munitions, and the operation of the economic structure of the state. However, with the airplane, said Mitchell, it would now be possible to fly *over* struggling armies and strike at the interior structure supporting the enemy nation. Billy Mitchell contended that if this kind of flying war were waged against the right targets and with an adequate number of aircraft, the results could culminate in a war-winning strategy.

Before Mitchell, American—and indeed most of the world's—military planners had only conceived of using air power in a *tactical* role, that is, to directly support surface forces in the field. Under the doctrine of *strategic* air power promulgated by Mitchell, air forces would use their unique ability to fly over the battlefronts and strike *directly* at an enemy's cities and industry, thus destroying both the enemy's *ability* and *will* to wage war.

After his departure from the service, Mitchell continued to speak out, with the Hearst newspaper chain and *Liberty* magazine being frequent venues for his byline. Having predicted the Japanese attack on Pearl Harbor in his 1924 report on Pacific defenses, Mitchell went on to predict the B-29 offensive against Japan. In his article *Are We Ready for War with Japan?* in the January 1932 issue of *Liberty,* Mitchell argued that Japan could be defeated in any future conflict, but only if the United States undertook the development of a long-range bomber with a range of 5000 miles and a service ceiling of 35,000 feet. A radical concept at the time, the idea was to become a reality a decade later when the B-29 made its first flight. Mitchell also went on to suggest basing these hypothetical bombers either in Alaska or at Midway Island in the Pacific.

I met Billy Mitchell only once. It was in 1930, when I was a second lieutenant with the Twenty-Seventh Pursuit Squadron at Selfridge Field, Michigan, and by that time he had been out of the Army for about four years. He was just passing through on a tour of Air Corps bases and had stopped to have lunch at the officers' club. I talked with him only briefly, to discuss a few things about the flying we were doing. He was held in very high regard by every one of us. We didn't say, "This is a very holy man"; we just believed in what he said. On the other hand, at higher levels in the Army and in the War Department, almost nobody agreed with Mitchell, or if they did, they were afraid to speak out. Of course, we had some people in the Air Corps who kept their mouths shut, too.

In 1932, Mitchell became an active supporter of New York Governor Franklin D. Roosevelt's campaign for the Democratic presidential nomination, hoping to be appointed Secretary of War for Air if FDR won in November. As it turned out, Mitchell had little clout within the Roosevelt camp, but the seeds of his far-reaching influence had already been sown among the young Air Corps captains a decade before.

By 1933, eight years after Billy Mitchell left the Air Service and three years before he died, the notion of strategic air power became a permanent lodger in the house of the U.S. Army Air Corps. Mitchell's disciples had multiplied like toadstools in the dark. Young officers like myself who'd gone through the Kelly Field, Texas, flying school in the 1920s when Mitchell was still in the service were now everywhere. Not only had we kept his memory alive, but by 1933 we were starting to reach important levels within the Air Corps. No longer mere second lieutenants and flying cadets, we were now captains and majors who were in a position to make the decisions that would shape and mold the Air Corps in the years to come.

Frank Andrews and Hugh Knerr were two of the many Air Corps officers who continued to advocate the need for strategic air power and the need for the type of aircraft necessary to support the air power concept. Major (later General) Knerr had commanded the Second Bombardment Group at Langley Field, Virginia, from 1927 to 1930. Summing up the attitude of his colleagues, Knerr described them as "still subject to the might of [their] none too appreciative parents." He went on to say that those "parents"— the War Department and the Army General Staff—were not "fully alive to the value of [their] Air Corps."

Those "none too appreciative parents" ruled their Air Corps like stern patriarchs refusing to accept their progeny's metamorphosis to adulthood. Like obedient youths, most airmen smiled, nodded, kept silent, and made future plans. Both Andrews and Knerr, however, were pulled out of good jobs and sent to the boondocks for speaking out. Eventually they were to be vindicated.

By 1933—though it was difficult to see at the time—tiny cracks were beginning to form in the strong countenances of the old horse soldiers who dominated the General Staff. There certainly was more military decorum in the clank of a cavalryman's spurs or the creak of saddle leather than there *ever* could be in the denture-jarring snarl of a Pratt & Whitney radial—but across the Atlantic, events were becoming just a tiny bit worrisome. In the beaten German Empire, a former infantry corporal suggested that the Great War may *not* have been fought to end *all* war.

Before his investiture as Germany's chancellor in January 1933, Adolf Hitler had garnered little more than an amused glance from the New World, but soon it was becoming clear that his goose-stepping legions were a genuine threat to world peace. Even though Chancellor Hitler's public relations apparatus portrayed him as a charming and amiable man of the people—much in the same way that Soviet Premier Mikhail Gorbachev is perceived today—his actual deeds were ominous: pulling Germany out of the League of Nations and beginning to rearm. Memories of the Great War, that conflagration that had swallowed the lives of nearly 9 million people, were still strong.

In the United States, by this time, those young Air Corps officers who were devotees of Billy Mitchell's theory of strategic air power had reached positions of authority within the Materiel Command—the Air Corps' research and development division—where they could really begin to develop those ideas. In July 1933, a carefully articulated blueprint for the future, known cryptically as "Project A," was drawn up. Originating at the epicenter of the Air Corps Materiel Command's engineering establishment at Wright Field near Dayton, Ohio, Project A was a feasibility study for a bomber that could fly 5000 miles with a ton of bombs. It was an amazing turn of events in an Air Corps that had never seen fit to produce a bomber with more than two engines.

On April 14, 1934, the cavalrymen on the Army General Staff gave their approval to the Project A outline that the whippersnappers at Wright Field had worked up over the winter. Officially, the new bomber was not to be thought of as an "offensive" weapon, but rather as a weapon for "hemisphere defense." The same abhorrence of "offensive" weapons that prevails today, pervaded the public mood in 1933 as well. Specifically, the Project A aircraft would be designed with sufficient range to reach Panama, Alaska, and Hawaii, the outposts of American influence in the Western Hemisphere.

The War Department—at the urging of the Navy Department—dictated that there be no mention of this revolutionary new aircraft in any maritime attack role. This was because the U.S. Navy had determined—despite Billy Mitchell's demonstration to the contrary—that airplanes would never be effective against warships. The Navy thought using aircraft against a ship of the line in wartime would be like a moth impacting the engine block of a Buick six. It didn't even make for a good laugh in the hallowed halls of the Navy Department.

Meanwhile, however, Project A had gotten over its highest

hurdle. The next step was the design. General Conger Pratt, head of the Air Corps Materiel Command, lost little time in getting requests for proposals into the mail to the nation's airplane builders. The two finalists in the Project A sweepstakes would be the Glenn Martin Company of Baltimore, Maryland, and the Boeing Aircraft Company of Seattle, Washington. Martin had recently been responsible for the Air Corps' B-10/B-12/B-14 series of twin-engine monoplane bombers, while Boeing had delivered the Air Corps' revolutionary B-9. First flown on April 13, 1931, the twin-engine B-9 monoplane quickly astounded the Air Corps by proving *faster* than most of that era's fighters. The Martin B-10 and its near twin, the B-12, had also gone on to prove themselves faster than the fighters that were supposed to intercept them. Thus, it was only logical that these two manufacturers should be entrusted with the responsibility of preparing preliminary designs for the plane with the 5000 mile range.

On May 12, General Pratt was authorized to commence negotiations directed toward those initial design concepts. Two days later, Martin President C. A. Van Dusen and Boeing President Clairmont L. Egtvedt were ushered into the general's office at Wright Field. Leonard "Jake" Harmon, General Pratt's aide, made an enthusiastic presentation to the two company presidents, in which he underscored the importance of Project A and the bomber that would be born of it. He then gave Egtvedt and Van Dusen one month to come up with their respective designs.

A month later, two revolutionary aircraft designs, Boeing's Model 294 and Martin's Model 145, were placed side by side on General Pratt's desk. From the two, the Materiel Division boss picked the Boeing design, thus initiating a line of four-motor heavy bombers that would culminate in the B-29. Originally designated as XBLR-1 for *experimental bomber, long range,* this designation was canceled and the nomenclature would follow the traditional *"B* for *bomber"* convention. The Boeing entry was redesignated as XB-15 and the Martin entry as XB-16.

The man who brought the $600,000 XB-15 mantle home to hang on the Boeing 294 was the earnest, dark-eyed Clairmont L. Egtvedt, president of Boeing for only a year. The 41-year-old former Stoughton, Wisconsin, farm boy had joined the company as a draftsman in 1917. He became chief experimental engineer within a year, and rose quickly within the growing Seattle aircraft company, becoming general manager in 1926. When he took the reins of Boeing's presidency in 1933, "Claire" Egtvedt had dreams for Boeing that paralleled those of the Army's airmen. He wanted to see his company building bigger and bigger airplanes. He wanted Boeing to become—in the words of a billboard he later had erected along Seattle's Airport Way—the "World Center of Four-Engine Airplane Development."

Against this backdrop, it was hardly surprising to see Claire Egtvedt back at Wright Field in August 1934 less than two months after winning the XB-15 contract. A new project was on the table this time. The Air Corps was now looking for a *second* bomber, an aircraft somewhat smaller and less breathtaking than the giant envisaged in Project A, though no less important. Because of its smaller, more conventional size, the airplane being discussed in the Materiel Command memorandum of July 18, 1934, stood a better chance of actually going into *production* sooner than the Project A bomber. Building an exotic behemoth like the XB-15 was exciting and would give Boeing a chance to push the limits of large aircraft technology, but getting a project on the *production* line meant cash flow. The Air Corps wanted a bomber that would carry a ton of bombs, the same capacity desired in the XB-15, but at a speed of at least 200 mph. The range would have to be at least 1,020 miles, though the desired range would be 2,200 miles, roughly double that of the best bombers then in service with the Air Corps. The plane would also, of course, have to be "multi-engined." To the Air Corps, "multiengined" meant two engines. To Claire Egtvedt, it meant four.

On August 16, 1934, Egtvedt instructed his designers to undertake the design of a low-wing monoplane bomber, which he designated Boeing Model 299. Except for the XB-15, the new Model 299 would be larger than anything the Air Corps had ever ordered, and it *would* have four engines. If anything, Egtvedt was more daring in the suggestion of the Model 299 than the Air Corps had been in its request for proposals. He sensed that by giving the Air Corps what it *really* wanted, though more than it *asked* for, he could win the development contract for this new bomber *and* establish Boeing as the leader in four-motor aircraft at the same time.

Under project engineer E. G. Emery, the Boeing designers began to flesh out the new bird of Egtvedt's dream. The clean lines of Model 299 were based on those of the sleek Model 247, a twin-engine airliner that Boeing had first flown in February 1933. In order to scale up the Model 247 into the larger Model 299, Emery's designers adopted many of the engineering innovations that had been developed by the Model 294 design team headed by Jack Kylstra.

Egtvedt, meanwhile, had decided to move forward with a four-engine airliner whose development would parallel that of the Model 299 and utilize some of its components. As E. G. Emery moved over to the project that would become the Model 307 Stratoliner—an airliner based on the Model 299—he was succeeded by his assistant, Edward C. Wells. At age 24, Ed Wells was now the project engineer on the airplane which, more than any other, would establish the reputation that Claire Egtvedt sought for Boeing.

By the time the first Model 299 was completed in July 1935, it was already being referred to as the XB-17, even though the project had not been officially adopted by the Air Corps. Because the larger XB-15 was still more than two years away from its first flight, the new airplane was the largest bomber yet unveiled to the curious American news media. Among the epithets that were devised to describe the huge aircraft, there was one that seemed to summarize nearly everyone's first impression, and the Model 299/XB-17 became Boeing's "Flying Fortress."

Having made its first flight on July 28, the plane with the unofficial designation and the colorful nickname flew east on August 20 to face the critical eye of the Air Corps at Wright Field. With project test pilot Leslie R. "Les" Tower at the controls, the XB-17 covered the 2100 mile distance nonstop at an average speed of 232 mph. The plane had satisfied two of the Air Corps' requirements before it had even arrived to be evaluated!

At Wright Field, the XB-17 would compete against the Douglas Model DB-1, which had also been developed in response to the Air Corps' August 1934 request for proposals. The DB-1 (Douglas Bomber, first) had been developed by the Santa Monica, California, plane builder, using the highly successful DC-3 commercial airliner as a pattern. The DB-1 had the same wing and tail surfaces as the DC-3, and while twin-engined, it was nearly as big as Boeing's Model 299. Like the Boeing bomber, the Douglas entry wore an unofficial Air Corps designation—XB-18. At Wright Field, the Materiel Division people picked both planes apart and found them to be among the best aircraft they had ever scrutinized, although the 2500 mile range of the four-engine Boeing plane was half again greater than that of its competitor.

Throughout August and September, Boeing's customers at Wright Field scrutinized the XB-17. As the flight tests continued into October, they only served to underscore the reliability of the big bomber. Word of an initial order for sixty-five aircraft was being circulated, and it began to look like the Boeing people would have a large tureen of good news to grace their table by Thanksgiving.

On the morning of October 30, 1935, the flight crew made their way to the prototype Flying Fortress. Taking his place in the pilot's seat was Les Tower, the 32-year-old Montana-born test pilot who had been first to fly the XB-17 and who represented the company throughout the flight test program. Beside Tower was Major P. P. "Pete" Hill, the Air Corps pilot assigned to monitor the Flying Fortress program from the "customer" point of view. As the rest of the crew took their places behind Tower and Hill, the two pilots went through the prescribed preflight checklist. They were quite familiar with the big bird by now and it went relatively quickly. What they did not—and would not—know, was that the ground crew had forgotten to remove a spring locking device that was fitted on the huge tail surfaces to keep them from flapping in the wind while the plane was on the ground.

Tower brought the Four Pratt & Whitney Hornet radial engines to life and began the takeoff roll. The XB-17 lifted into the air nicely but, once airborne, it was uncontrollable. Because of the ground crew's oversight, the important control surfaces in the tail were, in effect, frozen! The big plane had barely cleared the end of the field when it nosed into an adjoining pasture. Major Hill was killed on impact, but Les Tower—desperately battered and burned—survived for twenty agonizing days before he too died. Dragged from the burning wreckage, Air Corps Lieutenant Donald L. Putt was given little chance of survival even as he uttered what many feared would be his dying words: "Don't blame the airplane!"

(Not only did Don Putt survive, but he went on to be named—four years later—as the Air Corps project engineer for the B-29 program.)

The adoption of the Flying Fortress by the Air Corps, which had seemed a foregone conclusion, was now in question. For its part, the Air Corps still supported the Boeing bomber, noting that the crash was traceable to a maintenance error, rather than to a design defect, but still the Army General Staff was wary of making a decision in favor of the XB-17. In the face of the adverse publicity generated by the crash, the politically conscious General Staff couldn't see how the XB-17 could possibly be *justified* as being better than the XB-18 when both planes had done very well in their flight testing before the crash. And then there was also the question of the *price*—the dollars and cents numbers that Washington could understand. If ordered in equal numbers, the four-engine Boeing would cost almost twice as much as the twin-engine Douglas bomber. That settled it. On January 17, 1936, the General Staff authorized the purchase of 133 production model Douglas B-18s and only 13 of the longer-range Boeings under the designation YB-17. [The "Y" in official nomenclature is a step up from "X" (experimental), and denotes "service test" aircraft which may or *may not* precede production aircraft, which have no prefix before their type letter. At Boeing, the vortex of fear was on the *may not*.]

Redesignated Y1B-17 (because these planes were to be purchased out of F-1 fiscal year supplementary funds), the Flying Fortress went on the production line in Seattle, and on December 2, 1936, the first one was delivered. The final delivery took place on August 5, 1937, more than two months before the XB-15 made its first flight on October 15. While one Y1B-17 was retained by Wright Field for tests, the other dozen were all assigned to the Second Bombardment Group at Langley Field, Virginia, which was now under the direction of Brigadier General Frank Andrews of the General Headquarters (GHQ) Air Force, a newly established entity designed to be an umbrella for Air Corps operational units. Commanded by Lieutenant Colonel Robert Olds, the Second Bomb Group now had the job of developing techniques for long-range bombardment in wartime—techniques which literally had not been possible before the advent of the Flying Fortress. I was among the young pilots then assigned to Bob Olds' Second Bomb Group.

Billy Mitchell died in 1936, without having seen either the XB-15 or the Second Bomb Group become reality, but his memory was alive among the pilots associated with each. Soon there would be more B-17s, and the airmen who inherited Mitchell's dream would have the tools with which to demonstrate the real capability of strategic air power.

II

Getting the Tools
1938–1942

"THE FATHER OF THE B-29"

The Boeing B-29 Superfortress was certainly mothered by necessity, and, in some sense, fathered by the times, an inevitable ex-
tension of ideas at Boeing and within the Air Corps which had
begotten the B-17 and the XB-15 before it. But if one were to
attempt to point a finger to a single man as the "father of the
B-29," it would have to be General Henry Harley "Hap" Arnold,
the Air Corps' commander.

There were hundreds of people directly involved in planning
the B-29, and certainly Boeing had a well-established four-engine
bomber team long before the Air Corps asked for an airplane on
the scale of the B-29. Thus, the B-29 or something like it would almost certainly have come into being regardless of who commanded
the Air Corps. Nevertheless, it *was* Arnold who was in that critical
role during those critical years, and it was on Hap's desk that the
buck of future strategic air power stopped. Hap took the chances,
cut the corners, and ordered this unique airplane into production
before the prototype was even completed. He built the factories

and the command structure before the airplane itself came into being. Arnold took a calculated risk of unprecedented proportions—everything could have exploded in his face—and he won.

Arnold was born in Gladwynne, Pennsylvania, on June 25, 1886, the son of a surgeon assigned to the Pennsylvania Cavalry in Puerto Rico. Harley, as he was called by his family, had an older brother, Thomas, who had been preordained by their father to go to the U.S. Military Academy at West Point, just as Harley himself was pointed toward the ministry. When Thomas Arnold decided, against his father's decree, to follow the electrical engineering curriculum at Pennsylvania State University, it fell to Harley to take up the wearing of the gray.

Thus it was that the younger Arnold was diverted from the seminary and toward a career in the Army in which his father had served, and he went up to the Military Academy in the same year that the Wright brothers made their historic first powered flight at Kitty Hawk. At West Point, "Pewt" Arnold, as he was now dubbed, was remembered more as a prankster than a budding military genius. He acquired more notoriety for his exploits with the secret Black Hand society than for anything he ever did in the classroom. The crowning achievement of his cadet career seems to have been an unauthorized explosion of contraband fireworks to celebrate the arrival of 1907. Six months later, and eleven months before his twenty-first birthday, Pewt Arnold graduated from West Point and was commissioned a second lieutenant in the U.S. Army.

Arnold spent four years with the Infantry in the Philippines and at Governor's Island, New York, before being detailed to the Aeronautical Division of the Signal Corps at McCook Field near Dayton, Ohio, in April 1911. The young lieutenant had suddenly found himself on the ground floor of the Army's new air force. He became one of the Army's first flying cadets, learning to fly aboard one of the first Wright biplanes at a time when it was not unusual to have either Wilbur or Orville as an instructor.

June 1911 found Arnold—still a second lieutenant but already a flying instructor—at the Army's new Signal Corps Aviation School, which was located on a sylvan thousand-acre tract adjacent to College Park, Maryland. A year later, "Hap," as he was now known, distinguished himself by taking a rickety Burgess

Wright biplane up to a record altitude of 6540 feet. On October 9, 1912, Arnold was awarded the annual MacKay trophy for aviation excellence for a reconnaissance flight over the nation's capital from College Park to Fort Myer, Virginia. An outstanding navigational achievement for its day, it also enhanced Arnold's standing in the eyes of his superiors because of its venue.

In June 1916, after nearly three years in the Philippines, Arnold was promoted to captain and sent to organize the air defense of the Panama Canal Zone, which was where he was when the United States entered the First World War. Recalled to Washington with the temporary rank of colonel, he became the Army's *senior qualified pilot* in the nation's capital, as all the service's other pilots had gone to France to fight. Though it was his fervent desire to take an "air outfit" overseas, Arnold spent the duration of the war amid the men with the ideas from which would emerge the postwar air power movement. Arnold was assistant director of military aeronautics when the war ended, but he had spent those critical years an ocean away from the action in Europe. He finally arrived in France in November 1918 on an inspection tour just as the Armistice was taking effect. At last he had a chance to meet General Billy Mitchell and see firsthand what air power had done—and could do—in war.

After the war, reduced again to his permanent rank of captain, Arnold became a member of that coterie of captains that formed around Billy Mitchell as he became the rallying point of air power advocacy. As Mitchell's rising star glowed bright, faltered, and then plunged to earth, so too did the hopes, dreams, and careers of those around him. As one of Mitchell's closest confidantes throughout the court-martial, Arnold was one of the first airmen to find his wings clipped for his allegiance to the heretic. Arnold was exiled to an infantry unit at Fort Riley, Kansas, in March 1926 immediately after Mitchell's trial. Like so many of his colleagues, he spent the next several years as far away from the decision makers on the Army General Staff as they could banish him.

By the early 1930s, the young officers who still advanced the cause of Mitchell's brand of air power had moved high enough into the ranks of the Air Corps to begin making some small effect on policy. For his part, Arnold had made himself hard to ignore. In 1934, he led an Air Corps survey flight across both uncharted

25

and barely charted backwoods of the Alaskan wilderness. The navigational expertise required for the Alaska survey flight was no less an achievement than Arnold's MacKay-winning flight in 1912, and indeed this mission won him his second MacKay trophy for excellence in aviation achievement. Finally, on February 11, 1935, with the temporary rank of brigadier general, Lieutenant Colonel Arnold was given command of the First Wing of General Headquarters Air Force at March Field near Riverside, California—a posting so congenial to him that he remembered it most fondly to the end of his career. Eleven months later, he was posted back in Washington for the first time in nearly a decade—this time as assistant to Air Corps Chief, Major General Oscar Westover.

The next three years (1937–1940) were critical ones in the evolution of American air power. The four-engine monoplane bomber had become a reality, and the B-17 had entered service. Air power was, however, still taking its first tentative steps. The horse soldiers of the Army General Staff had allowed the airmen to experiment with strategic aircraft, but they still balked at permitting them to procure the number of B-17s needed to conduct a strategic air war, should that ever become necessary.

On September 21, 1938, General Oscar Westover died in a plane crash, and eight days later, Colonel (temporarily Major General) Hap Arnold found himself with the top job in the Army Air Corps. On the same day, September 29, 1938, a momentous event—an event whose repercussions would be felt worldwide—was taking place. Even as the new Air Corps Chief was being installed, Britain's Prime Minister Neville Chamberlain was sitting down across the table from Adolf Hitler in Munich to discuss the future of Czechoslovakia. Over the course of the next forty-eight hours, Chamberlain, desperate to preserve an uneasy peace at any cost, would fail in his attempt to appease the ruthless dictator, and pave the way for the outbreak, within a year, of the world's bloodiest war. Hap Arnold would soon face a task whose enormity was beyond his wildest imagination.

THE AIRCRAFT

By 1938, as the war clouds began to gather over the world, strategic air power had gained its converts, but still there were hardly any aircraft in the world that could execute Billy Mitchell's theory of "strategic air power." In the United States, the B-17 was the only strategic bomber that had actually been earmarked to go into multiple-unit production. The larger XB-15 was undergoing flight tests, but aviation technology was developing so fast that the XB-15's 1934–1935 design was rapidly becoming outdated. The Douglas XB-19, also larger than the B-17, was supposed to have flown in 1938, but it would not be ready before 1941 because of the company's other aircraft production commitments. Given the pace of developments within the industry at this time, it was generally accepted that any strategic bomber under development at the end of 1938 that was not yet *in production* (as the B-17 was) would be obsolete *before* it could go into production.

When he stepped into the role of Chief of the U.S. Army Air Corps, Hap Arnold presided over a force consisting of a mere fourteen B-17s. Billy Mitchell's teachings, largely ignored in Washington, seemed to have brought about little in the way of official reaction in other world capitals either. Despite the rearmament of Germany and the stirrings of a British response, the evolving European arsenals contained few strategic bombers in the Munich autumn of 1938.

In Germany, the Luftwaffe's advocates of strategic air power were few and they'd had even less luck in getting the ear of the German high command than had their counterparts in the U.S. Army Air Corps. Hitler firmly believed that a coordinated, tactical air/mechanized ground attack would overwhelm, not *some*, but *all* of his potential adversaries on the ground within eighteen months of the start of any conflict, and so he had instructed his Reich Air Ministry to bear that in mind and to invest no time in developing any new aircraft technology beyond what was already in the pipeline. In Japan, the emphasis in the projected Pacific war would be on carrier-based, tactical air power, which would prove devastatingly effective three years later. In Britain, the Air Ministry had been looking into long range four-engine bombers since 1936, a year after the advent of the B-17, but the first flight of the Avro Manchester (predecessor of the great Lancaster) was still almost a year away, as was that of the Handley Page Halifax and the full scale prototype of the Short Stirling.

In January 1939, President Roosevelt, having viewed his B-17s and other assorted air power at Bolling Field, made his now-famous call for "500 bombers a month." For Hap Arnold it was a question of *which* bombers. Later that month, Arnold asked Consolidated Aircraft to come up with a four-engine long-range bomber in the B-17 class, but exceeding B-17 performance. On March 30, 1939, the Air Corps gave the nod to Consolidated's Model 32 proposal, and the company began work on the project that would lead to the B-24 Liberator. Making its first flight on December 29, 1939, the Liberator would join the B-17 Flying Fortress as the staple of the American heavy bomber force in World War II.

Even as these two heavy bombers were moving forward toward their destiny, Arnold was thinking ahead toward a *super* strategic bomber, something that would be officially designated as a *very* heavy bomber. He assigned Brigadier General W. G. Kilner the task of determining and detailing the specifics of such an airplane. By June 1939, the report of the Kilner Board was on Hap Arnold's desk. It called for an aircraft with performance far in excess of the B-17 *or* the B-24—a virtual aerial battleship.

In the meantime, largely on its own initiative, Claire Egtvedt's Boeing Aircraft Company had been studying a similar concept. The Seattle plane maker had followed its Model 299—the B-17—with the commercial Model 307 Stratoliner, an airliner that utilized Model 299 components, but in addition introduced a pressurized fuselage. An attempt also to develop a pressurized B-17 resulted in the Model 322 design, a midwing monoplane with tricycle landing gear resembling a Stratoliner, but with a tail and aft fuselage design borrowed from early-model B-17s. This design was, however, deemed impractical, and it was abandoned. In the meanwhile, Boeing design engineer Lysle A. Wood had been assigned the parallel task of developing a successor to the XB-15 (Model 294), and it was on this limb of the Boeing family tree that the superbomber lineage would be grafted.

Wood began work on the advanced XB-15 in March 1936 under the Model 316 designation even before the XB-15 made its first flight. It featured the tricycle landing gear and the all-glass nose that would become well-recognized features of the eventual B-29. The Air Corps expressed interest in the Model 316 and even went so far as to assign a provisional designation—Y1B-20—to the study. No orders were forthcoming, however, and Boeing moved on, continuing to refine the advanced four-engine bomber project through the Model 330 study in May 1938 to the Model 333 in January 1939. Powered by four Allison V-1710 engines, the Model 333 design incorporated the radical innovation of having a large engine nacelle spanning each wing. There were, in turn, two engines in each nacelle—one pointing forward driving a conventional tractor (pulling) propeller and one on the trailing edge pointing backward and driving a pusher propeller. This idea was rejected by Boeing management because the unusual positioning of the engines had the potential for as yet unforeseen technical problems without providing enough in the way of increased performance. Thus, the Model 333 was followed a month later by the Model 333A, with the same four engines in a conventional configuration—all side by side on the leading edges of the wings.

These proposed designs were both rejected on the basis of the Allison V-1710 engines being inadequate for high-altitude operations, and a modified Model 333B with four Wright 1800 engines was presented in March. The Model 333B was, however, still in the same class as the B-17 and B-24, having a 2500 mile range with a 1-ton bombload. Boeing engineers felt that even more range could be had by further refinements, and so by the end of March, the project had evolved into the twin-tailed Model 334, which had a wing span of 120 feet and a proposed range of 4500 miles with a ton of payload. The Models 333A, 333B and 334 were all designed around flat liquid-cooled engines. Developed experimentally by such companies as Wright Aeronautical, these engines were intended to be so flat that they could be embedded completely within the wing so that there would be no nacelle or any other type of protrusion that could interrupt the airflow over the wing. They remained, however, impractical for use in an aircraft of this type because this necessitated a thicker wing than otherwise required, as well as a longer engine drive shaft, because the engine was submerged in the wing. The thick wing actually added to the drag so that the aerodynamic gains of submerging the engines were more theoretical than real. Other problems associated with these new and untried engines included the additional weight of the thicker wing and the fact that the submerged engines took up space that could otherwise be devoted to fuel tanks. The submerged engines also might cause overheating problems because they were entirely enclosed by the wing. Given the potential for problems and costly delays, the flat engines were stricken from consideration.

An interesting footnote to the Boeing Model 334 saga is that it reappeared almost intact toward the end of 1942 *in Germany!* Exactly *how* this happened is open to conjecture, but as early as 1940—a year after Boeing developed the Model 334—the Messerschmitt Aircraft Company in Germany began to develop a four-engine long-range strategic bomber that was specified to have sufficient range to bomb New York City from bases in Europe, and return. First flown in December 1942 (three months after the B-29) the Me-264 had a fuselage and tail that were identical to those of the Model 334 right down to the slight inward canting of the twin vertical stabilizers, the tricycle landing gear, and the all-glass nose that was to be a trademark of the B-29 series. Only the wings were slightly different, with four Junkers Jumo 211 radial engines in conventional cowlings. It is interesting to note that while the first Me-264 prototype had a wingspan of 127 feet 7½ inches, the second and third Me-264s had wingspans of 141 feet 1 inch—only *1 inch* different from the production model B-29! Though no specific German espionage project—to our knowledge—has ever been officially revealed which connects the B-29 and the Me-264, it is quite curious that two remarkably similar aircraft could have wound up *within 1 inch* of the same size *without* such an effort. While work on the Messerschmitt Me-264 paralleled that on the B-29, only three were ever built. The B-29 enjoyed immense support from the USAAF, but the Me-264 was not taken seriously by the Luftwaffe until late in the war when it was much too late to go into the production of the big aircraft.

In July 1939, even as the Kilner Board was making its recommendations to the chief of the Air Corps, Boeing's top engineers were huddling with the Materiel Command officers at Wright Field with the objective of molding their Model 333/334 series of design concepts into a real airplane that could answer the board's recommendations. On Boeing's side of the table were the men who had sharpened their skills on Claire Egtvedt's already successful four-engine aircraft such as the Model 307 Stratoliner, the Model 314 Clipper (a flying boat airliner for Pan American World

Airways), and of course the Model 299—the B-17 Flying Fortress. Egtvedt had assembled the finest group of four-engine aircraft engineers in the world, an ideal crew for the Army to entrust with what would soon evolve as its most ambitious—and most important—aircraft project ever.

The chief engineer would be Edward Curtiss Wells, a 28-year-old genius who had graduated cum laude from Stanford University and joined Boeing in time to put his considerable design talents to work on major components of the Model 299 program. Wells's assistant would be Lysle A. Wood, already a veteran of the Model 316 effort, while their boss would be Wellwood E. Beall, the dynamic former chief engineer who had just been promoted to vice president in charge of engineering. The 32-year-old Beall had come to Boeing's engineering wing by way of the university of his native Colorado and later New York University, landing a job as an instructor at the Boeing School of Aeronautics in Oakland, California, where he taught a diverse curriculum ranging from math and drafting to air commerce regulations. Later transferred to the Far East to help Boeing's efforts to sell fighter planes to Chiang Kai-Shek's Kuomintang air corps, Beall became interested in the notion of establishing airline links between the United States and China, an idea that was then under active consideration by Juan Trippe, president of Pan American Airways. When Beall returned to Seattle in 1935, shortly before Pan Am began its transpacific flying boat service, he transferred to Boeing's Engineering Division. There he spearheaded the development of the Model 314 Clipper, an enormous commercial flying boat much larger than the Martins and Sikorskys that Pan Am already had in service. The first Boeing Clippers had entered service with Pan American several months before in January 1939, and they were soon to become the last word in luxurious transpacific and transatlantic air service.

On the Air Corps side at the July meeting were Colonel (soon to be General) Oliver P. Echols, the powerful, fiery-haired commander of the Materiel Command; Lieutenant Colonel Frank Cook; and Lieutenant Colonel Donald L. Putt, the vociferous advocate of strategic air power who had survived the 1935 crash of the XB-17 prototype that killed Pete Hill and Les Tower. Don Putt was named as the Army's project engineer for the B-29 program, while Frank Cook would serve as the head of production engineering for the superbomber that would soon materialize from the vision of the Kilner Board.

By the time these men met to make that vision reality in the July of that last innocent summer before the war, the Boeing Model 334 had become the Model 334A. The new design was very unlike the series of four-engine bomber designs between Model 316 and Model 334, but its single tail and clean lines were a clear foreshadowing of the B-29 that was to come.

Two months later, on September 1, Germany invaded Poland. The long-feared, much-predicted Second World War was now a fact. On November 10, Hap Arnold formally requested that the War Department authorize him to ask the American aircraft industry to begin submitting designs for the superbomber recommended a half year before by the Kilner Board. That authorization was forthcoming three weeks later, on December 2, and Arnold's staff immediately began preparing Air Corps Data Request R-40B, and the accompanying specification XC-218, the historic documents that specified a giant bomber with a range of 5333 miles.

Even as the War Department was authorizing Arnold to start *looking* for designs, Boeing was putting the finishing touches on a full-scale Model 334A mock-up. Ed Wells, meanwhile, was not content that this plywood model be the final word on the subject, and since August he had been working on yet *another* design. Assigned the company designation Model 341 (Models 335 through 340 were design studies for other dissimilar aircraft), it was a superbomber with a high aspect-ratio wing that spanned 124 feet 7 inches. It was a case of the wing that made the airplane, for it was the unique Boeing Model 115 airfoil that set this wing—and the Model 341 itself—apart from the designs and proposals which had preceded it. The Model 115 wing was an important innovation because it could support almost twice as much weight per square foot of its area than could the wing types used on the B-17 and other earlier aircraft. In addition to this wing, other features were streamlined in the Model 341 bomber, and it was promised by the engineers as having the potential for unprecedented performance. No external vents or air scoops marred its lines. The radio's antenna was streamlined, and lights and deicers were designed to be made flush with the surface. Even the heads of the tiny external rivets that held the aluminum skin to the wing spars would be flush. Beall and Wells had demanded and had gotten the most aerodynamically efficient airplane possible. Every tiny, drag-producing detail that could be flattened and pushed beneath the Model 341's sleek surface translated into a few hundred feet of extra distance, feet which added up to miles and then, at last, to the range necessary for the superbomber to carry out its mission. On December 5, 1939, work began on the engineering mock-up of the Model 341.

Meanwhile, General Echol's Materiel Command in Ohio and General Arnold's Air Staff in Washington were going back and forth over the issue of how to define the superbomber recommended by the Kilner Board. Finally, on January 29, 1940, Echols finished Air Corps Data Request R-40B and posted copies to America's four leading manufacturers of large aircraft: Consolidated Aircraft of Fort Worth, Texas; Douglas Aircraft of Santa Monica, California; Lockheed Aircraft of Burbank, California; and the Boeing Airplane Company of Seattle, Washington.

On February 5, having been delayed by a blizzard en route, the copy of R-40B addressed to Boeing finally crossed its transom, landing square on the desk of Philip G. Johnson, the former airline executive who had stepped in as president of Boeing when Claire Egtvedt was elected to chair the Board of Directors.

A 45-year-old native of Seattle, Johnson had joined Boeing in 1917 at the same time that Claire Egtvedt had come aboard, and had served as president for several years in the late twenties. In 1931 when Boeing's fledgling airline, Boeing Air Transport, merged with National Air Transport, Pacific Air Transport, and Varney Airlines to form United Air Lines, Johnson became president of the new company as well. In 1933 he resigned as president of Boeing but retained his position at the helm of United until 1934.

In 1934 the Roosevelt administration decided that aircraft manufacturers could no longer own, or be owned by, airlines. Furthermore, it attempted—with disastrous results—to nationalize the airmail system by suspending contracts with commercial airlines and compelling the U.S. Army to fly the mail. A good many Army flyers were killed before it was determined that the airlines were better equipped than the Air Corps to handle the job, and the administration reversed itself. This exercise drew Roosevelt's attention to the Air Corps' lack of readiness, which ultimately benefited American air power. For Philip Johnson, however, the repercussions cost him his job. In order for United to regain its airmail contracts, it had to divest itself of its connection with Boeing, and the head that rolled was Johnson's.

By 1939, however, times had changed, and Johnson was back at Boeing, where he became an integral part of the leadership that made the B-29 possible. Claire Egtvedt was the visionary who dreamed of skies filled with four-engine Boeings, and men like Wellwood Beall and Ed Wells created them. Philip Johnson, on the other hand, would prove to be the production genius who would help mastermind the sprawling, nationwide industrial complex that would build until Japan's skies were black with the camouflaged underbellies of Boeing's masterpiece.

On February 5, 1940, however, the superbomber was still an elusive concept. Boeing had a plywood Model 334A and a paper Model 341 that would soon become a wooden mock-up. Now Boeing had a Data Request that called for performance that neither model could deliver. Data Request R-40B had been molded by the Air Staff's sobering observation of the first five months of World War II. As revised, the supplementary specifications that arrived at Boeing in March read "give us more airplanes, greater bomb capacity, leakproof fuel tanks and more defensive armament."

The fuel tanks could be leakproofed, but this added 3000 pounds to the weight, which in turn required another 2000 pounds of fuel in order not to diminish the airplane's range. Then too, the increased defensive armament added 2500 pounds and required yet another 1600 pounds of fuel. Simply put, the Air Corps' specifications demanded an airplane far heavier—and larger—than the Model 341.

The engineers who had presided over the evolution of the Model 333 into the Model 341 returned to their drawing boards. The Model 341 had been over 5 feet longer than the 334B, but they added yet another 6½ feet to make it an even 93 feet. The armament increased, and so did the gross weight. As the evolution made the aircraft heavier, the four Pratt & Whitney R-2800 engines were stricken from the blueprints and replaced with a quartet of Wright R-3350 Cyclones, which were themselves a new and untested quantity that nevertheless promised an increase in horsepower that was almost the equivalent of a fifth engine.

Midnight oil fueled the flickering lamps in Seattle, and decisions being made across the globe in Berlin would underscore the urgency of those efforts. On May 10, 1940, the horror of the German blitzkrieg was unleashed on the Netherlands, and World War II came to Europe's western front. As the Luftwaffe's Stukas were launching their attacks, a lone mail plane was humming across Montana's western mountains, following the Clark Fork up into Hellgate Canyon toward the continental divide. Beneath its corrugated metal skin were the papers that would translate into the final death knell of the Axis.

On May 11, the day after the invasion of the Netherlands, the first drawings of Boeing Model 345 reached the Air Corps Materiel Command at Wright Field. When General Oliver P. Echols unfolded the plans, he beheld an amazingly sleek four-engine bomber with a 141-foot 3-inch wingspan that promised a range of 5333 miles and a maximum bombload equal to that of a trio of B-17s. General Echols and his Wright Field engineers beheld the future, and they designated it XB-29, and named it *Superfortress*.

Of the four designs submitted to Wright Field in response to Data Request R-40B, the Boeing Model 345 was clearly the most revolutionary, the most favored, and the first to receive an official Air Corps designation. Neither the Lockheed XB-30 (a bomber version of the Constellation transport) nor the Douglas XB-31 made it off the drawing board. The Air Corps did decide to proceed with the Consolidated XB-32 program, however, if only as a measure of insurance against unforeseen problems in the future Boeing XB-29.

As the U.S. Army Air Corps was considering its superbomber designs, things were going from bad to worse for the Allies in the war in Europe. The German armies, supported by Luftwaffe tactical air power, smothered France, and were then poised for the short hop across the English Channel.

By June 14, 1940, the German armies were in Paris and the War Department had just authorized its Air Corps to write Boeing a check for $85,652 to begin work on the XB-29. The first steps meant further refinement of the basic Model 345 and wind tunnel tests. This in turn meant an evolution of the Model 115 wing into one with the ability to lift and support 50 tons. This task went to George Schairer, Boeing's chief aerodynamicist, who had come to the company straight from graduation from the Massachusetts Institute of Technology. For Schairer the task was not simply to make the wing larger and smoother. Rather it was dealing with subtleties and complexities brought about by the requirement that it be a structure capable of lifting an enormous airplane and supporting its own weight, as well as containing no fewer than twenty-two fuel cells. Thus, George Schairer's contribution to the XB-29 was the Model 117 wing, a creation that would earn him the same acclaim from the aircraft industry that the B-29 would earn for Boeing from the American people.

Schairer's Model 117 wing gave the Model 345 a span nearly 20 feet greater than that of the Model 341 and greatly increased the load-carrying capacity. It would define the B-29 in the same way that the Model 115 had defined the Model 341. It gave the B-29 just over nine times the wing area of a Piper Cub, yet with the ability to lift more than *ninety* times the total weight!

As the Air Corps placed a $3.6 million order for the first two XB-29s on August 29, 1940, waves of Luftwaffe medium bombers were ravaging English cities with nightly raids. There was every indication that England would soon be defeated, and for the first time, the War Department had to seriously consider future air operations against Germany from bases in the Western Hemisphere. Suddenly, the long-range bomber that had surfaced in the specifications of Project A six years earlier, and again in the Kilner Board report in 1939, was no longer just an esoteric toy for the Air Corps—it was a strategic necessity. Hand in hand with this realization was the sobering recognition of the massive production mobilization that would be required to produce adequate numbers of XB-29s on time. Once the design engineering had been completed, every conceivable shortcut would have to be taken to get the big birds into production and into service. In dollar terms, the project was now the largest single program *ever* undertaken by the Air Corps.

By April 1941, models of the XB-29 had been tested in the wind tunnels of the University of Washington, the California Institute of Technology, and the National Advisory Committee for

Aeronautics. In Seattle, a full-scale plywood mock-up had been built in complete secrecy, and the final refinement of the blueprints was being undertaken. Having inspected the mock-up, the Air Corps placed an order on May 17 for 14 service test YB-29s *and 250 production B-29s!* It was absolutely unprecedented for a huge aircraft of such revolutionary design to be ordered into production without the Air Corps having had the chance to conduct flight tests on a preproduction prototype. This meant that tooling would begin at the factory well before the first XB-29 took to the air.

THE PLAN

In contrast to the mood of the United States even two years earlier, the state of mind in the summer of 1941 reflected a nearly universal acceptance that an American entry into World War II was inevitable. Despite a cantankerous Congress—within which isolationist factions sought to prevent the war from spilling into the Western Hemisphere simply by refusing to prepare for the possibility—President Roosevelt's mobilization was proceeding apace, touted in the press under the newly popularized heading of "national defense." Shortly before General George Marshall became the U.S. Army's chief of staff in 1939, he came down to Langley Field, Virginia, where I was stationed with the Second Bombardment Group, and we took him out on a bombing mission in a B-17. Caleb V. Haynes was flying the airplane, I was navigating, and John B. "Jackpot" Montgomery was the bombardier. Jackpot wasn't any better than any of the other bombardiers when it came to normal practice, but when the chips were down and we had to hit a target, he hit it. So when the three of us took Marshall up, Jackpot dropped two water-filled bombs at a big battleship we had outlined on the bombing range. One bomb hit on the bow and one on the stern. It was a miracle. Normally, we would have been satisfied if only one had hit the target, but we scored two perfect hits. I think we made an impression on Marshall.

We were to make an impression on President Franklin D.

Roosevelt as well. The closest I ever got to Roosevelt was in 1939, at about the time he began worrying about our not having any air force. We flew a B-17 up from Langley Field and parked it at Bolling Field in the District of Columbia along with one of just about every kind of airplane that the Air Corps owned. There were eight or ten airplanes in a row, and we were standing in front of our B-17 when the President came by in an open sedan. Apparently our display was among the factors that helped to convince him of the importance of air power and the need for good aircraft, because right after that he got on the radio and started screaming for 5000 airplanes. Soon he was pushing it to 10,000 and finally after Pearl Harbor he got up to requesting that 50,000 be produced.

I'm sure General Hap Arnold and General Andrews had been trying to convince him to do that for a long time. Roosevelt overruled the reluctant War Department and ordered the B-17 back into production, after most of the order had been canceled by the War Department itself. I don't know if you could say that he was a convert to air power, but he *was* a convert to the power we needed to defend this country and eventually to whatever was needed to win the war.

In May 1941, Roosevelt had asked Army Chief of Staff Marshall and Chief of Naval Operations Admiral Harold Stark to begin to put together the production plans required to build the weapons needed not simply to defend the Western Hemisphere, but also to *defeat* the Axis. The building of the B-29 would ultimately be an essential part of these complex and farsighted production plans.

The initial groundwork for the mobilization of American air power in World War II began on June 20, four days after the first fourteen YB-29s went into the final round of engineering design in Seattle. On that day Roosevelt signed an executive order under the War Powers Act of 1941, authorizing Marshall to create the U.S. Army Air Forces (USAAF). This measure transformed the Air Corps and General Headquarters Air Force into a single self-governed body with its own *Air* Staff which was no longer at the mercy of the Army General Staff. Though not completely independent from the Army and the War Department, the USAAF would be operationally autonomous, and able to conduct training, procurement, and operations without its hands tightly bound by the Army red tape that had so frustrated the airmen under the previous organization. Within six months, Hap Arnold, who was now chief of the new USAAF, would also be a de facto member of the Joint Chiefs of Staff.

Two days later, on June 22, 1941, the war took an ominous turn as nearly 200 German divisions, backed by the bulk of the Luftwaffe, poured into the Soviet Union, achieving spectacular successes against the ill-prepared Russian defenders. These events lent an air of urgency to the American mobilization in which both the isolationists and the realists redoubled their conflicting efforts.

For Brigadier General Carl "Tooey" Spaatz, the boss of the Air Staff in Hap Arnold's new USAAF and a member of the 1939 Kilner Board, the urgency translated into the need for specific strategic planning. On July 10, Spaatz called in Lieutenant Colonel Harold George from his post as commander of the Second Bombardment Group at Langley Field to take charge of something even more important—the Air War Plans Division (AWPD). The USAAF equivalent of the Regular Army's War Plans Division, the AWPD consisted simply of Hal George; Lieutenant Colonels Orvil Anderson, Howard Craig, and Kenneth Walker; and Major (soon to be General) Haywood S. "Possum" Hansell, Jr., as a final addition. Spaatz entrusted them with a job to do, an enormous job. Spaatz wanted George and the AWPD to put together nothing short of an overall scheme to use air power to its fullest potential to defeat the Axis. He knew that the War Plans Division would be putting together its own plan and *that* plan would subvert air power to a supportive role. If air power was ever to demonstrate its fullest potential, there would have to be an *air* war plan, written *by* airmen, *for* air power.

Hansell was ultimately to be an extremely important player in the evolution of the strategic air war against the Axis. Not only was he a member of the AWPD at this vital juncture, but he would also serve as a combat commander in Europe, and as one of the first commanders of the B-29 force in the Pacific.

As General Hansell has recalled, both in his books on the subject (see the bibliography) and in his many postwar lectures at the Air War College, when World War II had broken out in Europe in 1939, Congress had taken the position that:

> The American military establishment should devote itself only to the defense of America against invasion. In seeking appropriations to build up our forces, neither the Army nor its Air Corps were permitted to discuss offensive operations, or four-engine bombers which were considered "offensive weapons." This was, of course, a very short-sighted national policy. If we were attacked, we would certainly need defense, but once *in* a war, it would be necessary to fight offensively if the nation intended to defeat the attackers.

As we've noted, concepts of American strategic air power, as developed from the ideas of Billy Mitchell, ran directly counter to the official War Department doctrine which contended that only land armies could win wars. This doctrine held that the role of air power was as an auxiliary to the land army—to support the army on the battlefield—and that it could have no other mission.

Thus, the Air Corps had felt compelled to fall back on a ruse in the 1930s and tell Congress,

> All right, if we are going to defend the Western Hemisphere, one of the things we must defend against is enemy air power. We must therefore be able to destroy enemy air bases that might be established in the Western Hemisphere. This hemisphere is a big area and it would take a long-range aircraft to do this. We therefore need four-engine bombers, not for offensive operations in Europe or elsewhere, but for defense of the Western Hemisphere. Only long range, four-engine airplanes can reach all of the places where bases might be established.

This was essentially the situation until June 1941, when Germany, having lost the Battle of Britain, turned on Russia. The Nazis were so immediately successful that it appeared to General Hansell and his colleagues on the newly formed Air Staff that Russia would collapse. There was a genuine fear in this country that Hitler might actually win the war, and that we would be faced with a world in which Germany was dominant.

Prompted by apprehension of German successes, President Roosevelt took a very powerful step. In two highly secret letters, one to Secretary of War Henry L. Stimson and one to Secretary of the Navy Frank Knox, Franklin Roosevelt wrote, "I should like to have your estimates of the production requirements needed to defeat our potential enemies." That was a tremendously important request. He didn't say, "I should like to have your estimates of the requirements to defend ourselves," nor, "to prevent an attack against the Western Hemisphere." He said, "to *defeat* our potential enemies." That allowed the Air Staff to talk openly about offensive operations for the first time.

Under Lieutenant Colonel George and Major Hansell, the Air War Plans Division was authorized to determine the air requirements in response to the President's letter. As they went to work during July of 1941, they were also instructed to abide by a secret agreement reached with the British six months earlier called the ABC Agreement. That agreement, incorporated into Joint War Plan Rainbow V, called for the defeat of Hitler and Mussolini *first*, with just a defensive posture in regard to the Japanese in the Pacific. This agreement also included plans for an initial massive air offensive against Nazi Germany. Fortunately, members of the Intelligence Branch of the Office of the Chief of Air Corps—where Major Hansell had served before being assigned to the AWPD—had been working on this same idea for about a year. They had come up with the strategic air intelligence on which to base a plan for offensive air operations against Germany. They had also, of course, studied plans for the defense by air of the Western Hemisphere and support of naval operations for an initial defense against possible Japanese aggression in the Pacific.

As General Hansell recalls,

> The primary starting point in developing a plan for an air offensive against Germany was the adoption of an air objective. What were we going to try to do? Were we simply going to support the Army ground forces in the invasion of Europe, or were we going to try to *win* the war by air power? We decided on a compromise. We would *try* to win the war with strategic air power, but we'd also recognize the fact that nothing like this had ever been done before, and it might be necessary for a land invasion of the continent *as well as* an air offensive. As it evolved in the

41

AWPD, the basis of the overall Air War Plan was to destroy the capability and willingness of the German people to continue the war. It was our hope that this would be decisive, but we were also committed to provide additional tactical air forces for support of the invasion should that also be necessary.

In determining the size of force required to conduct a decisive strategic air offensive against Hitler, Hansell and the other members of the AWPD reasoned that Nazi Germany, like any other major power, was dependent upon vital industrial and economic systems, such things as electric power, transportation, fuel and raw materials, and certain production facilities. Those essentials that were susceptible to destruction from the air were selected as a potential target list.

The AWPD analyzed these systems, selected strategic targets, and determined the number of bombs that would have to be dropped to destroy each of those targets. Then the AWPD adopted a 90 percent probability of destruction as a requirement. This meant that the USAAF personnel would have to be 90 percent sure that a target was destroyed before it was written off the target list, and that they'd have to be prepared to keep attacking until they *were* 90 percent sure. The AWPD selected types of aircraft with adequate ranges to reach and destroy those targets from various bases, and this determined the bomb loads that could be carried on each mission. These calculations enabled the AWPD to determine the number of missions that would have to be flown to destroy each target and keep it out of service.

As General Hansell recalls,

We sought to paralyze the German electric power, transportation and fuel systems, selecting a total of 124 individual targets. We also concluded that we would also need to cripple the German air force as an intermediate objective. This called for 30 additional targets. Thus we worked out the number of heavy strategic bomber sorties required to destroy 154 selected targets, which we figured would completely cripple the German war machine. We were then faced with the question of how much time we had in which to do this. We found that the Army's ground forces were struggling with their side of the problem, and that their bottleneck was in shipping. They would need to move about 5 million men overseas and keep them supplied, but they did not have nearly enough shipping tonnage to do it. More ships would have to be built, and that would take more than two years. Thus, the USAAF had a period of a little over two years in which to create air forces, deploy them, and conduct the air offensive, before the Army would be ready to attempt an invasion of Europe.

We figured that it would take about nine months to begin to build up our air forces and to start construction of 100 air bases in England. Another nine months would be required to bring these air forces up to full strength at those bases, and complete construction. This would leave about six months in which to carry out a sustained and unremitting strategic air offensive, with our strategic air forces at full strength, before the Army would be ready to make a final decision on invasion. Typical weather over Europe permitted five missions per month, and that meant we would have 30 missions in which to destroy those 154 pre-selected targets. We determined the size of the force necessary on that basis. The result was a pretty staggering requirement. Excluding combat attrition, which would be heavy, we came up with a requirement for about 7500 four-engine strategic bombers, 1000 medium bombers, and 3500 fighters in the offensive force against Germany. In addition, we provided 5000 aircraft for tactical support of the Army's ground forces in case of an invasion of Europe.

In the aggregate, the AWPD plan called for about 12,000 combat aircraft allocated to the air offensive against Germany. About the same total would be required for the other three missions: (1) defense in the Pacific (which had been considered a Navy responsibility before Pearl Harbor; (2) hemisphere defense; and (3) tactical air support of an invasion of Europe. After the defeat of Nazi Germany, the strategic air forces would then be directed against Japan. That effort called for a total of about 24,500 combat aircraft, of which nearly 10,000 would be four-engine and six-engine bombers. (Development of the latter was ultimately postponed in order to concentrate on production of four-engine bombers.) These combat aircraft were to be supported by 37,000 trainers, bringing the total to about 61,500 military aircraft. To operate this force would require over 2,165,000 men and women in uniform operating and supporting 251 groups, and enormous quantities of supplies, including of course, gasoline and bombs. Replacement combat aircraft to meet six months of operations were calculated to reach 19,000 combat types.

The air war plan, AWPD-1, was completed and submitted to the War Plans Division of the Army General Staff at about midnight on August 12, 1941. The General Staff was struggling to meet its own deadline for its own war plan, and so there was no time for review. General Marshall and General Arnold had been absent from Washington during preparation of AWPD-1. Together with Admiral Ernest King, they had been with President Roosevelt at Argentia, Newfoundland, for a secret meeting with British Prime Minister Churchill and the British Chiefs of Staff, and so the final decision really took place on August 30 when Marshall finally had a chance to sit down with his General Staff. General Arnold was also present, as was William Signius Knudsen, director general of Roosevelt's Office of Production Management.

As General Hansell told me later,

We approached this presentation with considerable apprehension because we were flying in the face of all earlier War Department doctrine. I know of no one other than Lieutenant Colonel Harold George who might have had the effrontery to propose to General Marshall in the presence of the general officers who headed the General Staff that we should (1) expand the Army Air Forces *forty-two-fold*, (2) scrap all our existing airplanes and replace them with *ten-fold* new ones [including 10,000 four-engine and six-engine bombers which the Army's General Staff had just told the Congress were not needed at all], and (3) recommend that primary reliance for victory be placed on untried air power.

During the presentation there was a series of vigorous objections by members of the General Staff, but Marshall said nothing at all. When all the evidence had been discussed, he simply said, "Gentlemen, I think the plan has merit, I should like for Secretary of War Stimson to hear it." We were over the biggest hurdle that the USAAF had yet encountered.

If General Marshall had said—as he so easily might have— "This is interesting, but completely out of step with the whole Army plan," then our proposal would have been thrown in the waste basket. He was, however, a very farsighted and broadminded man. I know of no other Army general who would have taken this step against the advice of most of his General Staff.

BLUEPRINT FOR PRODUCTION

On September 11, 1941, when General Marshall officially accepted AWPD-1, the B-29 was prominent among the nearly 70,000 aircraft that the USAAF projected it would need.

However, the *production planning* that would make the strategic bomber element of this force possible actually dated back to a telephone conversation on the night of May 7 between Hap Arnold and Boeing President Philip Johnson. Johnson was visiting Wright Field for discussions on the B-17 and XB-29 programs and had just returned to his hotel in Dayton when Arnold tracked him down by phone from Washington to say: "I would like for you to recommend how America can build the greatest number of heavy bombers in the shortest time."

Johnson said he'd think about it and that he'd call Arnold back in the morning. At the crack of dawn, as Johnson and his team, which included company attorney (and later president) Bill Allen, treasurer Harold Bowman, and sales manager Frederick B. Collins, were getting ready for their day at Wright Field, Collins reminded Johnson to make the call. Johnson grabbed a tablet, jotted a few notes, and picked up the phone. This hastily scribbled memo, the product of a largely sleepless night for Johnson, was the cornerstone of the production effort required to build Arnold's huge air force.

Still preserved in Boeing's archives, the memo reads simply:

1. Establish the principle of one or two proven production models of heavy bombardment airplane.

2. Arrange for the models selected to be built in factories having facilities now used for other purposes.

3. Give first priorities to such factories from materials and machine tools.

4. Continue the development of replacement types for the models selected, so that in time they can become the production model.

As a result of this recommendation, Arnold established the BDV Committee, a joint production organization consisting of

Boeing, Douglas Aircraft, and the Vega Aircraft subsidiary of Lockheed. The purpose of the BDV Committee was to coordinate all the production efforts for the B-17 Flying Fortress, which would be built not only by Boeing, but by the other two firms as well.

It would seem that such an arrangement between competing firms would be a blueprint for disaster, but it *actually worked!* It worked so well, in fact, that Consolidated, North American, and Ford entered into a similar production organization to build the B-24, the other standard American heavy bomber.

Johnson had said that replacements for production types should be developed, which in turn would themselves become production types. With this in mind, it is little wonder that the BDV system would be considered a model for B-29 production as well.

A B-29 Liaison Committee, similar to the BDV Committee, was set up to coordinate what would soon be the most ambitious aircraft production effort of the war, involving not only Boeing, but (as of December 22, 1941, two weeks after the Japanese attack on Pearl Harbor) Bell Aircraft as well. The production capacity of these two firms was in turn to be supplemented by General Motors, the nation's leading industrial giant. The Liaison Committee worked out the details during a historic three-day series of meetings that began on February 10, 1942, chaired by Undersecretary of War Lovett, but really starring the dynamic Materiel Command boss, General Oliver Echols.

Echols had brought the Ford Motor Company's Willow Run plant into the B-24 consortium, and he was determined to see some of the magnificent production performance of the American automobile industry brought into the B-29 program. He wanted General Motors involved as well, but the latter insisted that it was too overcommitted to other war-related activities and could not participate. The B-29 Liaison Committee had timidly agreed with GM, but Echols would have nothing of it. "General Motors is going to be in this program because General Motors *has* to be in this program." On February 12, Echols demanded, "I'm directing it to remain in our plans and to assume its full share of this greater burden."

Chaired by the Air Corps and headquartered in Seattle, the B-29 Liaison Committee was made up of representatives of the three major manufacturers to be included. Among them were Fred Collins from Boeing, B. A. Winter from Bell Aircraft, and A. P. Ripley from General Motors' Fisher Body Division.

Boeing was to supply the engineering data, blueprints, and templates to the prime contractors as well as tooling and manufacturing procedures and technical expertise. Because Boeing's Plant 2 at Boeing Field on the south side of Seattle was committed to B-17 production, the USAAF decided also to designate General Motors' Fisher Body plant at Cleveland, Ohio, and the North American Aviation factory at Kansas City, Missouri, as B-29 airframe facilities. The USAAF also decided to build two factories at Marietta, Georgia, and Wichita, Kansas, to be managed by Bell Aircraft and Boeing, respectively. Subcontractors that were lined up to produce major B-29 subassemblies included Cessna in Wichita, Kansas; Chrysler in Detroit, Michigan; Fisher Body in Cleveland, Ohio, as well as in Lansing and Grand Rapids, Michigan; Goodyear in Akron, Ohio; McDonnell in St. Louis, Missouri; and Republic in Farmingdale, New York.

In Seattle, where the first three XB-29 prototypes were being built (a third XB-29 was ordered in December 1940), Plant 2 would become a major B-29 production facility when (and if) it became feasible to phase out B-17 production. (Eventually, Plant 2 was designated as the "B-29C" facility, but the "C" series was canceled in 1945.) Meanwhile, however, North American was relieved of its B-29 commitment in order to concentrate on building B-25 bombers of its own design in Kansas City. Boeing had a new factory, just a few miles south of Seattle, at Renton, near the foot of Lake Washington, which it had constructed in anticipation of the production of 500 PBB-1 Sea Ranger flying boats that the Navy had ordered in June 1940. When the Navy canceled the Sea Ranger program, the Renton factory was quickly earmarked as a B-29 production facility.

Boeing's need for more engineers for its part of the project put it into conflict with the Selective Service in the spring of 1942. Draft boards were eyeing new engineering school graduates the same way they looked at everyone else, while Boeing saw them as an integral part of the effort required to get the B-29 off the ground. Despite the secrecy surrounding the B-29 project, the USAAF was able to reveal enough to the Selective Service for Boeing to get the people it needed.

The participation by General Motors in the B-29 consortium (which Echols so fervently demanded) was, however, doomed. In September 1942 the company advanced a peculiar scheme to create a hybrid fighter plane based on the V-3420-19 water-cooled engine being developed by its Allison engine division. The proposal called for an airplane with Curtiss P-40 wings, a Douglas SBD tail, and Vought F4U landing gear. This strange creation, nicknamed "Eagle," in which the body parts of three dissimilar aircraft would be brought together around a new engine, was contracted for by the Materiel Division and given the designation XP-75. In June 1943, the USAAF approved plans to build 2500 "Fisher Eagles" at General Motors' Fisher Body plant in Cleveland, which had heretofore been earmarked for the B-29 program. Ultimately there were only six P-75s completed, but the essential fact in this aside is that the effort thrown into the Fisher's mongrel Eagle had permanently removed the Cleveland plant from the B-29 production consortium. General Motors was in turn replaced by the Glenn L. Martin Company, with its 84-acre plant at Omaha, Nebraska. Ironically, the Martin Omaha site was to become the USAAF's Offutt Field in 1946, and the headquarters of the Strategic Air Command.

Having laid out an elaborate blueprint for the production of the B-29, the members of the B-29 Liaison Committee faced no small task in putting together all the pieces. Not only would they have to design and build an extremely advanced and complex aircraft under wartime conditions, but they would first have to design and build the most complicated network of factories ever dedicated to a single aircraft.

Irving Brinton Holley, Jr., would write in *Buying Aircraft: Materiel Procurement for the Army Air Forces*, the official Department of the Army history of this era:

> The B-29 program was the most complex joint production undertaking of the war. This in itself made effective co-ordination a requisite of the utmost importance. The many changes in contractors along the way only served to emphasize the need for the closest kind of production control. So too did the highly experimental character of the bomber itself, which meant that design changes were numerous in every stage of the program. There

INSET: Clairmont "Claire" Egtvedt, president of Boeing. The B-29 helped to realize his dream that Boeing would become the "World Center of Four-Engine Airplane Development." (*Boeing photo*)

TOP: The team that made the Superfortress possible: (*left to right*) George Schairer, Ed Wells, Wellwood Beall, N. D. Showalter, and Lysle Wood. (*Boeing photo*)

BOTTOM: The B-17 Flying Fortress, Boeing's first four-engine, full-production bomber, provided the valuable experience that would make the B-29 possible. (*Boeing photo*)

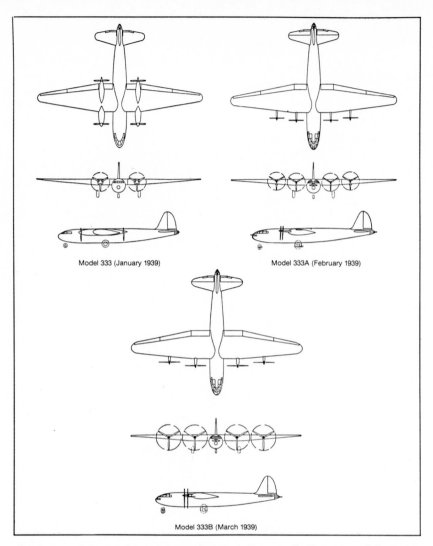

Model 333 (January 1939)

Model 333A (February 1939)

Model 333B (March 1939)

The design of the Model 333 series departed dramatically from that of the B-17. Several radical engine placement concepts were tried and rejected, including the "pusher-tractor" layout of the Model 333 and the flat, totally flush Wright engines on the Model 333A that were actually retained in the Model 334. (*Boeing photo*)

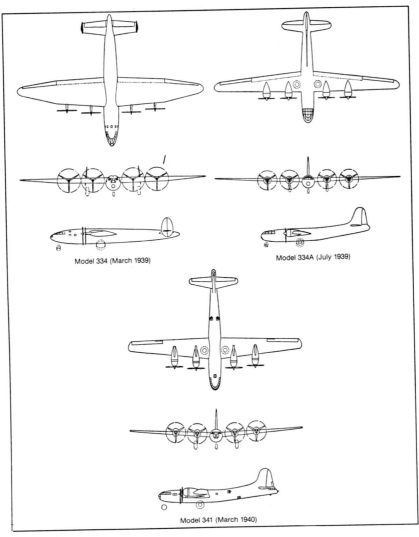

Model 334 (March 1939)

Model 334A (July 1939)

Model 341 (March 1940)

The Model 334 was little more than a twin-tailed Model 333B, but the Model 334A had many features that appeared on the B-29 as it went into production. The Model 341 featured George Shairer's Model 115 wing, a precursor to the Model 117 wing that was to help give the B-29 such outstanding load-carrying ability. (*Boeing photo*)

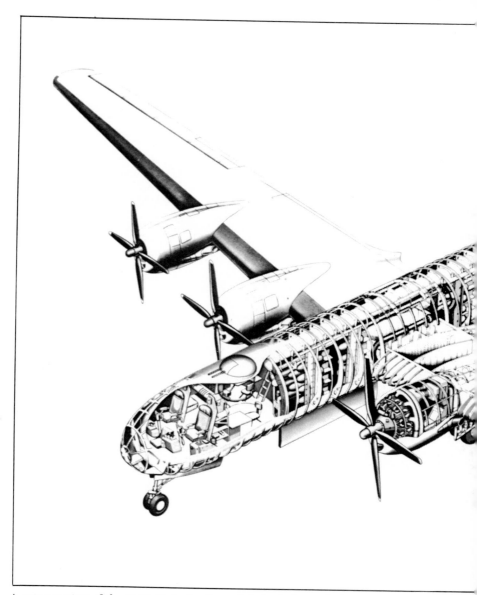

A cutaway view of the B-29. Note the forward flight deck in which pilot, copilot, and bombardier were all positioned *together* in a single large "greenhouse." In earlier bombers, such as Boeing's B-17, the bombardier was located farther away from the pilot, making communication difficult. The navigator's station is immediately behind the pilot. Both the "greenhouse" and the navigator's station were in a single pressurized cabin so that crewmen no longer had to wear clumsy flight suits and oxygen masks during high-altitude missions. The crewmen in the aft portion also occupied a pressurized cabin, and the two were connected by a tube-like crawl space that can be seen above the bomb bays. The ladder leading to the forward end of this tube is behind the navigator's chair.

The B-29 had two bomb bays, one ahead of and one behind the wing roots. When dropping the bombs, the bombardier had to keep the weight of the two bays roughly

equal because if one were to become lighter than the other the plane would be hard to control.

Another feature that set the B-29 apart from earlier bomber types was the gun turrets which, except for the tail turret, were handled by remote control from a gunner's station visible here beneath the small plexiglass bubble, immediately ahead of the rear top turret. The gunner sighted the guns through a periscope system.

This drawing is of an early production-model B-29, because later Superfortresses had four .50-caliber machine guns in the forward top turret. All other turrets contained two such weapons, while the tail turret also had a 20-mm cannon between the two machine guns. For the low-level raids conducted after March 9, 1945, General LeMay had the guns removed from all but the tail turret on many B-29s to save weight. (*Boeing photo*)

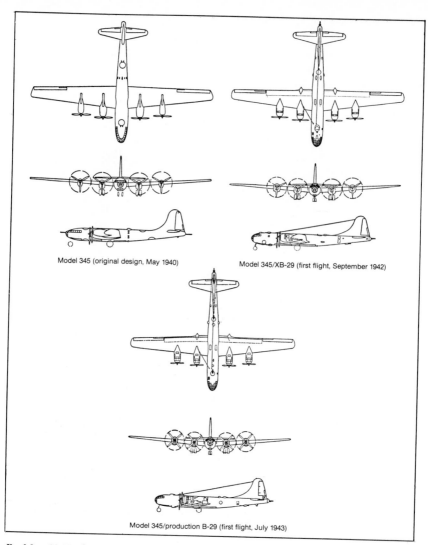

Model 345 (original design, May 1940)

Model 345/XB-29 (first flight, September 1942)

Model 345/production B-29 (first flight, July 1943)

By May 1940, the Model 341 had evolved into the Model 345. Only minor design revisions now separated the basic drawings from the production blueprints of the Superfortress. After the first XB-29 flights in the fall of 1942, the only major changes were a slightly redesigned tail turret and the replacement of three-bladed props by four-bladed ones. (*Boeing photo*)

TOP: On July 21, 1942, the highly secret XB-29 prototype was barged up the Duwamish River to its final assembly point in the sprawling Boeing Field complex. The U.S. Army stood guard with Garand and Thompson submachine guns as two Navy sailors and a private guard stood by. (*Boeing photo*)

MIDDLE: The first prototype XB-29 takes off from Boeing Field in Seattle for its maiden flight on September 21, 1942, with Eddie Allen at the controls. (*Boeing photo*)

BOTTOM: Test pilot Eddie Allen contemplates the second prototype XB-29 Superfortress. On February 18, 1943, a few weeks after this photo was taken, Allen met his death aboard this same aircraft. (*Boeing photo*)

TOP: When the first YB-29s to be built at Boeing's Wichita, Kansas, plant began their service test cycle on June 26, 1943, they were the same dark olive green as the early B-17s and the first XB-29. When the Superforts went into production, however, they had a natural metal finish because there was no longer any need for them to be camouflaged. (*Boeing photo*)

MIDDLE AND BOTTOM: The arsenal of democracy: B-29 Superfortresses undergo final assembly at Boeing's Renton, Washington, factory. (*Boeing photos*) were, for example, 1,174 engineering changes introduced even before the first item was officially accepted by the Air Forces. Some 900 of these had to be rushed through at the last minute as a result of findings made during flight tests.

Before the end of the war the various participating contractors turned out 3,628 B-29 Superforts for the sustained aerial assault on Japan. All this was possible only because tens of thousands of diverse details in factories all over the country were successfully harmonized into a single effective program.

THE CATALYST

With a date like December 7, 1941, burned into our historical memory, there is a tendency to forget that the B-29 planning that went on before December 7 during 1941 in Seattle, in Washington, and elsewhere was theoretical—the United States was still neutral and no one knew *when* we might actually enter the war. Through the "phony war" period in the winter of 1939–1940 it was easy to joke about World War II. Many called it a "sitzkrieg"— a declared war in which no fighting was taking place. However, by the summer of 1940, France and most of western Europe had been gobbled up in a matter of ten weeks, and only Britain was left—hanging by a thread. World War II was suddenly no laughing matter.

No crystal ball was needed to predict that the United States would inevitably be drawn into the conflict alongside the British with whom the Americans had stood in the previous world war a quarter century earlier. The questions that could not be answered, however, were *when?* and *how?*

Planners such as the AWPD group used a theoretical "M-day" pegged to April 1942. Other dates were also theorized but few could conceive that the United States would remain on the sidelines throughout 1942.

When the question arose of *how* the United States would enter the war, most people thought back to events of April 1917, the "wolf packs" of German submarines that prowled the Atlantic and the sinking of the liner *Lusitania* that catalyzed the American declaration of war in World War I. There had already been so many parallels between the two world wars that it was logical to predict that the backbreaking straw would be laid upon American neutrality by German hands. A surprise, however, was in store.

Billy Mitchell had not been alone in predicting that a war with Japan would begin one day with an attack on the United States naval facilities at Pearl Harbor, Hawaii. This notion, however, was a distinctly minority view. By mid-1941 Imperial Japan was deeply enmeshed in its pillage of China. While it certainly had designs on the riches of Southeast Asia, most analysts considered it absurd to think that Japan would cross thousands of miles of Pacific Ocean to attack a major naval base in the American backyard.

The events of December 7, 1941, were a bitter vindication of Billy Mitchell. The Japanese not only fulfilled his prediction of an attack on Pearl Harbor, but also proved that air power could sink battleships—the heaviest of combat vessels—in wartime. Of the American battleships anchored on Pearl Harbor's "battleship row," four were sunk and one was beached in sinking condition. (Three of these ships were later raised and recommissioned, but had the battle taken place at sea rather than in a *shallow* harbor, all five would have been lost.) It was the worst American naval defeat in modern history, and every bit of damage had been rendered by *aircraft!*

Three days later, on December 10, across the international dateline off the east coast of the Malay Peninsula, Japanese air power underscored the lesson it had inflicted at Pearl Harbor. The British battleship *HMS Prince of Wales* and battle cruiser *HMS Repulse*, sailing north from Singapore in response to a Japanese attack on Malaya, were located by Japanese bombers and sunk.

Simultaneous with the attacks on Pearl Harbor and Malaya the Japanese launched attacks on British and American positions throughout the Far East and the Pacific. Hong Kong, Guam, and Wake Island were in Japanese hands by the end of December 1941, and Singapore and the Philippines were taken in the dark opening months of 1942.

April 18, 1942, was the 167th anniversary of the "midnight ride" of Paul Revere, and the fortunes of the United States in World War II were about as low as they had been when the minutemen faced the British at Lexington and Concord. It had been a little more than a week since the American defenders of the Philippines had surrendered at Bataan. A Japanese invasion of the western United States was feared at any moment. Then suddenly, when Americans needed it most, their morale got an enormous boost.

Launched from the deck of the carrier *USS Hornet,* sixteen USAAF B-25 Mitchell bombers led by Colonel (soon to be Brigadier General) Jimmy Doolittle had bombed the heart of Japan! The raiders did little in the way of physical damage, but they demonstrated to the Japanese—as well as to the Americans—that Tokyo, like Hawaii, was vulnerable to air attack, and dealt a severe blow to Japanese morale. This one-of-a-kind operation could easily have failed, but it demonstrated that long-range bombing was possible, and implied the likelihood of a repeat performance. It gave Americans hope just as it gravely worried the Japanese.

Hap Arnold knew, however, that this mission could not be repeated. The Doolittle raid had stretched existing technology to the limit. B-25 bombers were not designed to operate from carriers. It had taken extensive practice to train the crews for this hazardous operation and it was a near-miracle that all of them successfully took off from the *Hornet*'s rain-swept flight deck. The Japanese had known that there were no bases from which existing long-range American bombers (B-17s and B-24s) could attack Japan. At the same time they knew the range of conventional short-range carrier-based aircraft. What they hadn't figured on was that the Americans would split the difference and risk a carrier-based attack from a farther distance with *medium*-range bombers that were technically too large for carrier operations. Even so, the *Hornet* had had to venture deep into Japanese waters to launch the Doolittle raid, and "once bitten, twice shy," the Japanese Imperial Navy would widen its defenses to make another such attack impossible. The very reasons that had made the attack such a surprise were those that mitigated against its repetition.

From the American military point of view, the Doolittle mission simply hadn't inflicted enough substantive damage to risk repetition, and the morale-boosting potential of a *second* raid wouldn't justify taking another chance. From a practical standpoint, so much fuel had to be carried that the effective bomb load was greatly reduced. Furthermore, *none* of the B-25s had managed to reach the bases in China where they were supposed to land. Fifteen crash-landed in China short of the intended landing sites, and one landed in the Soviet Union, where it was confiscated and its crew interned. Most of the crewmen survived the daring mission, but 100 percent losses of aircraft on missions with small bomb loads would be hard for the fledging USAAF to support. Before Tokyo could be bombed a second time, the USAAF would need bigger, longer-range bombers and secure bases. The USAAF would need the B-29.

In August 1942, four months after the Doolittle raid, the President went back to the Air Staff for an estimate of the airplanes that should be produced in 1943 in order for the USAAF to obtain air supremacy over the Axis air forces. The Air War Plans Division developed a new plan which was very much like AWPD-1, but which profited from the war experience that had been accumulated. The air objective of AWPD-42, as the new plan came to be designated, was the same as that of AWPD-1: destruction of the will and capability of Germany to continue the war, combined with the air support of an invasion if that should still be necessary. Two targets were added to the primary target list: submarine construction yards and synthetic rubber production plants.

The Air War Plans Division also made some major changes in deployment. In the first plan, forty-four groups of six-engine—as yet unbuilt—very long range aircraft had been allocated to the strategic air war against Axis Europe, because at that time it was impossible to tell whether England was going to survive. If Russia collapsed—as the intelligence people were estimating would occur in the summer of 1943—German armies and air forces would be released to attack England. The Nazis would have had the production capacity of all Europe to back up their military requirements, and bases in England would almost surely have been made untenable. If that had been the case, the USAAF would have had to fight from bases located within the Western Hemisphere. The USAAF had a preliminary design on the boards for a six-engine bomber—the Consolidated B-36—with a range that would be even greater than that of the B-29. It was because of the uncertainty of bases in England that the B-36s had been included in the first plan. By August 1942, however, it was apparent that England was going to survive, and so in AWPD-42, the B-36s were eliminated and ultimately postponed until 1946. Meanwhile, the Air War

Plans Division knew that the B-29s wouldn't be ready for two years, and it was reasoned that by that time the fortunes of war in Europe would have gone against Hitler, so that the USAAF could then afford to turn attention to the Japanese.

With the arrival of early autumn 1942, the fortunes of war had finally changed. England would survive, and although the United States wasn't winning yet, neither were we on the run. In May, the line had been held on Guadalcanal, and the Japanese advance had been blunted in the Battle of the Coral Sea. In June, American air power had defeated the Japanese fleet at Midway in our first major victory of the war. In August, American B-17s bombed Nazi-occupied Europe for the first time, and it was starting to look less likely that either the Germans or the Japanese would ever be able to launch air attacks against the continental United States.

THE ORGANIZATION

The U.S. Army Air Forces were growing rapidly to meet the expanding needs of a nation at war. From 51,165 men in 1940, the air arm grew to 764,415 in 1942. It was an expansion unprecedented in history, but it nevertheless would be dwarfed by the planned growth to a strength of over 2 *million* in 1943. With this in mind, the Air Staff reorganized the USAAF by establishing the numbered Army Air Force (the airmen preferred to use the term *Air Forces*) as its major component. The Army's ground forces had done the same sort of thing some years earlier by establishing four *numbered* armies in the four geographical quadrants of the continental United States.

To some extent, the USAAF followed this pattern by replacing the Northeast, Northwest, Southeast and Southwest Air Districts with the First, Second, Third and Fourth Air Forces. In February 1942 the former Far Eastern Air Force, once headquartered at Clark Field in the Philippines (but driven south to Australia by the Japanese invasion), became the Fifth Air Force, while the former Caribbean Air Force based in the Panama Canal Zone, and charged with its defense, became the Sixth Air Force. The Hawaiian Air Force, based at Hickam Field, adjacent to Pearl Harbor, was the first USAAF component to see action in the war. Its losses were much less than those suffered by the Navy at Pearl Harbor, but 163 airmen lost their lives, and 152 out of 231 aircraft were destroyed. Nonetheless, several Hawaiian Air Force fighters were able to engage the enemy, and Lieutenant George Welch shot down four Japanese aircraft. In February 1942, the Hawaiian Air Force was redesignated as the Seventh Air Force, and by September the bulk of its aircraft had been rotated to the South Pacific where it would begin striking back at the Japanese.

The first numbered air force *specifically created* for offensive operations against the Axis was the Eighth Air Force, which was based in England. The Eighth became identified exclusively with heavy bombers and their supporting units and fighter escorts. The Ninth Air Force (also in England) was created in November 1942 as an umbrella organization for light bombers, ground support, and other tactical air power.

The Tenth Air Force was established in India to oversee operations in South and Southeast Asia, and the Eleventh Air Force was created around the former Alaskan Air Force in response to the Japanese invasion of the Aleutian Islands. The Twelfth Air Force was an amalgam of the USAAF units in North Africa and the Mediterranean area. In December 1942, the USAAF units in the South Pacific, which were not part of the Seventh Air Force, were designated as the Thirteenth Air Force, the so-called "Jungle Air Force."

In June 1944, the Fifth and Thirteenth Air Forces would be placed within a structure called the Far East Air Forces (FEAF) under the command of General George Kenney, who answered directly to General Douglas MacArthur, the supreme Allied commander in the Pacific theater. (In July 1945, the Seventh Air Force would join the Fifth and Thirteenth as part of the FEAF.)

Thus it was that there were thirteen numbered air forces in place within the USAAF by the end of 1942. In March 1943, the China Air Task Force of the Tenth Air Force under General Claire Chennault was elevated in status, becoming the Fourteenth Air Force. (The China Air Task Force was created before U.S. entry into the war and was known as the American Volunteer Group— the "Flying Tigers"—of the Chinese Air Force.) In November

1943, in light of USAAF offensive operations against Italy and Axis positions in southern Europe, heavy bomber units in the Mediterranean theater would be consolidated under the Fifteenth Air Force, which thereby became the southern European counterpart of the Eighth Air Force in England. In December 1943, in fact, an entity called the U.S. Strategic Air Forces in Europe (USSAFE) was established to coordinate the strategic bombing activities of the Eighth and the Fifteenth.

By the end of 1943, the USAAF personnel strength had risen to 2,197,114, and was spread around the world within an organization composed of fifteen operational numbered air forces, which were in turn supported by the Air Materiel Command, the Air Transport Command, and the USAAF Training Command. In terms of manpower and number of aircraft—and indeed in terms of its global scope—it was the largest air force the world had ever seen, or would ever see. And it was growing even larger—by the end of 1944, the USAAF would have 78,757 aircraft and 2,372,292 personnel.

Yet, despite being the largest air force in history, it was still part of the Army, and its archipelago of numbered air forces were all under the jurisdiction of theater commanders! The Eighth, Ninth, Twelfth, and Fifteenth Air Forces were under General Dwight D. Eisenhower, while the Fifth, Seventh, and Thirteenth answered ultimately to General Douglas MacArthur.

Hap Arnold had realized as early as the fall of 1942, when he toured the Pacific theater, that placing the B-29s under a theater commander would be a mistake. Such a commander was concerned only with what was going on in his own theater of operations, and would feel obligated to divert the B-29s to tactical targets as needed rather than allowing them to concentrate on conducting a continuous, unrelenting strategic air offensive outside his theater against Japan—which was the B-29's ultimate purpose.

Thus the notion was conceived by Arnold and his Air Staff that Arnold should command the B-29s *himself*. A new air force—the Twentieth—would be set up directly under the Joint Chiefs of Staff, with Arnold serving as its commander as an *agent* of the Joint Chiefs. Arnold was reluctant to take on yet another chore—certainly, running the world's largest air force in a global war was no small task—but he recognized the need. There was no way that the Twentieth Air Force could be allowed to become just the Pacific equivalent of the Eighth or the Fifteenth.

The B-29 force, as Arnold later recalled,

> would operate directly against the Japanese homeland, which influenced the movements of both MacArthur and Nimitz. Yet with operating areas set up as they were, I could do nothing but retain command of the B-29s myself—something I did not want to do. I could not give them to MacArthur because then they would operate ahead of Nimitz's command; I could not give them to Nimitz since in that case they would operate ahead of Mac-Arthur's advance. So, in the end, while everybody wondered why I kept personal command of the Twentieth Air Force—the B-29s—there was nothing else I could do, with no unity of command in the Pacific. I could find no one out there who wanted unity of command, seemingly, unless he himself was made Supreme Commander.

Everything about the Twentieth would be special. It would be a new and separate numbered Army Air Force designated to manage *all* the B-29s and *only* the B-29s. Even its name was special. With fifteen air forces in place, it should have become the sixteenth, but Arnold went to the next round number and called it the *Twentieth*. And Arnold would control it directly from his seat on the Joint Chiefs of Staff, just as though it were *itself* another theater of the war! There was the European theater, the Mediterranean theater, the Pacific theater, and the Twentieth Air Force!

Just as the other air forces were composed of specific commands, so too was the Twentieth. The Eighth Air Force had its Eighth Bomber Command, its Eighth Fighter Command to escort the bombers of the Eighth Bomber Command, and the Eighth Air Support Command to take care of everyone else; so the Twentieth would also have commands—bomber commands!

The new Twentieth Air Force was not officially "constituted and activated" until April 4, 1944, and General Arnold did not officially assume command until April 6. As such the Twentieth Air Force was actually *preceded* by its first bomber command, the appropriately numbered Twentieth Bomber Command formed at Smoky

Hill Army Air Field on November 20, 1943, and which at that time was composed only of General K. B. Wolfe's Fifty-Eighth Bomb Wing. The Fifty-Eighth would, in fact, be the only wing ever assigned to the Twentieth Bomber Command. The Twentieth Bomber Command had actually been born in August 1943 as the First Bomber Command of the Second Air Force, and was composed at the time of all the assets that had once belonged to the USAAF Antisubmarine Command, which was closed down when the USAAF had agreed to transfer all such activities to the Navy.

The headquarters of the Twentieth Bomber Command remained at Smoky Hill Field until General Wolfe took the advanced echelon to New Delhi, India, in January 1944. The Twentieth Bomber Command was not, however, officially assigned to the Twentieth Air Force until April 19.

The second bomber command assigned to the Twentieth Air Force was the Twenty-First. It was originally established on March 1, 1944, at Smoky Hill Field, under the Second Air Force, and over the 73d Bombardment Wing, which had been earmarked for the Twentieth Bomber Command, but was diverted in order to build up the strength of the Twenty-First at a faster pace. The Twenty-First Bomber Command was assigned to the Twentieth Air Force on August 28, 1944. General Hansell was given command, and he took it out to Saipan on October 12. Eventually it would have five wings, *including* the Fifty-Eighth.

When plans for the Twentieth Air Force were originally drawn up, it was envisioned as being composed of *four* bomber commands, each one driving at the heart of the Japanese Empire from a different point on the compass. The Twentieth would be based in China, and the Twenty-First in the Marianas, while the Twenty-Second would be based in the Philippines or Formosa, and the Twenty-Third would be based at Shemya Army Air Field at the tip of the Aleutian Islands. As a practical matter, the Marianas turned out to be by far the best place to base the B-29s for the final assault against Japan. Thus, Arnold decided not to activate the Twenty-Second or Twenty-Third Bomber Commands but instead to pour all the wings, groups, *and* B-29s into the Twenty-First alone.

The unique organizational structure that had been created for the B-29 force gave American airmen the long-awaited opportunity to demonstrate the war-winning potential of strategic air power. The Twentieth Air Force was the beginning of Billy Mitchell's dream come true, but before that dream could truly be fulfilled, the men of the Twentieth Air Force would need an airplane which itself was without precedent—the Boeing B-29 Superfortress.

III

The Birth of the Superfortress
1942–1944

September 21, 1942, was clear and warm as fall days in the Pacific Northwest often are. The big hangar doors at Boeing's plant 2 were pushed open, and out it rolled, a huge olive-drab monster, its Wright Cyclones adorned with three-bladed props. The plane was a dream come true, the culmination of efforts dating back to Billy Mitchell's concept of American air power, Claire Egtvedt's vision of Boeing leadership in the genre of four-engine strategic bombers, and Hap Arnold's dogged determination that *his* air force should have the very best that could possibly be built. Designated XB-29-B0—experimental bomber, type 29—and built by Boeing in Seattle, the plane was so big that the USAAF refused to call it a "heavy bomber," and so the appellation "*very* heavy bomber" was born.

With its swan-graceful vertical stabilizer, a feature that had been an innovation created for the B-17E the year before, it was clearly a true descendant of the older Flying Fortress. As on that day seven years before at this very field when the XB-17 was named Flying Fortress, the given name for this new bird could be nothing else—it was the *Superfortress!*

The test pilot for the Superfortress's maiden voyage was himself the stuff from which legends are made. Edmund T. "Eddie" Allen was a small man with thinning hair and a Clark Gable mustache. A vegetarian who practiced yoga, dabbled in Egyptology, and enjoyed poetry, he was nothing less than the world's greatest test pilot.

Born on January 4, 1896, in Chicago, he had been at the University of Illinois for a year when the United States entered the First World War. Enlisting in the Army Signal Corps, Allen found himself in England observing aircraft test procedure. After the war, he left the Army to become a test pilot for the new National Advisory Committee for Aeronautics (NACA). In 1920 he entered the Massachusetts Institute of Technology, and in 1923 he began his career as a free-lance test pilot and consulting engineer.

Over the next two decades Eddie Allen designed gliders, led the American glider team to Europe, flew air mail across the Rockies, and tested airplanes for nearly every airline and aircraft manufacturer in the United States. He became a recognized expert in the flight testing of large aircraft, and soon he had found a natural home at Boeing. After Les Tower was killed in the first B-17, Eddie Allen took over the controls of the Flying Fortress program. He test-flew the XB-15, the Model 307 Stratoliner, and Wellwood Beall's Model 314 Clipper. When Lockheed was ready to test its huge Constellation transport, it sent to Seattle to borrow Eddie Allen from Boeing.

By the time he urged the first XB-29 off the Boeing Field runway at 3:40 p.m. on September 21, 1942, Allen probably knew as much about the big plane as anyone. He had been one of its most thorough students, and as chief of Boeing's flight test and aerodynamics staff, he had played an active part in its development.

At 4:45 that afternoon, Allen brought the XB-29 back safely to Boeing Field. Stepping from the cockpit, he was greeted by Wellwood Beall, everyone from the Model 345 engineering staff, and a million questions.

"She flew," he grinned.

Considering the source, nothing more really needed to be said, but Wellwood Beall's memo to Washington at 5:25 p.m. that afternoon was slightly more verbose: "Eddie Allen reports we have an excellent airplane."

By December 2 the XB-29 had logged five minutes short of eighteen hours, and the test team was ready for flight testing at 25,000 feet. The Superfortress itself was performing perfectly, but there were problems with the Cyclone engines. On December 28, two of the four engines failed at 6800 feet. They were replaced, but within the week another engine had failed. On December 30, Eddie Allen took the second XB-29 on its first flight, and once again there were engine problems, the most ominous to date. The number four engine had *caught fire* at 3000 feet. Unable to extinguish it, Allen quickly returned to Boeing Field where ground crews finally doused the flaming engine.

No one knew better than Eddie Allen that the Superfortress *had* to work. Boeing had its reputation on the line, and so did Hap Arnold. The chief of the USAAF had already ordered the plane into production. This action was verging on the reckless, but Arnold had made sure there were 1664 orders for B-29s on the books before Allen took the first one into the air. He knew that the program had to be accelerated if the Superfortress was to get into service as soon as possible. There was no turning back now. Not only must the B-29 itself work, but the Wright Cyclones with which it was born would also have to work.

On January 31, 1943, however, the number two engine on the second XB-29 failed at 20,000 feet, and on February 17 a serious fuel leak was detected just aft of the number four engine.

The next day, Thursday, February 18, dawned overcast and cold in Seattle—the very opposite of that day in September when the first XB-29 made its historic flight. Eddie Allen was in the cockpit of the big, silver second prototype at 10:40 a.m., and the crew began to go through the routine preflight check. That day the crew included Robert Dansfield in the copilot's seat, Fritz Mohn as flight engineer, Robert Maxfield observing engine monitoring instrumentation, Barclay Henshaw as photorecorder observer, and Harry Ralston as radio man. Vincent North was the aerodynamicist, and the four flight test engineers were Raymond Basel, Charles Blaine, Thomas Lankford, and Edward Ireland Wersebe, a highly regarded aerodynamics engineer and the world's third-ranking airman in point of flying hours spent above 30,000 feet altitude. Because of this expertise, Wersebe was a key member of the test team for the Superfortress, an aircraft whose operating environment would be at higher altitudes than any bomber before it.

At 12:11 the XB-29 took off and climbed to 5000 feet. At 12:16 a fire broke out in the number one engine nacelle. Allen feathered the prop and closed the throttle while Fritz Mohn closed the cowling flaps and engaged the carbon dioxide fire extinguisher. Allen made the decision to return to the field. "Fire in number one engine," he reported. "Coming in. Had fire in engine and used CO_2 bottle and think we have it under control."

"Tell us if at any time you think you need fire equipment," came the reply.

Then, at 12:21, Allen made contact with Boeing's field at Renton. "Renton, 2400 feet descending. Request immediate landing clearance. Number one engine was on fire. Propeller feathered and trouble not serious. Order crash equipment to stand by."

Allen knew that he had a problem, but in his usual calm, deliberate way he was certain that it could be handled. The tower immediately cleared the XB-29 to land, giving wind speed and runway, and at 12:24 the plane was over Lake Washington and just minutes from safety when Allen told the tower: "[We're over the] Lake Washington Bridge, 2500 feet—correction: 1500 feet."

Just then the tower overheard a crew member on the intercom "*Allen!*" The man was heard to exclaim, "Better get this thing down in a hurry—the wing spar's burning badly!"

For the great test pilot, an engine fire was a serious concern in the testing of a new aircraft, but this was suddenly a major crisis. At 12:25 came the bad news from Eddie Allen as he made a last desperate dash toward Boeing Field, Seattle. "Have fire equipment ready. Am coming in with a wing on fire."

By this time the doomed bird was at 1200 feet over downtown Seattle and losing altitude rapidly. The wing was engulfed in flames that were now licking at the fuselage and into the cabin within. Harry Ralston bailed out, but the plane was already too low. He struck a key power-line on the way down and was killed instantly. Electricity in southern Seattle flickered out. Ed Wersebe followed him out, but there wasn't even time for his parachute to open. Fifteen seconds later the faltering XB-29 struck the top of the five-story Frye meat packing plant. W. J. Yenne, a welder working at the nearby Todd Shipyards was at work in the forward end of the *USS Fletcher* Class destroyer when the power suddenly went out. He recalls that "without waiting a second, I went up to the main deck. A couple of fellows at the top of the stairs immediately pointed out the Frye Packing Company building across the waterway, where the plane had crashed a few seconds before. It rested on the packing plant's roof like a hen sitting on her nest. Even though the building was very large, both ends of the plane extended a small distance past the sides of the building. All of us wondered at first if it might be a passenger plane because of its bare aluminum color. Since this was Seattle, where Boeing had been producing the familiar B-17 for some time, everyone was familiar with the lines [shape] of that plane. The plane we were looking at had a similar, though longer and more slender appearing, shape. It was only a matter of minutes until every window became a fire-red square. Soon the building was swallowed by billowing black smoke. The man I rode to work with, Byron Moran, had been an employee of Pacific Power & Light, and still had his pass for being allowed into disaster areas. After work we drove to the area, where the sentrys let us pass into the cordoned-off area without question when Moran showed them his PP&L pass. A few short blocks before reaching the packing plant we passed the place where the men who had been on the plane had parachuted out. Of course their parachutes had not had time to open, and their bodies were still where they had landed, covered with blankets."

Inside the packing plant, the men on the building's lower floors feared that the cataclysm above was a Japanese air attack. Fortunately it was lunch hour and only a few men were on the top floor. Had the crash come an hour later, over 30 people would have been killed.

Eddie Allen and all the members of the test crew were dead, along with many of the Frye employees and several firemen. It was a test program disaster of unparalleled proportions. At the time, many people compared it to the October 30, 1935, crash of the XB-17 that had taken the life of Les Tower, but in many ways it was far more serious, since it had the potential to delay or destroy the USAAF's most important program. It was the equivalent of the *Apollo 1* fire on January 27, 1967, that nearly derailed the American lunar landing program, or the Mission 51-L/*Challenger* disaster (nineteen years and one day later) on January 28, 1986, that crippled and grounded the space shuttle program.

Unlike the situation with the space shuttle in the 1980s, however, there could be no turning back and no second thoughts. Arnold had committed himself to the B-29 project, and it *would* go forward. There were problems inherent in the decision to move into production without a flight test program, but they would just have to be overcome. Specific problems with the engines would have to be carefully diagnosed and quickly modified. The USAAF needed the Superfort, and it was going to have it. On time.

Beyond being the most ambitious and important USAAF development project, the B-29 program had also been one of the most secret. The loss of the lives of Eddie Allen and ten other key personnel, along with a costly prototype, was one thing, but the XB-29 had come down in the heart of a major urban area, its demise witnessed by perhaps tens of thousands, not to mention the dozens of firemen who fought the fire and the passersby who helped pull injured people from the burning Frye Packing Plant.

Fortunately—from the standpoint of secrecy—the second prototype (unlike the first) was unpainted, and many people mistook the big silver bird for an airliner. Witnesses had also had only a short glimpse of the XB-29 before it was enveloped by smoke, and so when wire services referred to it as a "four-engine bomber," it was inferred that the plane in question was simply a familiar B-17. The FBI descended upon the scene to further pull a veil of confusion around the doomed bomber, interviewing witnesses and emerging generally confident that no one had garnered more than a fleeting impression. The FBI had an ironic ally in the conflagration itself. So hot and furious were the flames that they consumed not only the lives of the XB-29's crew and a half dozen firemen, but the aircraft itself was reduced to a dustbin of charred aluminum fragments. In the still-classified photos that rest in Boeing's vaults, only the twisted hulks of the Superfort's Cyclones bear even a passing resemblance to airplane parts, as furrowed-faced FBI agents, clad in fedoras and Bogart-style trench coats, are seen sifting their way through the ruins of the erstwhile packing plant.

Their diligence came within a hair's breadth of being for

naught, however, as a Seattle city bus driver had taken some clear photos of the plane and submitted them for publication to his employee newspaper. The G-men managed to intercept that issue of the *City Transit Weekly,* and to recover every last one of the 500 copies that had been distributed before they reached the *Weekly*'s offices. The secret remained safe.

Meanwhile, work was moving ahead at full clip on the construction of the YB-29 service test Superforts at Boeing-Wichita. The first of these rolled out on April 15, with the periscopically sighted Sperry gun turrets originally planned for the Superfortress series now replaced by General Electric turrets, which were sighted directly from plexiglass blisters. The engines were the Wright Cyclone R-3350 Series 21 engines, upgraded from the R-3350 Series 13 used in the first two prototypes. The turbosupercharger overheating problem that had been the culprit in the February 18 crash was diagnosed and corrected. The major observable difference between the XB-29 and the YB-29 was that the latter was fitted with four-bladed Hamilton Standard propellers, rather than the three-bladed props that had characterized the first Superforts. The first YB-29 began flight tests at Wichita on June 26 shortly after the rollout in Seattle of the third and last XB-29 which itself was used to test many of the hundreds of engineering detail changes that were made in the aircraft's subsystems as the Superfortress program evolved.

Meanwhile, the USAAF had begun to design the operational plan for putting the B-29s into service. The questions of *when* and *where* had already been answered. As early as 1941, the Joint Chiefs had recognized that the Superfortress would not be in full production until June 1944, but having the service test YB-29 aircraft in June 1943 meant there would be twelve months to train the crews, work out the bugs, build the bases, and get enough of the early B-29 aircraft overseas to make a start. The question of *where* overseas that start would be had also been answered. As General Arnold put it:

We did not consider Germany as a possible target for the B-29s because we figured that by the time they were ready, the intensive bombardment schedule we were planning with our B-17s and B-24s would have [already] destroyed most of the industrial facilities, the communications systems, and other military objectives within Germany and German-controlled Europe. On the other hand, we figured Japan would be free from aerial bombardment until we could get the B-29s into the picture.

In mid-May 1943, three months after Eddie Allen's death and a month before the first flight of a service test YB-29, the Trident Conference was convened in Washington. At the Trident Conference, President Franklin D. Roosevelt, Prime Minister Winston Churchill, and the Anglo-American Combined Chiefs of Staff took up the question of the B-29's potential role in the war against Japan. Essential to the discussion was the issue of where the Superforts could be based. A quick glance at the geography of the region showed that the only places then under Allied control were in China, and a plan called "Setting Sun" was drawn up whereby the B-29s would be based near Changsha, about 1500 miles from Tokyo.

Under careful scrutiny, however, it became clear to the planners that maintaining complete bases in central China would be virtually impossible because they would be, essentially, behind enemy lines. The Japanese controlled all the sea and land access to the region and the only way in would be by air across the Himalayas. The *B-29s themselves* could be flown into such bases, but the problem was that the *bases* would have to be flown in as well. Setting Sun thus evolved into a plan code-named "Twilight" that included, among other provisions, the notion of basing the B-29s at locations in India that could be supplied more easily and then staging the bombing missions through *advanced* fields in China.

While Twilight itself was rejected at the Quadrant Conference at Quebec in August 1943, the India-China basing idea was not, and this element of the old plan became the cornerstone of a further plan which was taken up in September. The new plan envisioned the Japanese-held Mariana Islands in the mid-Pacific as the ideal B-29 base, but recognized that by the time the Superfortress was ready, the Mariana Islands would not yet be under Allied control. The invasion of the Marianas, which was originally scheduled for early 1946, was recommended to coincide with the target date for full-scale production of the B-29 in mid-1944. In the meantime, the India-China basing scenario not only would soothe the Chinese, whose foreign minister T. V. Soong had been at Quadrant pressing for more Allied military aid, but also would mean that the B-29s would be able to hit Japan at the earliest possible moment—with or without the Marianas.

General Arnold, in turn, asked that the B-29 basing plan be reconsidered at the Sextant Conference which was set to be held at Cairo in November 1943. President Roosevelt liked the plan. He had made many promises to Chiang Kai-shek without yet being able to live up to them, but here at last was an opportunity to do something that would enlist the enthusiasm of Chiang Kai-shek and his Chinese Nationalist forces in the war at a time when it was quite possible they might collapse. The President took up the idea with Chiang Kai-shek and with British Prime Minister Churchill, and sold it over the objections of the American Joint Chiefs of Staff, the Joint Logistics Committee, and the Joint Plans Committee. It was a military-political plan at the most, but its objectives *were* political: to keep Chiang Kai-shek in the war, to initiate B-29 operations against the Japanese home islands, and to avoid committing the B-29s to areas from which they might not be rediverted to the strategic air offensive against Japan.

At Cairo, Possum Hansell and members of the Air Staff persuaded the Joint Chiefs of Staff to direct the Navy-dominated Pacific Ocean Area Command to capture the Marianas as bases for the B-29s. The Marianas were within range of the Japanese home islands and could be supplied by sea much more easily than the advanced bases in China could be supplied by airlift across the treacherous Himalayas.

General Hansell received permission from General Arnold to discuss command arrangements for the B-29s in the Pacific with Admiral Ernest J. King. As commander of the U.S. Fleet, chief of Naval Operations, and a member of the Joint Chiefs of Staff, Admiral King controlled the Pacific Ocean area, where the Marianas would be used as B-29 bases. Hansell told him that the USAAF had a problem that was very similar to that pertaining to the Navy. In the Navy, combat ships may be stationed in ports anywhere, but the port commanders and the frontier commanders do not command them. Each ship has a captain, and is under a chain of command that goes all the way back to the chief of Naval Operations, or the commander of the United States Fleet, both of whom were, at this time, Admiral King himself. This allowed King to concentrate the warships in the areas of critical combat without having to go through lengthy arguments with local commanders about releasing them. Naval base commanders and area commanders were required to supply and protect and provide administrative support for combat ships in port, but they had no jurisdiction over the employment of the ships in combat.

General Hansell asked Admiral King whether he thought it might be reasonable to set up an air command somewhat like the Navy system. The Twentieth Air Force would control the B-29s wherever they might be, while at the same time requiring theater commanders to defend them, to build bases, and to provide heavy supplies. Hansell explained that the chain of command would go from the combat units all the way back to the Joint Chiefs of Staff, with General Arnold commanding the force as its executive agent. "To my enormous relief," General Hansell recalls, "he thought a moment and said, 'I could find such an arrangement agreeable.'"

President Roosevelt had in fact given his approval to the China-India B-29 basing plan—now code-named "Matterhorn"—on November 10, 1943, in Cairo, just before he met with Prime Minister Churchill and Chiang Kai-shek. The title page of Matterhorn called for the "early sustained bombing of Japan." At last there was a blueprint for a strategic air offensive against Japan. This also gave Roosevelt a bargaining chip to use with Chiang at the conference, but as a practical matter the Combined Chiefs didn't give their final nod to the plan until April 10, 1944, after the first echelons of the B-29 force were already in China.

While the Allied leadership was concerning itself with the B-29's place on the war's global chessboard, the USAAF tackled the job of transforming the Superfortress from a skittish test bird into a combat-ready warplane. Soon after the Eddie Allen disaster, General Arnold assigned the task of troubleshooting this transition to Brigadier General Kenneth B. "K. B." Wolfe of the Materiel Command. Arnold told Wolfe to expedite B-29 production and pull in needed personnel from *anywhere* in the USAAF.

Wolfe moved quickly. Even before the Trident Conference back in May 1943 had decided what to do about the Setting Sun plan, he had laid the groundwork for the first B-29 operational training units. On June 1, 1943, the first flight of a YB-29 was still three weeks away when he established the 58th Bombardment Wing at Bell's Marietta, Georgia, Superfort factory. On September 15, as production B-29s began spilling out of the factories on the heels of the service test YB-29s, Wolfe relocated his headquarters to Smoky Hill Army Air Field near Salina, Kansas, and activated five *Very Heavy* Bombardment Groups—the 40th, 444th, 462nd, 468th, and 472nd—as components of his 58th Bomb Wing.

The only problem now was that the planes pouring into Smoky Hill were not ready for combat, and they were still plagued by engine problems. In normal times the assembly line would have been shut down and the problems corrected before planes were built, but these were anything but normal times. Modification centers were set up from Alabama to Colorado to fix the B-29s before they got to Smoky Hill.

In November 1943 while Franklin Roosevelt was in Cairo promising B-29s and asking Chiang Kai-shek to start building airfields, Colonel Leonard "Jake" Harmon, the Materiel Command's B-29 project flight test officer, was filing a report with Wright Field detailing the defects that still persisted in the Superfortress. It read virtually like a parts list, from carburetor airduct baffles to fuel cells, from exhaust cylinder heads to exhaust valves. On top of this, the planes were coming in from the modification centers with nonstandard equipment and incomplete inspections. In the meanwhile, Chiang Kai-shek had said he could promise to build airfields at Chengtu if Roosevelt could promise that there would be B-29s on them by April 15, 1944. No problem, said Roosevelt.

This meant that the first combat-ready B-29s would have to start flying out of Smoky Hill on March 10. Assuming that this three-month deadline could be met, Arnold sent General Wolfe out to the Far East in December to prepare for the arrival of the B-29s. On March 8, two days before the B-29s were scheduled to start following Wolfe's trail to India, Arnold flew into Smoky Hill to see how things were going. When Arnold inquired how many B-29s would be ready to leave for India on March 10 and was told "none," he became livid.

"I was appalled at what I found," Arnold said later. "There were shortages in all kinds and classes of equipment. The engines were not fitted with the latest gadgets; *the planes were not ready to go*. It would be impossible for them to be anywhere *near* China by the 15th of April unless some drastic measures were taken."

And drastic measures they were. During the next five weeks, in what would be called the "Battle of Kansas," Arnold stood the whole program on its head. If the Chinese could build the airfields—by hand—by April 15, then the Americans could build the bombers and deliver them to those airfields by April 15.

For Hap Arnold, the Battle of Kansas was no clever euphemism applied to a logistical setback—it was Stalingrad. It was a battle that *could not* be lost. If it were lost, there would be no tomorrow for the dream of autonomous strategic air power in World War II. In a grand global conflict in which logistics proved again and again to be the critical factor in narrow—yet decisive—victories, the Battle of Kansas was a major turning point.

The logistic problems inherent in producing a plane as complex as the B-29 would have been monstrous under the best of conditions, but the B-29s had to be produced quickly, and this led to their starting to roll off the assembly line before all the engineering changes were made. There were fifty-four major modifications that had to be made to every B-29 that came off the line in 1944. The areas affected included the electric system, the fire control system, the propeller-feathering system, the tires, and of course the engines, the most complex part of an incredibly complex aircraft. Eventually it would be possible to make these changes on the assembly line, but in March 1944, they would have to be made on the flight line, and the necessary parts were spread out in subassembly factories and warehouses all over the country.

Arnold's first step was to assign Major General Bennett E. "Benny" Meyers, then in charge of aircraft procurement for the USAAF, as his field commander for the Battle of Kansas. In the wave of second-guessing that followed the war, Benny Meyers would find himself called on the congressional carpet for holding stock in companies from which he procured goods or services for the USAAF, but in the Battle of Kansas, his gift for cutting a deal came down squarely on the side of the B-29 program.

Meyers spent the next five weeks on the telephone, begging, threatening, and sweet-talking the firms—in many of which he owned stock—whose cooperation meant the difference between success and failure for Billy Mitchell's posthumous dream. At the modification centers across Kansas—at Great Bend and Pratt, at Walker and Salina—people went on double shifts as the trickle of parts and critical subassemblies became an avalanche. Benny Meyers demanded, and the vast archipelago of suppliers responded.

The Battle of Kansas was typical of a great many efforts waged by Americans at home and abroad during World War II, when the chips were really down. The work went on night and day— with much of it completed outdoors on flight lines in subzero weather and howling snowstorms. One B-29 was flown to England to be tested on a long-range overwater flight. This well-publicized British diversion also helped to boost morale in England and to give the Germans the erroneous impression that the B-29 effort might be directed toward them.

Finally, on March 26, 1944, less than three weeks after the Battle of Kansas began, Jake Harmon led the first B-29s out of Smoky Hill, bound for Gander, Newfoundland, and points east. On the flight across North Africa between Marrakesh and Cairo, however, the Wright Cyclones developed serious overheating problems. Despite its apparent victory in the Battle of Kansas, the B-29 was still beset by bugs. Once again there would have to be flight-line modifications, but this time it was in the parched desert outside Cairo, 7630 air miles from the blizzards of the Kansas prairies. The B-29 force was grounded in Cairo for a week while technicians were flown in to overhaul the bombers. The basic problem was traced to the fact that the engines were not designed to operate at ground temperatures above 115° F, and the cylinders were literally melting in the blistering North African heat. Flying out of Cairo on the 2400 mile hop to Karachi, however, was literally a case of exchanging the frying pan for the fire. Temperatures on the ground in Karachi reached 120° F, and inside the B-29s they approached 200° F. Some engines even came within 20° of overheating while they were standing still. Engine baffles were redesigned literally overnight and rushed to the stricken planes, and crossover tubes were hastily designed by the globe-trotting technicians that had earlier raced to Cairo. These tubes were, in turn, retrofitted on the spot in Karachi to pump more oil to the rear cylinders most susceptible to overheating.

Meanwhile, K. B. Wolfe sat in the sweltering tropical heat of the base in Chakulia, outside Calcutta, watching and waiting. The bomber force was scheduled to arrive between April 1 and April 15. April 1 came and went without a sign of the airplanes and no word about their progress. The following day, however, Jake Harmon roared down out of the blue, delivering the first Superfortress to India. By April 15, there were 32 B-29s at their bases in India, and by May 8 the number had grown to 130. In the meanwhile, General Wolfe and Fifty-Eighth Bomb Wing commander General LeVerne "Blondie" Saunders had flown the first B-29s across the "Hump" into China on April 24. Of this first group of 150, 5 Superforts were lost to engine failure and 4 were seriously damaged. With the engines modified, however, only 3 more B-29s were lost in the next wave of 275 planes sent to India.

It was a grueling hell, climbing the big bombers over the rugged Himalayas—the roof of the world. It was 1200 miles of the worst flying imaginable. The mountains were a veritable smorgasbord of meteorological treachery—violent downdrafts, high winds, and sudden snowstorms—all served up in temperatures 20° below zero. As if they needed any reminding, the crews could frequently glimpse the 29,028 foot peak of Mt. Everest thrusting up through the clouds just 150 miles from their flight path.

Nothing, except perhaps the green hills of home, looked better to the crews than the airfields across the Hump in China's Chengtu Valley. As Captain William O'Malley, navigator aboard Blondie Saunders' B-29 on the April 24 flight, described it:

> We took off at ten in the morning with General Saunders as command pilot, Colonel Blanchard as pilot, and Major Berton H. "Tex" Burns as copilot. On the way up we flew directly over the Japanese lines in the vicinity of the Kohima Road and the Imphal Plain, without incident. The flight over the Hump was by-God-amazing; perfect weather, incredible mountain valleys and gorges, tiny villages on the lesser mountains. We sighted three huge peaks about 200 miles distant. An Air Transport Command (ATC) safety pilot told us nobody knew how high they were.
>
> After finally getting over the Hump, we flew above an overcast through which we let down into the Yangtze Valley. And there was China! A most amazing landscape of thousands of cultivated rice paddies. For the first time in my life I had the feeling of being in a different world—one that could not be described with a "Well this looks like Texas," or "This looks like Iowa."

The airfield at Kwanghan looked wonderful from the air. The landing was apparently quite an event. Thousands of coolies lined each side of the runway. After getting out of the plane, we lined up and motion and still pictures were taken. General Chennault and his staff greeted us, as well as Chinese officials and American engineers. Everywhere the Chinese would smile and yell "Ding Hao"—which means "very best."

The first contact with the Japanese over the Hump came on April 26, when a northbound B-29 piloted by Major Charles H. Hansen observed twelve Nakajima KI-43 fighters (Allied code name "Oscar") about 2000 feet below, near the border of India and Burma. Half the enemy formation broke off and climbed to the bomber's altitude. They observed the Superfortress from beyond its gun range for several tense moments, awestruck by so huge an airplane flying so fast and so high. When the Oscars finally pounced on the B-29, the attacks were tentative—the Japanese pilots were testing the big plane's defensive armament.

The response was disappointing—no doubt to both sides. Three of the Superfort's turrets jammed as the enemy aircraft pressed their attacks. Most of the fighter passes came from below, but as one of the Oscars roared in from the rear, tail gunner Harold Lanham pumped a stream of tracers into the attacker, who plummeted into the overcast below furiously trailing a plume of black smoke.

The B-29 took several hits but nothing that affected its performance as it climbed to an altitude above the capability of the Nakajimas, which in turn broke off their attack and disappeared into the clouds.

With its baptism of fire, the Superfortress was fast on its way to becoming a legend among Japanese fighter pilots. Stories quickly spread through the Japanese airfields concerning the airplane that was being described as a "stupendous giant" or a "monstrous bull."

To the bomber crews that had begun to arrive in India on April 2, everything that lay behind them now—the Battle of Kansas, the overheating engines, and the grueling trip across half the globe—was the easy part. Ahead of them lay the six to eight flights across the Himalayas to stock up fuel and supplies for each mission they would fly, and beyond that lay World War II.

IV

On Destiny's Doorstep
India and China,
August–December 1944

When I'd first taken the 305th Bombardment Group to England in the spring of 1942 as part of the Eighth Air Force that was being assembled to begin bombing Germany, I had just thirty-five pilots. Of course, we were also supposed to have thirty-five airplanes, but we had only three. We had no navigators, no bombardiers, and no gunners.

We had three months to get ready, three B-17s, and only a couple of people who knew how to fly them. We had been in tents with no hangars up on Muroc Lake at what is now Edwards Air Force Base, California. By the time we had to go overseas I had worked with the navigators for only about a week or two, but I'd gotten them one training flight out of Rome, New York, in the B-17s we were going to take to England. The bombardiers came into Muroc a couple of weeks before we were due to go. They had never dropped a live bomb in their lives—because we had no airplanes to allocate to bombing training. All the training the bombardiers had was with a few sand-filled bombs dropped from a twin Beechcraft we had rigged up. The gunners were supposed to have gone through a gunnery school, but they had never shot a gun from an airplane. They would mount a gun on a truck, run it up against a bank out in the boondocks someplace, and blast away. At Muroc I gave each of the gunners one ride in an airplane, and they fired their guns as we went across the desert. That was about it.

In Europe, the navigators discovered that flying over England was not like flying over Kansas, where all the section lines run north and south, east and west. In England—as in continental Europe—towns were butted up against each other, with railroads and roads running in every direction. They had a hell of a time at first.

We had never flown formation until we got to England simply because we didn't have enough airplanes. The first day that we *could* fly over there I got the planes up and tried to assemble a formation. It was a complete debacle. We couldn't do it. During the next flight I got up into the top turret of the lead B-17 with a radio and brought the pilots as close together into formation as I could. The third flight was an actual mission across the English Channel. That's how we got started in Europe.

I hadn't been in on the earliest development of the B-29 because I was overseas with the Eighth Air Force from early 1942 until the middle of 1944. The B-29 project was top secret, and I knew nothing of it until I got orders to go over to India in July 1944 to take command of the Twentieth Bomber Command of the new Twentieth Air Force. I didn't get much detailed guidance from General Arnold, but I sure got the message about what he expected to do with the B-29s in the Far East. For all the developmental effort that had already gone into the B-29 program, the aircraft had only been in combat for a month and the USAAF was still getting only minimal results. That wasn't enough for Arnold. He made it clear that we finally had a chance to prove something with strategic air power, but in order to do this, I would have to go to India and see to it that the B-29 lived up to its potential.

I left Europe about three weeks after D day and arrived back in the States during the first week of July 1944. I stopped in Washington for a couple of days and then went on to Cleveland to see my wife. I loaded her and our daughter into a B-25 and flew out to Nebraska, where the B-29s were being prepared to go overseas. We had three or four weeks together while I was getting checked out in the cockpit. At the end of that time I was ready to go to India and go to work, but there was no B-29 that was ready to be taken. I waited for two days trying to get a plane. When I finally got tired of waiting, I got a C-54 transport and flew that out to India by way of Brazil and North Africa. I arrived and took command of the Twentieth Bomber Command on August 29.

The Twentieth Bomber Command, the first of two bomber commands to be set up under the Twentieth Air Force, had already hit the Japanese before I got over to India. Its first mission had been against Bangkok, Thailand, on June 5, 1944, and the B-29s had flown their first attack on Japan proper (the first since Jimmy Doolittle's mission in April 1942) against the Imperial Iron & Steel Works in Yawata, just ten days later. However, those raids had achieved only marginal results. It was great to finally be able to bomb Japan, but we would have to do better—a lot better.

General Wolfe had selected Japanese-held Bangkok for the shakedown mission because the attack could be launched from India, and as such the crews wouldn't need to dip into the precious supplies that had been so painstakingly carted over the Hump. It was also an overwater approach to a land target which simulated an attack on Japan. Beyond these considerations, Bangkok was a legitimate strategic target. Its Makasan rail yard was one of the most important transportation hubs in Southeast Asia and a critical part of the Japanese war effort in Burma.

The attack was launched at sunrise on June 5, with Colonel Jake Harmon leading. Of the hundred aircraft scheduled to make the mission, one was forced to abort because of a mechanical failure and a second crashed just after takeoff, leaving only one survivor. Eighteen aircraft suffered mechanical failures and had to turn back, and so Harmon arrived over Thailand's capital at 25,000 feet with 80 percent of his original force. Nevertheless, all but two of these dropped their bombs in the target area, and there were no losses due to the action of the Japanese, who had been taken largely by surprise.

Returning home, the fuel-short bomber force ran into heavy storms over the Bay of Bengal. Four ditched at sea or landed at alternative RAF bases in India, with seventy-six of the original one hundred completing the round trip to Bangkok and returning back to Twentieth Air Force fields.

The Yawata raid ten days later was richer in morale value (although the Bangkok strike had played very well in the headlines at home). Because of the enormous logistics problem, fewer B-29s took part, and out of sixty-eight that were successfully launched from the Chengtu Valley base at Pengshan, only forty-seven bombed the Imperial Iron & Steel Works. As with the Doolittle raid on Japan twenty-six months before, the physical results of the Yawata mission were minimal, and they were greatly overshadowed by the psychological impact—on both sides.

The firsthand account of a Yawata journalist told the story from the enemy perspective:

> Now all the city is black. Suddenly in the north we heard the sound of plane engines. The orders were flashed everywhere and all the sounds on the street stilled. The propeller noise of the enemy planes spread over the whole sky. Minute by minute the noise approached. At this moment there was a shot, like a skyrocket, into the air. Several tons of shots. I could see clearly the figures of the enemy planes. At once antiaircraft began to shoot. The guns shouted like lightning. But the hateful enemy planes flew on. Suddenly fire dropped from them—one, two, three. These were the flares. The whole city could be clearly seen in reddish light. Then came big black things from the white bodies of the planes. Bombs! And boom! boom! boom! The devils, the beasts! Again boom! boom! boom!...

On the other hand, Colonel Alan Clark aboard one of the Superforts later reported:

> The results of the mission were poor. Of the bombs dropped on the Yawata area, only a very small proportion came within the target area, and some were as far as 20 miles away. The reason was that our radar operators had not been trained to do blind bombing [bombing by radar]. As a result of this mission, the Twentieth Bomber Command put in a training schedule for ra-

dar operators, and radar bombing improved somewhat in subsequent missions.

It had been a logical choice to send General K. B. Wolfe out to India with the B-29s because he knew more than anyone else in the USAAF about their operational quirks. This was probably a good idea because the B-29 was in pretty bad shape insofar as being ready for combat. There were all kinds of mechanical problems with the engines. In fact, there were over 3000 changes that had to be made in the engine alone during the first few months we were flying out of India and China.

The major technical problem we had with the B-29 when I got to India was with the big Wright Cyclone R-3350 air-cooled engines. They had a tendency to swallow valves. A valve would burn, and then the head would go off and chew up one of the engine's eighteen cylinders. Sometimes the cylinder would, in turn, fly off and chew up the whole engine. If we lost some of the hydraulic fluid and couldn't feather the prop, then the prop would fly off. You would be lucky if *just* the prop flew off, because sometimes the whole damned engine seized and twisted right out of the wing.

We were also flying the airplanes at a higher gross weight than they were designed for. Of course, there was a safety figure and a design figure, but the safety figure didn't make it into every operation. We were flying at about 40,000 pounds over the recommended gross weight, since we needed to carry extra fuel for long missions. If we got detonation in hot weather, the plane lost power and didn't make it off the runway. Once I had to sit up in the control tower in China and watch a fire burn at the end of a field because an airplane didn't make the takeoff. Usually if a plane crashed on takeoff, the bomb load went off with it.

The technical problems that first cropped up happened, of course, because the factory had gone into production of the B-29s before flight testing was completed. Boeing had all the problems that you would ordinarily have with a new airplane. However, normally you build an airplane prototype more or less by hand. Then you fly it, shake it down, find out the design changes you have to make, and clean those up. When it looks like you've got it, then you go into production. But even after a plane goes into production under these circumstances, you will find things that have to be changed.

In this case, the factories started grinding out the B-29s much sooner than they would have under any other scenario because the B-29s were so badly needed. When the technicians started finding things wrong with them, Boeing started producing the kits to modify the B-29s in the field. The USAAF had finished B-29s scattered all over the United States awaiting kits, and not necessarily in factories where they were supposed to be. We'd find airplanes in Kansas at 20° below zero and no hangars. People were being brought off the Boeing production line at Wichita to make some modifications on the planes and get them overseas to us in India. It had been quite a hassle.

By the time I got to the Far East, Boeing was even sending kits to India to modify the planes. Engineering teams, including people such as Eric Nelson—who was one of Boeing's top troubleshooters—also came out to help us. The main thing that Nelson was working on at the time was engine detonation.

We were correcting these problems as we went along. After a while we just traded airplanes. So many things were being added to the newer B-29s that we would just take one of these new ones and let a crew take the old plane back to the States to have it modified. We also had what were called "tech orders" coming out of Materiel Command telling us which things to change. These were mostly modifications that we could do out in the field.

We were conducting a test program as we fought, doing the modifications that would have been done in the test program at the factory during peacetime. If times had been normal, the factory would have tested the B-29s before they went into production, but we were doing it in combat, and we were still modifying the plane twenty years later when we finally retired it in the early 1950s.

In addition to the mechanical troubles we were having, and the massive logistical problems that we encountered in the Far East, I found problems with the troops as well. The status of training wasn't as bad as it had been when we went overseas to Europe in 1942, but it was bad enough.

The units were formed with better people because, as the

USAAF was expanding and graduating classes from the flying school, half of the graduates would go into a combat unit and the other half would stay in the Air Training Command to expand our training capability. By 1944 we had a lot of guys who had been flying the hell out of training airplanes back home in the Air Training Command. They had a lot more flying time than the 200 hours my people had when they went overseas to Europe in 1942, but they hadn't seen any combat. We did have a few people sprinkled around in the Twentieth Air Force who had been in combat in Europe or in the South Pacific between 1942 and 1944, but not very many of them. As for cohesive training, we had none because there hadn't been enough B-29s with which to conduct squadron training exercises. Pilots were flying B-17s and B-18s while they waited for the B-29 to arrive, and as soon as a B-29 came along, bang, the crew went overseas with it. In fact, their first flight in a B-29 was likely to be the overseas run. They probably had a little more flight time than that, but certainly no more scheduled operational training because it was rush, rush, rush to get the men into combat.

As in England, I got the crews out of bed at three o'clock in the morning, fed them some breakfast, and got them down to the briefing room before daylight. I would run them in there, pull back the curtain covering the blackboard, and say "Here is the target for the day."

They couldn't even pronounce the names of the targets, let alone know where they were or what was there. Navigators and bombardiers had about an hour to look over some target materials that in England we would get from the British. Usually there would be a photograph or a map of the area. But these didn't mean very much to the crews, because they were largely unfamiliar with the country over which they'd be flying; and so when they got over enemy territory, they had a hell of a time finding the target and then approaching it. (The bombardier would expect to see it in one place, but instead of appearing there it might appear somewhere else.) Then came the problem of trying to get the whole formation turned, get the equipment leveled, and bomb the target.

Finally, I picked out the lead crews—not necessarily the best crews, but people I had learned would be the ones who were most

TOP: A B-29 built at Boeing's Wichita, Kansas, plant climbs above the cumulus and sets course for Asia. (*Boeing photo*)

BOTTOM: A Twentieth Bomber Command B-29 high over the Himalayas en route from Kharagpur, India, to one of the advanced bases in China's Chengtu Valley. (*USAF photo*)

Brigadier General Haywood S. "Possum" Hansell (*left*) and Colonel Curtis E. LeMay (*right*) in front of a B-17 at an Eighth Air Force base in England on May 13, 1943. (*USAF photo*)

In April 1944, USAAF B-29s began to arrive at advanced bases in China's Chengtu Valley. The bases had been literally constructed by hand by thousands of Chinese laborers, some of whom are pictured resting beside a mound of stones used in the tedious task of leveling the airstrips. (*USAF photo*)

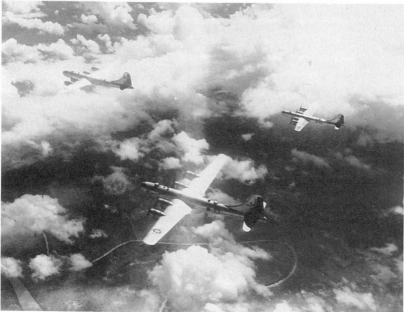

TOP: The B-29 named for test pilot Eddie Allen and assigned to the Fortieth Bomb Group of the Twentieth Bomber Command, shown nearing its target during the November 3, 1944, bombing raid against Rangoon, Burma. (*USAF photo*)

BOTTOM: Boeing B-29 Superfortresses of the 462nd Bomb Group, Twentieth Bomber Command, returning to home base after bombing enemy installations at Rangoon, Burma, on November 3, 1944. (*USAF photo*)

Superfortresses of the Twenty-First Bomber Command's 314th Bomb Wing parked at hardstands along the taxiways of Guam's North Field, later renamed Andersen Air Force Base after Brigadier General James Roy Andersen, who was lost aboard a B-29 in February 1945. During the Vietnam war this base was the headquarters of the Eighth Air Force (which has been part of the Strategic Air Command since 1946); numerous B-52 strikes were launched from here against enemy targets in both North and South Vietnam between 1965 and 1972. (*USAF photo*)

When Curtis E. LeMay (*left*), now a major general, took over command of the Twentieth Air Force's Twenty-First Bomber Command in the Marianas in January 1945, he left Brigadier General Roger Ramey in command of the Twentieth Bomber Command in India. (*USAF photo*)

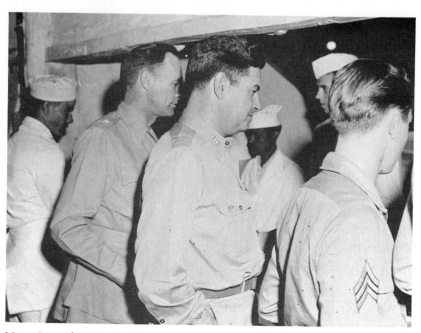

Major General Curtis E. LeMay (*center*) and his Chief of Staff Brigadier General John E. Upston (*left*) stand in the chow line along with the enlisted men. (*USAF photo*)

TOP: A Marianas-based Boeing B-29 Superfort on its way to rendezvous with its formation for a bombing run over war production centers in Japan. (*USAF photo*)

BOTTOM: An old Japanese stronghold was converted for use as base operations for the Twentieth Air Force, Isley Field, on Saipan in the Marianas Islands. The USAAF Air Transport Command and Transport Air Group planes also used this strip until completion of nearby Kobler Field. (*USAF photo*)

Twentieth Air Force B-29 Superfortresses depart from Guam on their strategic mission against Japanese industry in May 1945. (*USAF photo*)

likely to hit the target regardless. "You're a lead crew now," I'd tell them, "but all that means is you're going to stay over here longer. You're only going to fly your 25 missions, but it's going to take you longer doing it."

I put them in the operations center with the intelligence people, and they would spend all their time studying targets. I started out by giving each one of them an area in which we were operating. "Take this area," I would say, "and study the maps and pictures and everything you can get hold of. I want you to be able to draw your area freehand in your sleep."

When we got that done, I would start picking targets that I thought we might hit in their area and get them to study the targets in minute detail. If the navigator could draw his target freehand in his sleep, he had a better chance of enabling the bombardier to really do *his* job. That's the reason the 305th Bomb Group had gotten more bombs on German targets than anybody else in the Eighth Air Force. We were getting even better by the time I left for India in the summer of 1944 and were able to operate as a cohesive unit, knowing what we were doing and knowing what everyone else was going to do.

While we were conducting our combat training in India during the summer and early fall of 1944, we bombed a few targets in Burma, or wherever we could find them. We even went as far as Singapore on November 5, 1944. These were training missions more than anything else, but as long as we were running missions, if we could drop some bombs on the Japanese at the same time, we'd do it. These missions were designed to teach some of the tactics that had been successful in Europe, such as the idea of massing large numbers of bombers against a target.

Another thing I did in India was to improve aircraft maintenance. When we went into the war in 1942, we used one type of maintenance system throughout the USAAF. Each airplane had its own crew chief and a staff of maintenance personnel. Among them, they could fix anything that needed fixing on the airplane. We'd have a sheet metal worker, an electrician, an engine mechanic, and so on, but no one in the service crew was part of the combat group. If you turned an airplane over to the service crew, the plane was transferred. When the men in the service crew got the thing fixed, they turned it back to you. The combat commander didn't have any control over how long the service crew would have the plane, and so when a commander needed every one of his airplanes to do his job, he was damned careful about turning one of them loose. The same was true in 1945 when I arrived.

In India in 1944, as in England in 1942, each squadron had its own supply sergeant. If you had a good supply sergeant, he scrounged and he would have a dozen generators stacked way back under his shelves, and the next squadron wouldn't have any. Would he turn one of them loose? Over his dead body. He might need it later. I couldn't do much about that when I was just a group commander in Europe, but in India where there was nobody looking over my shoulder, I could operate differently. I combined all the supply sections so that the supplies were in one place, not stashed in some squadron supply area.

This squadron crew business was all right in peacetime, when you had a lot of people who were trained. However, when you didn't, it was a misuse of such people to have them working on just a single airplane. I set up a production-line maintenance program for the whole base. We could take the people who knew what they were doing and let them supervise the less skilled personnel so we could get a lot more done. Everyone worked on the airplane that needed to be worked on. In the old system, when one squadron got shot up and had a lot of holes to patch, the sheet metal guys in that squadron would be burning the midnight oil while the next-door squadron would be down at the pub having a beer. The maintenance system that I set up in India in 1944 got everyone working. I did the same thing when I got over to the Marianas in 1945.

Because of all these problems, when I got out to India in August 1944, I found a pretty desperate situation. The B-29s were based at six airfields in Bengal, about 90 miles west of Calcutta. These fields—at Kharagpur, Chakulia, Charra, Dudhkundi, Kalaikunda, and Piardoba—were British-built, but they were better than the usual British airfields in India because a normal RAF field wouldn't take the weight of a B-29 and these fields could. There wasn't much British Royal Air Force flying activity around the Calcutta area, and so we didn't have much contact with them. Their logistics people, however, were helpful. The British theater commander in the area got no credit for our success or blame for our failures, yet we took his lifeblood in the way of supplies.

Our forward bases—those from which we flew the actual missions against Japan—were located at Hsinching, Kiunglai, Kwanghan and Pengshan, 1200 miles north in China's Chengtu Valley. We were not able to supply these bases by surface transportation, because the Japanese held all the ports, the railroads, the highways and the lines of communication to the big cities. The Allies were trying to get the Ledo Road built into China at that time, but it was a slow process. The USAAF Transport Command had its hands full flying supplies into China to Chennault's Fourteenth Air Force and to Chiang Kai-shek's forces, and so we found that we had to practically supply ourselves.

We were flying seven trips over the Himalayas with every B-29, off-loading as much gas as we could to still get back to India. On the eighth trip across the Hump to Chengtu, we would finally take a load of bombs and fly a bombing mission against the Japanese. Because it took so many flights to get our fuel and bombs to China, we could fly only one mission a week against the Japanese.

Those of us in command knew what target we were going to bomb before we left India, but we never said anything to the crews about it while we were still down there. They wouldn't know what they were going to bomb until they got up to Chengtu. On a typical mission we would fly up to Chengtu with the bombs loaded on the plane. Once we had a good night's sleep, we would give the crews a briefing, get gassed up and checked out, and we'd be off. We would fly across China in a pretty loose formation, because we didn't get any attacks from Japanese interceptors based there. We'd make a run on the target and come back in the same way.

We would usually loosen up on the formation coming back to save gasoline, because we didn't get intercepted on the way back either, and anybody who had engine problems could land someplace. The main force of B-29s would get back to Chengtu, and then the crews would go to bed for the night. The day after a bombing raid against Japan, we would fly back to India and start all over again. How soon we'd go back to Chengtu for a bombing mission always depended upon how much gasoline we had up there. It was at least a week, normally, but we'd make flights up there with fuel all the time. We could only make one flight a day in a B-29, but there were B-29s flying up there almost every day. Everything that we used in Chengtu, except the food we ate, had to be hauled in this way.

As we've noted, Chiang Kai-shek had built the airfields in western China by hand with internal labor. The materials and machinery were flown in by the USAAF Transport Command, but most of the construction work had been done *literally* by hand. All around the airfields there were cones of various heights sticking up, which showed where the ground had been before the Chinese work crews started to level it. They left the cones to show how much they'd removed because they were paid by the amount of dirt they moved. After they removed the dirt, they brought stones out of the riverbed and carried them up to the fields by hand. They put big ones down, then smaller and smaller ones. Finally they pounded them into gravel with a hammer and added a slurry that was made of clay and tung oil. There had been about 10,000 workers building each one of the fields, and afterward there were still a couple of thousand people maintaining each one. It later became a major problem to have such large numbers of maintenance workers on the field while we were conducting flight operations.

The main road to Chengtu ran between the field and my headquarters, and had a constant stream of wheelbarrows going along it all the time. There were also workers pulling wagons with rubber automobile tires on them that they had taken from cars, which were now useless because there was no longer any gasoline. Their load might have been a big hog lying on his back tied to a wheelbarrow, with his eyes sewn closed so he wouldn't see anything and struggle. The Chinese would wheel such vehicles 20 miles to market.

All these conveyances had wooden axles that screeched like mad. One day a mechanic couldn't stand the racket any longer. One of the Chinese had dropped a wheelbarrow nearby and was looking at the airplanes and resting a little bit, and the mechanic climbed over the fence with an oil can and oiled the axle on the wheelbarrow. When the fellow started up again, it didn't screech and scare any dragons away, and so he left the whole damned thing right there. He wouldn't have anything to do with it. We had to learn to back off and not be so helpful with things. Once we began to understand the Chinese, we began to have a little more appreciation for what they did for us.

The Japanese controlled the big Chinese cities and all the major lines of communication throughout China, but there were large areas, particularly in the southern and western parts of China, that Chiang Kai-shek's forces controlled. If we had an airplane go down in one of those areas, his people, the Nationalist government troops, would hear about it and help to get our men out; aside from this, I didn't have too much direct contact with Chiang Kai-shek. I saw him a couple of times when I would come up to China to run a mission.

In the northern part of China, however, the Chinese communist leader Mao Tse-tung was in control. In the early part of the century, Chiang and Mao had been disciples of Sun Yat-sen, and when the latter died in 1925, there was a clash between the two of them over who was going to replace Sun. They wound up fighting a very bitter civil war that lasted until 1949, when Mao finally pushed Chiang out of China completely and into Taiwan.

When World War II began, Chiang had been in control of the central Chinese government while Mao was in Yenan, in northern China, where he controlled large areas that the Japanese hadn't conquered. Of course, Chiang and Mao weren't speaking to each other even though they were both technically at war with the Japanese. They had stopped fighting each other, but they both planned to start up again after the Japanese situation was clarified. Chiang even had some old warplanes that were not being used against the Japanese. They were stashed around Chengtu, off the fields and down the road with guards on them. He also had caches of other supplies that he was hoarding for use against Mao when the Americans finally drove the Japanese out.

Because Mao controlled nearly as much territory in China as Chiang did, I decided that it would be useful to have some contact with him. I sent a couple of staff officers up into Yenan in a C-47 transport plane, not knowing for certain how well they would be received. They were greeted cordially, however. I was asked to establish a radio station up there and send in the people to operate and supply it if he would get help to any of our crews that might go down in his area. He not only agreed, but even volunteered to build some airfields for B-29s up there if we wanted them. We had a hard enough time supplying the fields we had down at Chengtu, and so we couldn't use any more, but I appreciated his offer.

I sent up a C-47 load of medical supplies to keep Mao happy. The truth was that if his men picked up any of my fliers, I wanted to be sure that our guys would have access to any medical supplies they might need. When the C-47 arrived, their doctors stayed up all night with tears in their eyes. They had never seen any of this stuff. They didn't know anything about sulfa drugs because sulfa had been developed since the doctors had been up there with Mao, and so we had to label everything with instructions on how to use it. In return, Mao sent me a Japanese sword and some woodcuts, and we got along fine.

The first plane that Mao helped was a B-29 that had just barely made it back across the Yellow Sea from a raid on Anshan in September 1944. The crew bailed out right on the shore. We got a message from Mao saying that his men had picked up all the crew except one—the Japanese had fatally wounded him. Mao also told us that his men had all four of the engines from the airplane. I said to throw away the engines and bring the crew out. I received periodic reports from Mao as his men made their way across northern China. From what I heard, I knew that they had anywhere from 10 to 3000 people with them at any given time. If they had to punch through an occupied area, or if they were in danger of getting picked up by the Japanese, they had enough troops. They were riding horses and cattle and anything else they could. One of our men died en route, but the Chinese finally got the others out through Iran.

North of the Himalayas there was a pretty wide area of western China that was inhabited by tribes that were not Chinese, and of whom the Chinese were scared to death. These tribes, whom the Chinese called Lolos, were said to be wild, uncivilized, and cruel. Some of our intelligence men finally went in there and found a pretty miserable bunch of people. They also found evidence that some of our aircrews had gone down in there, but we had very little contact with the Lolos.

We tried to convince the tribes in the remote corners of China that if they brought our crews out, they could get paid. We finally met some people from the extreme west who agreed to help our men, but they didn't want to be paid in cash—they wanted opium. One of my officers came in and said, "What am I going to do? They don't want money, and I haven't got any opium."

I said, "We have to get the crews. Get the opium. Go buy it."

"I can't put that down on the accounting," he said.

"I don't give a damn what you put down," I told him. "Get our men out. Pay these people, and let them know they are going to be paid in anything they want if they help our men."

When this officer came back later, he told me that he'd entered "fertilizer" on the manifest for the amount of money he'd paid for the opium. He pulled it off, and we got a little bit of help out of these tribes.

Most of the men who crashed in the Himalayas never came back. I had one crew who did walk out, but they weren't too far in. The weather over the Hump is usually stinking, particularly in the monsoon season. The mountains are extraordinarily high— the highest in the world—and we had none of the sophisticated navigation aids that are taken for granted today. The Japanese fighter bases were also within range, and so we always ran the risk of being attacked.

Weather was probably our greatest problem in attacking Japan. There were, of course, no weather reports coming out of Japan, and the Russians refused to give us any weather reports out of their stations in Asia. I received reports from my people at Mao's headquarters in northwestern China, and once in a while I would get a report from a detachment that the U.S. Navy had set up— for what purpose I never knew—in the Gobi Desert.

Our problem was to forecast the weather over an area 1700 miles away with no information for thousands of miles to the west where the weather originated. Our only solution was to send airplanes up to Japan to look at the weather and report back what they observed. From this meager information, our weather people would try to draw a weather map and make a forecast. I'm sure that they felt that they were carrying most of the load in deciding whether or not we launched a mission, and so I tried to take some of this pressure off by asking what they thought the degree of reliability was on a scale of one to ten. I would then toss this information in the pot along with all the other factors involved. I don't know whether this relieved any of the pressure they felt, but I hope so.

I personally flew only one B-29 combat mission. When we had first gone to England at the start of the war, there had been no rules about commanders flying combat missions. Every commander flew them when, and as often as, he considered it necessary. For instance, I flew the first five missions with the 305th Bomb Group before I would let anyone else lead. Very soon, however, someone at USAAF headquarters discovered that the RAF had lost over half their experienced commanders in the first few months of the war. To prevent this from happening to the USAAF as well, an order was sent down forbidding commanders to fly in combat. It took some effort, because in our view, while a commander could not and should not fly *every* mission, he *had to* fly enough to know what was going on within his outfit during the missions.

When I was sent to the Far East, General Arnold had expressly forbidden me to fly any more combat missions. I presented all my arguments and finally got permission to fly one mission. I accepted that, expecting to argue a little bit later on and get some more, but before I got a *chance* to argue again, I was briefed on the atomic bomb and any possibility of my flying another combat mission went out the window.

The combat mission I picked was the ninety-eight-plane raid that we flew on September 8, 1944, against the big coke ovens at the Showa Steel Works in Anshan, Manchuria. Our A2 (intelligence) people said the best fighter outfit in the Japanese air force was stationed there, and I wanted to get a look at it. When we arrived over Anshan, the Japanese were up in force. They were out in front, and in perfect position to make a frontal attack on our B-29s, but they turned the wrong way. They managed to take a few shots at a couple of airplanes at the rear of our formation when we went by, but the bulk of the Japanese fighter group never were able to shoot at us. I didn't see much of what they were doing, but I realized that they didn't know much about the B-29, and that they had misjudged our speed.

Our plane was hit by anti-aircraft fire as we were flying over the target, though. The radio operator got on the intercom and said he was wounded, and the top turret gunner called in that he was hit also. I said to hold on until we got a look at the fighter attack, and then I would come back with the first aid kit.

When the attack was over, I went back to the radio operator and found him with his flak vest on his lap and a silly look on his face. He'd been hit in the back with a piece of flak about 3 inches long and an inch wide. It got stuck in the vest and he wasn't hurt. I went back through the tunnel to the top turret gunner. A piece of flak had hit his gun grip which stung his hands and he had a little white scratch on his knuckle. That was his wound.

We also had a few holes in the airplane, the biggest one about 8 inches across. We stuffed an old pair of coveralls in it and some rags in another one and managed to keep the pressure up all right. We made it back to Chengtu with no further problems.

At Chengtu we would occasionally get a night attack from Japanese bombers. We got one the night after the Anshan raid, in fact. The raiding party usually was not big, just a half dozen enemy airplanes at the most. As the bombers came over, fires would suddenly spring up, like beacons, all around the fields. The Japanese had agents in Chengtu that paid some of the Chinese to start these fires so that the Japanese bombers could locate the blacked-out B-29 bases in the dark. In the village closest to the airfields, the Japanese even had a radio homing device. We never could find whoever was starting the fires and we never could find any radios. Chinese troops would ransack the village and never find anything.

One day, one of my group commanders, Albert Kalberer, heard from a Chinese officer that the Chinese had caught one of the guys who was building fires. I told Kalberer to go and see if he could find out anything. I soon got a telephone call from him saying, "I went down there and they hadn't gotten anything out of him; he was dead."

"What happened?" I asked.

"We didn't kill him," they had told Kalberer. "We just hung him up by the thumbs and were asking him some questions when he died on us."

The bombing that the Japanese did against the bomber bases was never very good. The raids were light and annoying rather than seriously damaging. We never did lose a B-29, but we lost a C-54 cargo plane once, and we would occasionally lose some gasoline. After October 6, 1944, we had a fighter outfit with some Northrop P-61 Black Widow night fighters that were supposed to protect the air bases, but the outfit only had a few planes available then, and didn't have any gasoline to practice. As a matter of fact, the outfit said it couldn't protect us unless we provided some gasoline, and so we had to furnish gasoline.

With no radar the night fighters never did any good, except one night. That night the Japanese made a mistake and bombed the fighter field instead of one of our bomber fields. The Japanese could bomb the bomber fields without a loss, but as soon as they hit the fighter field, the Black Widows flew into a frenzy and shot down one of the attackers. After that, Russ Randal, who commanded the fighters, never got me off his back.

General Joseph "Vinegar Joe" Stillwell, the U.S. Army theater commander in China, came up to Chengtu to see us. He arrived one day when we were right in the middle of trying to launch the B-29s, so I said, "Come on, follow me around until I get the mission off and then I can talk to you."

I stayed up practically all night talking to Stillwell about what we were trying to do, but I didn't get to first base with him. He just barely admitted that the wheel had been invented and farther than that he wouldn't go. His position was that in war the infantry was the queen of battle—the same old Army line.

The next time I saw Stillwell was aboard the *USS Missouri* in September 1945 at the time of the Japanese surrender. Two days later I was back at my headquarters in Guam when Stillwell stopped to visit me. He came into the office and said, "LeMay, I'm on my way back to the United States and I just had to stop and tell you that when I got up to Yokohama for the first time I understood what you were trying to tell me back in Chengtu Valley last year. I was a language student in Yokohama before the war, and I know what was there. Seeing what was left standing when your B-29s were through, I understood. I just wanted to tell you that before I went home."

General Chennault, meanwhile, was always heckling us to do something in China to help him out, especially after he managed to get Chiang Kai-shek to convince Washington that western China would fall if we didn't. General Albert Wedemeyer, who had succeeded Stillwell as the American theater commander in the China-

Burma-India theater, was also badgering me in China to help the theater operations. Their intelligence said there was a Japanese build-up being made for a drive on western China aimed at capturing Chungking, and he wanted me to stop this with the B-29s. I, of course, refused because it wasn't in line with my orders. He finally did get the Joint Chiefs to order me to get Hankow. So we hit Hankow with a pretty good wallop on December 18, 1944, and stopped a major Japanese drive against western China.

In the Hankow raid, 84 Superfortresses (out of 89 launched) teamed up with 33 Fourteenth Air Force B-24s and 149 fighters in an attack on what were essentially tactical targets, but which nevertheless proved to be a major milestone in the evolution of our plan for the strategic air offensive against Japan. December 18, 1944, marked the first large-scale attack on Japanese positions using incendiaries, and its success gave us a great deal of useful information about the effects of incendiaries on the highly flammable wood and paper construction common to the housing stock in the Far East. We realized that because of these types of building materials, incendiaries would be more useful than they had been against targets in Europe built of stone and masonry.

Despite some modest successes and the lessons learned from the Hankow raid, we really didn't accomplish as much in China as we had hoped. That would come later when we moved the B-29 bases to the Marianas. In the meantime, I recommended that Arnold not send anymore B-29s to India after November 1944, because we really couldn't supply them adequately at the bases up in China. So as soon as American forces captured the Marianas, we closed the Twentieth Air Force operations in India and China and moved over to Guam. The Marianas would be the beginning of the end of the road to Tokyo.

V

Preparing the
Final Assault

The Marianas,
August–December 1944

Even as we were struggling with the logistics of staging the Twentieth Bomber Command's B-29s through the bases in China, General Hansell was moving into the Marianas with the Twenty-First
Bomber Command. The American recapture of this important island chain had begun on June 15, 1944, with Marine amphibious
landings on Saipan. Exactly one week later, the first USAAF aircraft arrived at American-held airfields on that island to help support Marine assaults on Guam and Tinian which began on July 21
and July 24, respectively. By the end of the first week in August,
organized Japanese resistance on the three islands—resistance
which had been ferocious—all but collapsed.

By the middle of August the Marianas were being transformed
into major American bases. Guam, ruled by the U.S. Navy from
1898 until its capture by the Japanese in December 1941, returned

to Navy administration as its Advanced Headquarters, Pacific Ocean Area. Hap Arnold would point out in his postwar autobiography, however, that—while the Navy owned and administered Guam and the Marianas—neither the Navy nor its Marine Corps could attack Japan from there because of the distance. It would be the USAAF Superforts—and *only* the USAAF Superforts—that would be able to strike Japan from the Navy's Advanced Headquarters.

The original plan had been for me to take over the Twenty-First Bomber Command in the Marianas, while General Hansell was to have the Twenty-Second, to be based in the Philippines. However, the Twentieth Bomber Command got off to such a rocky start in the India-China theater during the spring of 1944, that General Arnold decided to send me out *there,* giving the Twenty-First to General Hansell. On August 24, 1944, the advanced air echelons of General Rosey O'Donnell's Seventy-Third Bomb Wing headquarters—the combat unit of the Twenty-First Bomber Command—arrived by ship in the Marianas. This was the first contingent to arrive there, as the ground echelons of the bomber groups would not arrive by water until September 16, and Possum Hansell himself didn't arrive with the first B-29 until October 12. The Twenty-First Bomber Command initially had its own headquarters located at Isley Field, Saipan, along with the Seventy-Third until New Year's Eve, when it moved to a more permanent setup on Guam.

As I had discovered in China, however, the state of training was deplorable. As General Hansell has described it,

> Our people had no gunnery experience, and the gunnery equipment for the B-29 was extremely sophisticated. It was so complex that the average individual simply couldn't operate it. A gunner had to take care of three motions at once, which is extremely difficult for anybody, especially in combat. The gunner's problem was about like cutting a spiral gear on a hand lathe. It was one of those cases where technology really did outrun itself. As a result our gunnery was very bad and the crews got little experience with the gun sights, which controlled the remote turrets. Bombing operations were also poor. The 73rd Wing had been relying on night operations, using radar against area targets, so the bombardiers were not trained for daylight operations.

Navigation was poor as well. As a matter of fact, training all across the board was deplorable.

Before he went out to the Pacific, Possum had met with General Marshall on the first of October. Marshall told Possum that the operation Possum was about to launch would be part of a joint operation. "It's not *just* a B-29 operation," Marshall said. "It's to be geared into the operations of the entire Pacific Ocean Area. As a matter of fact, a carrier task force will accompany you on your first attack on Japan in order to protect your forces from fighter attacks."

Hansell hadn't known about this, but it certainly sounded good to him at the time. Marshall continued, "The schedule of operation calls for the first attack in the second half of November." Then Marshall asked whether the Twenty-First Bomber Command would be ready to carry out its part on schedule. Possum told him that it would. This meant that Possum had just six weeks in which to move the B-29s of the Seventy-Third Bomb Wing to what he hoped would be prepared bases in the Marianas, to fly a few shakedown flights, and then to launch an operation against Tokyo.

General Hansell began to make the plans for the move to the Marianas. Because the Twenty-First Bomber Command had almost no experience in long-range formation flying, he asked Arnold for permission to move the outfit out to the Marianas in squadron units under Air Transport Command Control. It was the normal procedure for the Air Transport Command to take responsibility for the movement of all forces overseas. The only unusual part of General Hansell's request was that the Twenty-First Bomber Command be moved by squadron, which would offer a priceless opportunity to learn something about cruise control in formation. The Air Transport Command refused. Even when Hansell said he would personally take the responsibility if anything went wrong, the command still refused, saying that the B-29 lacked the range to fly from Sacramento to Honolulu in formation!

As General Hansell told me later:

I was incredulous. I was going to have to take these same airplanes and immediately fly them 50% farther than the distance to Honolulu—with a bomb load, in the face of opposition, without any weather information, and with very poor bases. The Air Transport Command reasoning defied logic. I appealed to General George, an old friend of mine, who was the Commander of the Air Transport Command, hoping to convince him. However, he was so certain that it was impossible, that he went to General Arnold and threatened to resign his command if we insisted on flying B-29s to Honolulu in formation.

I took the first B-29—*Joltin' Josey, the Pacific Pioneer*—out to the Marianas myself. My co-pilot was Major Jack Catton, who later became a four-star general. When I stopped at Honolulu, I called on Admiral Chester Nimitz, the Commander in Chief for the Pacific Ocean Area (CINCPAC), who was also preparing to move to Guam, and I discussed the Twentieth Air Force command arrangements with him. I found that he was not thoroughly familiar with those arrangements. Apparently he didn't realize that he was to have no control of the B-29 operations. I had brought along a set of Joint Chiefs' papers on the subject, so I showed these to him. He shook his head and said, "If I had known this, I would have opposed it vigorously. I didn't understand it this way, but since the Joint Chiefs of Staff have set up this method, I will abide by it and I can assure you I will give you all the help I possibly can." Which he did. He was wonderful about it, but he added, "I think I should tell you that my commander out in the Forward Area, Admiral Hoover, breaks my admirals and throws them overboard without the slightest compunction. And God knows what he is going to do to you." I learned later that Admiral Nimitz had a very acute sense of humor, but he deliberately concealed it at the time of our meeting at Pearl Harbor in October 1944.

As General Arnold was to say after the war,

At first, the Navy opposed our B-29 operations, and opposed them violently; then they tolerated them, and then the whole Navy was back of them, but *they* wanted control of all the Superforts.

General Hansell proceeded to Saipan with some misgivings, and as he described it:

When I got out there on October 12, I was horribly disappointed. I had been told that I would have two bases, each with two 8,500-foot paved runways, operations buildings, crew quarters, maintenance facilities, and engineering shops—all of them ready to operate—but we had none of these things. We had one runway—8,500 feet long, to be sure—but only 5,000 feet of it was paved! We had only 40 hardstands [protected parking spaces for the bombers] instead of 80. The other runway was unusable because there was a hill about 500 feet high a couple of miles beyond the end of the runway that couldn't be cleared by a B-29 with a full bomb load. I had no shops and no facilities except tents. I had a bomb dump, a vehicle park and gasoline storage, but the rest of it was the most miserable shambles I had ever seen. We soon had B-29s coming into Saipan's Isley Field, but we had to double-park them on the hardstands, and try our best to provide some kind of facilities for ourselves. The regular air echelon of the Seventy-Third Bomb Wing arrived in Saipan soon after I came in. It was followed during October and the first week of November by four bomb groups and four air service groups.

We built a rough looking camp, but it worked and people did live in it. They spent 24 hours a day working, trying to get ready for the first mission. The aviation engineers who built the bases were the finest bunch of people I ever knew—they just worked all the time. When they had no camp, they slept under their trucks wherever they parked them. By the time of our first mission in November, the construction battalions had completed paving two runways on Saipan and were close to finishing two more on Guam. Once they got started, they did a magnificent job.

Before going out to the Marianas, General Hansell had also carefully planned for a whole maintenance depot, including supplies, to be set up in the States, then disassembled. These components were then boxed and labeled, and arrangements were made to load them in a U.S. Navy transport ship at a West Coast port. They were to be put aboard in a precise order, so that as they came out, they could be trucked to the depot hangar and unloaded, giving the Twenty-First Bomber Command a complete inventory and a complete depot in very short time. However, the Japanese were still fighting when the ship arrived, and so the harbor master (or in this case, the beach master), a very powerful guy in the Navy, said, "I'll give you 24 hours to get that goddamn ship out of here." The depot was unloaded helter-skelter, and dumped into the jungle. No part of it was ever used—it was simply lost. General Hansell's supply officer, Bill Irvine, who later also served me so well, somehow managed after that to maintain the Superforts on a shoestring from the depot at Sacramento.

In the frantic environment of a fast-moving and unpredictable war, supply operations were anything but routine. Not long after General Hansell arrived on Saipan, he was called upon one morning by a colonel in sort of an outsize uniform. As Hansell recalled, there was nothing quite right about it. The pockets were too big, the lapels were too wide, and the colonel was wearing cowboy boots. He introduced himself to Hansell and said, "Sir, I have brought you a ship."

Possum asked him, "What are you talking about?" The colonel answered, "If you could come out to the harbor, I would be honored if you would come and visit my ship. It's a full machine shop, all of the latest equipment on it."

Then General Hansell remembered something that had happened months before in Washington when he'd had a supply officer on the Twentieth Air Force staff named Sol Rosenblatt. Possum had been so displeased with the way the supplies were moving to the B-29s that he read the riot act to Rosenblatt. Possum stated emphatically that he was more than a little fed up with the Navy always getting the best of everything and the USAAF having to get along on what was left. Possum went on to tell Rosenblatt that the USAAF was going to have the finest fighting force in the world and that he wanted it correspondingly supplied and equipped.

Rosenblatt, it turned out, had been the secretary of the Democratic Party of the state of New York and was a man of considerable power. When General Hansell turned him loose on this mission, he used that power. He used General Arnold's name, General Hansell's name, and the name of anybody else that was necessary. He organized a fleet of six ships, and got them assigned to the Twenty-First Bomber Command. And now one of them had finally arrived. When Possum went aboard this ship that was anchored off Saipan, he found it very well established. He asked the colonel how he had gotten it out to the Marianas, to which the man proudly replied,

I brought it out from New York. Just before we sailed a fellow came out in a Merchant Marine uniform, and he said he was the captain of the ship, and I told him that couldn't be so, because I was in command. So we worked out a deal. He said, "I'll be in command, but you tell me what to do and I'll do it." I said, "The first thing I'm going to tell you to do is take this ship to Saipan." And on this basis we got along just fine.

In the end, Possum didn't get to keep his fleet. Admiral Nimitz found out about it and commandeered it, but the ships were used to the advantage of the Twenty-First Bomber Command in the meantime.

As the day approached for the bombing operation against Japan, the Twenty-First Bomber Command ran a few training flights out against Truk to get some experience bombing, but time was very, very short. On October 27 the crews flew their first combat training missions, in which fourteen of the B-29s attacked Japanese submarine pens on Dublon Island—part of Truk Atoll. Four other B-29s, including the one flown by General Hansell, had to abort the mission because of mechanical problems. Only about a quarter of the bombs that were dropped fell in the target areas.

These training flights were interrupted late in October when the Japanese fleet made a foray into the Philippine Sea, causing a tremendous commotion. The Navy didn't have any idea where the Japanese fleet was, or what it was doing. The Twenty-First Bomber Command had about thirty combat-ready B-29s, which was not enough to launch a diversionary attack against a Japanese city, but General Hansell felt he ought to do *something*. In a compromise to the Twentieth Air Force agreement with the Joint Chiefs of Staff, it had been determined that any time a theater commander declared an emergency, he could take command of the B-29s and notify the Joint Chiefs of Staff. In this instance, General Hansell was afraid that Admiral Nimitz would declare this an emergency—which it certainly was—and take over the B-29s. Possum also feared that he would then have a difficult job of trying to get them back, and that could take months. In hopes of avoiding a takeover, he voluntarily went to the admiral and placed the thirty B-29s at his disposal, asked for Navy officers to be assigned to the command to act as identification officers, loaded up the force with 2000-pound bombs, and stood by ready and willing to do anything he could to help. General Hansell reasoned that if he voluntarily placed his forces at Nimitz's disposal, it would preclude the necessity or excuse for the admiral to take over the Twenty-First or make a formal request to the Joint Chiefs of Staff. In turn, after the emergency, this would make it easier for Hansell to withdraw his forces from Navy control. Fortunately, the B-29s were not called upon, and after a few days the Twenty-First Bomber Command was able to go back to its job.

On November 5, twenty-five Superfortresses from the Twenty-First Bomber Command bombed two airfields on Iwo Jima, starting the tactical operations against the island in preparation for the invasion which the Twentieth Air Force had requested earlier and which was to come in February. Three days later, on November 8, seventeen B-29s went to bomb the airfields on Iwo Jima again. Six managed to bomb through a hole in the cloud cover, but the others failed to get the target. Enemy aircraft dropped phosphorous bombs on the formations, damaging one of the B-29s, whose crew was forced to ditch. It was the first aircraft lost by the Twenty-First Bomber Command on a combat mission. On November 11, they flew the last of the preliminary training missions against Truk Atoll, as eight B-29s bombed those Dublon Island submarine pens again.

A lot of things that happen in wartime are attributable to luck. If the loss of General Hansell's entire supply depot had constituted good planning destroyed by bad fortune, then another experience that he had was exactly the opposite. When he arrived on Saipan, he had been assigned the task of destroying the Japanese aircraft industry, but he did not have a single specific target, and he didn't know where a single target was. The Japanese had maintained such tight secrecy that USAAF planners knew almost nothing about the location of the industry. They knew the names of some factories, and they knew in general where the factories were, but they didn't know the locations well enough to launch an attack. On October 13, 1944, however, a photoreconnaissance airplane, a modified B-29—designated F-13—arrived. It wasn't the only F-13 that we'd have in the Marianas; it just happened that this one, with the auspicious name of *Tokyo Rose*, arrived on an extraordinarily auspicious day—one of those rare days that occur only "on the birthday of the seventh son of a seventh son."

Captain Ralph Steakley, the F-13 aircraft commander, said that he and his crew were ready to take off right away for a reconnaissance mission over Japan. Possum told him that he ought to give his crew a rest, because they had been flying straight through from Kansas. Streakley said no, that he was ready to go, and so General Hansell said, "Okay, go ahead."

It was the luckiest thing that ever happened to the Twenty-First Bomber Command. It was a rare day in Japan when it was clear, but on October 13 there wasn't a cloud in the sky. The *Tokyo Rose* covered a great deal of Japan's urban area, and spent thirty-five minutes flying over Tokyo itself, taking thousands of absolutely priceless photographs. Streakley brought them back, they were developed, and there were the Twenty-First Bomber Command targets! It was the first time an American plane had been over Tokyo since the Doolittle raid in April 1942. The plane flew high enough that it went unchallenged and possibly undetected. Indeed the Japanese were seldom to send interceptors after single Superforts, reserving their efforts for large formations.

General Hansell thought the Navy would be interested in these photos too, since the operation there was supposed to be a combined one. He had an extra set of prints made and asked a staff officer to take them to Admiral William F. "Bull" Halsey, the commander of the Navy's Third Fleet. The next thing he heard was that Admiral Halsey complained to Admiral Nimitz that the Twenty-First Bomber Command was just stirring up the Japanese by flying over Japan, and he requested that the Joint Chiefs of Staff direct that Superfortress operations be grounded. Fortunately that didn't happen, but the whole affair was a shock to General Hansell because he thought he was doing the Navy an enormous favor.

At the end of October, the Navy declared that as a result of the operations of the Japanese fleet, it would be unable to conduct the planned joint mission against Tokyo with the Twenty-First Bomber Command, which was scheduled for the third week of November. The Navy requested that the Twenty-First Bomber Command be grounded until such time as the Navy was prepared to conduct the joint operation. This, along with Halsey's reaction to receiving the photos, alarmed General Hansell, who observed that if he were not permitted to operate except with the blessing of the Navy, he didn't have any separate Twentieth Air Force and that "we might just as well turn everything over to Admiral Nimitz."

He notified General Arnold that he was prepared to bomb Tokyo without Navy support. He realized that this was a brash thing to do:

> I wasn't really prepared yet to do a damn thing, but I was so afraid that the command situation would erode and rob us of our independent operations against the Japanese home islands that I offered to go ahead alone. I never heard anything more about the Navy's request, so we continued with our plans.

General Hansell had submitted his plan for this first operation to General Arnold, and without consulting Possum, Arnold sent a copy to General George Kenney, the commander of the Far East Air Forces, which was an amalgam of nearly every USAAF combat unit in the Southwest Pacific *except* the Twentieth Air Force. Kenney responded by saying that Hansell's plan was totally unfeasible, that all the airplanes could not make the mission, and that those that got there would be shot out of the sky by the Japanese fighters. General Arnold sent this comment back to Hansell and he added under Kenney's statement,

> My people in Washington are inclined to agree with General Kenney and I'm inclined to agree with him too. But, if you feel the operation can be carried out, good luck.

As General Hansell put it,

> This left me saddled with a responsibility which I didn't mind. I was glad to have the authority to go ahead with a mission against Japan. I think I figured out why it had been done that way. If the mission failed—and there was a very good chance that it *would* fail—and General Arnold had ordered it, then the whole scheme of an autonomous Twentieth Air Force might collapse. This would certainly destroy its credibility. On the other hand, if it failed and I had done it against Arnold's advice, I would get fired and the onus would not be on the Command as a whole. It

was a big responsibility, but I really was not too much disturbed by it.

A couple of days after that, however, something else happened that *did* disturb me. I was forbidden to fly on the first mission, which I had planned to lead personally. There was a good deal of apprehension among the crews, for two reasons. One of them was the Japanese opposition, which we knew would be bitter. In defense of Tokyo, and of their emperor's palace, they would do everything they possibly could to stop us. The other was the range of the airplanes, about which we were still concerned. For the sake of morale, I thought that this was a time for the commander to get aboard. I thought I'd had this cleared, so I planned to ignore the order not to fly, but Arnold sent a message through Navy channels and a couple of Navy officers came out and called on me and demanded my signature acknowledging it.

I had to turn the operation over to General Emmett "Rosey" O'Donnell, the Seventy-Third Bombardment Wing commander. I don't think General Arnold was prompted primarily by concern about losing me. When I thought about it afterwards, I remembered that I did have knowledge of our having broken the Japanese codes, and people who knew about this were prohibited from entering into combat areas.

Using the reconnaissance photos that were taken on October 13, General Hansell and his staff made mosaics from the photos of the aircraft factory complex at Musashino near Tokyo. They then stipulated that every bombardier and every navigator memorize those mosaics with the initial point on them, and then draw them from memory, over and over, again and again. Hansell wanted to be damned sure—as sure as he possibly could be—that there wouldn't be any foul-up, at least from the standpoint of recognition.

In the meantime, however, General O'Donnell sent Possum a private handwritten letter in which he said that his outfit was incapable of carrying out the mission as directed. He recommended instead that the first attack by the Twenty-First Bomber Command against Japan proper be a nighttime raid on a coastal target, which would have been much easier.

The two men had a private meeting, in which Hansell told O'Donnell that "I recognize your right to tell me this. As a matter of fact, if you hadn't told me that you felt this way, and the mission had failed, I would have had reason to criticize you. Our orders, however, call for us to attack an aircraft factory, and attacking a seaport at night is certainly not going to do the job. Furthermore, this would indicate immediately that the Twenty-First Bomber Command of the Twentieth Air Force is incapable of carrying out its mission. I am determined that we are going to carry out our mission. If you don't want to lead it, I've got other people who do."

General O'Donnell replied, "No, I want to lead it all right, but I thought I owed it to you to tell you that I don't think it will work."

"If I'd had a little more time," Possum recalled, "I think I would have tried to find somebody else to lead it. It's a very bad idea to give a dangerous, difficult mission to a guy who says he can't do it, but if I had put somebody else in his place, I think the effect on the morale of the Seventy-Third Bomb Wing would have been very bad. They liked Rosey O'Donnell, and had confidence in him." On November 24, 1944, the Twenty-First Bomber Command flew its first mission against Japan. Thirty-five of the one hundred eleven B-29s that Rosey O'Donnell took up to Japan hit the primary target, the Musashino plant, while fifty bombers hit secondary targets in the urban areas and docks. Due to various mechanical difficulties, twenty-six of the bombers had to abort the mission en route or were unable to drop their bombs after they reached Japan. One B-29 crashed off Honshu with all aboard when a fighter rammed it, shearing off the elevator and the right horizontal stabilizer. It was the only plane to be lost to Japanese action, but one other B-29 ditched after running out of fuel. The crew of the latter survived, however. In all, the B-29 gunners claimed to have shot down seven Japanese fighters.

The bombing was poor, but the Twenty-First Bomber Command had gotten over its first major hurdle. The mission had proved to the crews that they could do it—get there and back. Now they would have an opportunity to work on their bombing proficiency. The same mission was repeated on November 27, with eighty-one B-29s, but the target was completely covered by clouds, and so the Musashino plant was attacked again on November 29.

On its way back from that third mission the bomber force was hit by something we always dreaded in the Marianas. At eight o'clock, a tropical storm moved in. For those standing in the wooden tower overlooking the runway, all that could be seen through the rain were the smudge pots. As General Hansell recalls, they couldn't even see the outlines of the runway itself. The air was full of pilots reporting, "Sixty miles from Saipan and out of gasoline. Request landing instructions."

Hansell had a sergeant who was the controller, and he did a magnificent job. "He used his head," Possum remembers. "He didn't lose his voice, he was calm and precise in giving instructions by radio to the bombers on their final approach to the storm-shrouded runway. I realized that, for those few hours, the real commanding general of the Twenty-First Bomber Command was wearing sergeant's stripes! The best I could do was to stay out of his way which I did."

They lost one airplane, though. The pilot ran out of fuel just as he arrived back at the base. He saw some lights which he hoped was the runway, but they turned out to be a vehicle park, and he put the B-29 down on top of the trucks. Big fuel tank trailers were scattered all over the place. The wings were cut off the bomber, and it was folded up like a tin can. The whole area was about 3 inches deep in gasoline, but all the men got out of the B-29 and nobody got hurt. Somehow, miraculously, there was no fire. As Possum said, "It was by the grace of God, with no help from us."

General Hansell realized that those early operations against Japan from the Marianas were not good. They were dependent on optical bombsights, because the AN/APQ-13 radar sights simply were not adequate for bombing noncoastal precision targets. The weather was so damned bad that time after time the B-29s went up to Japan and found nothing but solid undercast.

It's an understatement to say that the weather *forecasting* system was inadequate—it simply wasn't there. We did have an excellent weather officer, though: Colonel Seaver, who had been with General Hansell in England. Possum felt that he was one of the heroes of the war because he did the best interpreting he could without adequate weather intelligence. He gave his best opinion, and it was accepted. He knew very well that if he said he thought the weather was good enough for bombing, the Twenty-First Bomber Command was going to go. He was really carrying the command decisions in his hands, but he never welched it. When the weather was bad, we all knew he had done better than anyone else could have done.

Though the Twenty-First Bomber Command attacked the Japanese airfields on Iwo Jima, its efforts in November and December 1944 were, for the most part, directed at the primary objective, which was the Japanese aircraft industry. The crews bombed the Mitsubishi factory in Nagoya three times between December 13 and December 22. Then on January 9, 1945, they sent seventy-two bombers against the Musashino aircraft factory at Tokyo again, but high winds coupled with cloud cover disrupted the bombing and only eighteen of the B-29s could bomb the primary target.

General Hansell was very disappointed with his results. As he remembers,

The only decent operation that we flew during this series of high-altitude attacks was the last one I ran. It was a 62-plane raid against the Kawasaki aircraft factory at Akashi on January 19. For once we obliterated an engine and aircraft factory! The bombing was not as good as it should have been by standards established in the European theater, but we had so many bombs that we were able to simply obliterate the place. The Japanese never even tried to rebuild it. That is what we wanted to do with the rest of the factories, but weather and ineptitude on our part kept us from doing so. This was my last mission. The next day, the 20th of January, 1945, General LeMay took over from me.

I think the major factor in the decision to move General LeMay to the Marianas had to do with General Arnold's dissatisfaction with my rate of operations. I wasn't satisfied with it either. I knew it would improve over time, but he was very impatient. He was also aware that if the Twentieth Bomber Command were moved to Saipan there would then be two commanders—General LeMay and myself—when we only needed one. General Arnold had asked me to stay on as vice-commander to General LeMay, but I didn't think that was a good idea. It wasn't that I didn't have confidence in General LeMay—in fact I had *every* confidence in him. I simply felt that he didn't need a second-in-command, especially one who was in effect being relieved from first-in-command. It is a difficult thing and probably a bad idea, to take the commander of an outfit and keep him on in a subordinate position, so I asked Arnold that I be relieved and I was.

VI

A Change of Command

The Marianas, January 1945

When I had gone into China in August 1944, it was with the basic understanding that the Twentieth Bomber Command would get out of there as soon as the better bases in the Marianas became operable and capable of supporting large numbers of B-29s. By January 1945, General Hansell had demonstrated that the Marianas were finally ready to support the long-planned B-29 strategic air offensive against Japan. China had proved to be a horrible, almost impossible, logistical situation, and we knew it. The Marianas meanwhile had turned out to be better bases than we had thought; eventually there would be room for the Fifty-Eighth Wing to move over from the China-India theater.

In the meantime, Colonel John H. "Skippy" Davies had already arrived in the Marianas from the States on December 27 with the 313th Bomb Wing. This bomb wing was, after the Seventy-Third,

106

the second B-29 wing to be assigned to the Twenty-First Bomber Command. This wing was directed to have one of its groups develop techniques for aerial mining of harbors. The wing crews flew an operational bombing training mission against Pagan Island on January 16, but they didn't fly against targets in Japan until after I took over the Twenty-First Bomber Command.

I never knew the exact date that General Arnold made the decision to move me out of India and China to replace General Hansell as commander of the Twenty-First Bomber Command, but I got a message on January 1, 1945, to come over to the Marianas to consult with General Hansell. I was told to go by way of Australia, and I spent a day or so arguing about flying around that way. I finally got permission to go straight through to Guam by way of Kunming. I flew a route that was a little south of Formosa, and arrived on January 7.

I went to Guam simply for a twenty-four-hour visit to be briefed by Hansell and General Lauris Norstad, Hap Arnold's deputy, about the ongoing plan to destroy the Japanese aircraft industry by high-altitude precision bombing. When I flew back to India, I was accompanied by Brigadier General Roger Ramey, an old flying school classmate of mine. He had been Hansell's chief of staff in the Marianas, and he would now take over from me as the new commander of the Twentieth Bomber Command. I stayed at Kharagpur only long enough to familiarize him with what was going on. I went back over to the Marianas on January 18, relieved Possum two days later, and we went on from there.

The Twentieth Bomber Command remained headquartered in Kharagpur after I went over to the Marianas, but it soon stopped bombing the main islands of Japan; and on January 27, it evacuated the advanced fields in Chengtu Valley entirely. It had been ordered to fly all its missions from India to relieve the logistics problems for Chennault's Fourteenth Air Force in China, because the Japanese had overrun Luchow in November and were now threatening Kunming. For the next two months, the Twentieth Bomber Command ran training missions and bombed Japanese targets in Southeast Asia. There were a number of pretty substantial raids against Bangkok and Singapore, as well as throughout Burma and the Malay Peninsula until the end of March, when the Twentieth closed up shop and the Fifty-Eighth Bomb Wing moved to the Marianas.

We shared the Marianas with the Seventh Air Force B-24s that had been island-hopping up from Australia for the preceding two years as MacArthur moved forward. Eventually they were to get bases in Okinawa from which they could reach Japan, but in early 1945 the B-24s in the Marianas were still being used in the same way as they had been in the Southwest Pacific. They were flying against island targets they could reach like Truk and Iwo Jima, and against shipping targets, because they lacked the range to get to Japan.

Iwo Jima was a key target, however, because the Japanese had bombers based there. After November 2, 1944, when the Seventy-Third Bomb Wing—Rosey O'Donnell's outfit—got to Saipan, the Japanese on Iwo Jima launched some air attacks on the Marianas, but only five attacks amounted to anything. On the last raid, however, which took place on Christmas, the Japanese managed to send twenty-four planes. They destroyed eleven B-29s and damaged forty-three more, but after the Seventy-Third Bomb Wing hit Iwo Jima a couple of times, the attacks stopped. After January 2, 1945, there were no Japanese air attacks on the Marianas.

Iwo Jima was the only place from which the Japanese *could* have launched an air raid against the Marianas, and B-24s and B-29s from the Marianas had taken care of them there. The Japanese didn't have anything at Truk at that time, and so there was no danger of a Japanese attack of any magnitude. This meant that by the time I arrived, our crews could work all night and put up all the lights they needed.

Life in the Marianas was pretty rugged in January 1945, but we got American food and we didn't worry about malaria after the area was sprayed with DDT. To start with, we were in tents. Gradually, along a bluff on the north side of Guam, we set up headquarters buildings constructed mostly of wood because wooden buildings could be put up quickly. We also had a good hospital made out of quonset huts. We even tried to run a little senior officers' mess at the headquarters.

Life was made bearable by the mild weather, which was generally pretty good because the intertropical front stayed roughly 150 miles south of us. It would move slightly, and usually *stayed* to the south, but we never knew when it might run north on us. If it did, it would come up *very fast,* and we couldn't forecast it. When we sent our airplanes out, we always worried about the front moving over our bases before the planes could get back, as happened that time at the end of November 1944, when Possum Hansell was still there.

We finally built a road down to the beach on the north shore, and so if you were a beach fanatic, you were in heaven. I was the fly in that ointment, though, because I got the men to work—I told them that they were going to fly 120 hours a month. *That was work,* so they really didn't have time to wonder too much about what kind of environment they were in.

Even though the Americans had taken Guam five months before, and had turned it into a major air and naval base, Japanese troops that had never surrendered were *still* hiding in the jungle. The Marines just gave this jungle the "once over lightly" and moved on. We had lights along the bluff near our headquarters, but if anyone went there during the night, he would be sure to make a lot of noise so that the guards would see him. Otherwise he might be mistaken for a Japanese soldier coming back up and be shot. As the theater commander, Admiral Nimitz was responsible for base security, but if there were ever any Navy security people around, I never saw them. We would put our own sentries near our tents and in the places that we had people.

I only know of one case in which one of the Japanese was actually killed, but there were other instances where several shots were fired. I never heard of any sabotage, but frequently the Japanese would sneak in to steal food or anything they could get their hands on without being seen by a sentry. There was a joke about a Japanese soldier getting in the chow line, and then getting in the paymaster's line and getting paid. Some of our people did actually get carbines and go hunting the Japanese. I don't think they hunted very hard, but they would comb the jungle around the base.

The Japanese troops that ran out of ammunition would fight like animals to the last man. Their persistence showed the strength of their belief in the code under which they lived, and it helps explain some of the cruelty to our people who were captured, especially in the Philippines. To the Japanese, being captured was a very degrading experience, to be avoided at all costs. They either fought until they were killed or else committed suicide. We only captured a handful of Japanese on all the Pacific islands, and they were either incapacitated or unconscious when they were found.

When I settled into my new command on Guam at the end of January, I went down to call on Admiral Chester Nimitz, who was Commander in Chief for the Pacific (CINCPAC). I had to stop in to say hello to these people—protocol demanded it. About three days later, though, I got a dinner invitation from Admiral Nimitz. I was pretty busy, but of course I had to go. I put on a clean pair of pants and a clean shirt—it hadn't been ironed very well, but at least it was washed—and I went over to the admiral's quarters. The Seabees had built him a house on the highest hill in the southern part of Guam. It looked like a fairly big civilian residence with a huge dining room. It wasn't such a bad place to be.

I went in to find chandeliers glowing and all the lights ablaze, the dinner table set with a white tablecloth, sparkling silverware, and so forth. Everyone was standing around in starched white uniforms having a drink. I felt like a skunk at a family reunion, but we had a really nice dinner with soup, roast beef, and salad. We had the whole works, including ice cream. When it was over I thanked him very much and told him that I had to get home.

A few days later the same thing happened again. This time the invitation came from Admiral John Hoover. He had a house on the *second* highest hill, but he had a tennis court, because he was a tennis player and liked a little recreation. We had the same thing for dinner there.

Finally, I got an invitation from Admiral Charles Lockwood, who was at sea aboard what used to be Vanderbilt's yacht. Navy regulations forbade alcohol aboard its ships, and so there was no liquor at this dinner party. However, Admiral Lockwood had all the houseboys running around, just the same as at the other places. Filipino houseboys were standard equipment in the Navy then.

Of course, I had to return this hospitality, and so a week or two later I invited them all up to dinner on Guam's north shore. We had drinks in my tent and went over to the quonset hut that we had set up as a senior officers' dining room for the meal. We opened up flight rations and had canned turkey for dinner. Having dinner at the quonset hut made an impression on Nimitz, but his attitude seemed to be "that's good enough for the Army, or in this case, the Army Air Forces." Nothing was ever said about it. The Navy was supposed to supply and support us, but it took them a very long time to get things done for us out there.

I was supposed to be supplied by Nimitz, but he was too busy supplying himself and the fleet to think about my operation, which had started off little, but grew, like the camel getting his head under the tent. The Navy always treated us rather like stepchildren in the Marianas.

After the war, Hap Arnold put it into perspective when he said: "Before we got the Marianas, the columnists, commentators, and newspaper reporters had all talked about the *Naval* capture of the Islands. The *Navy* would take the Islands and use them as a base. No one had mentioned using them as bases for the B-29s, yet it was the B-29s and the B-29s only that could put tons and tons of bombs on Japan. The fleet couldn't do it; the Naval air couldn't do it; the Army couldn't do it. The B-29s could." And we did.

Down at the second-echelon level, we got along pretty well with the Navy. The Seabees finally built us a row of five or six little bungalows for some of our staff to move into, with open living rooms and patio area, a little kitchen, and two or three bedrooms. This wasn't part of their construction program, but they did it on their own for us.

Throughout the rest of the war, I would meet with Nimitz once a week on the average. Relations were always very cordial; he was a fine old gentleman.

Before World War II the Air Corps had an organization consisting of a combat group, a service group, an air base group, communications, and a few other dogs and cats. These entities existed in parallel rather than being arranged in a chain of command that made sense from an operational point of view. The base was usually commanded by the base commander, as it was with ground forces. The other people were, let's say, tenants on the base, and so the combat group commander was just a tenant under the base commander. Naturally if the base commander wanted to mow the grass on the field and the combat commander wanted to fly his airplanes, the grass was mowed. If the combat commander wanted the service group to work on his airplanes, the group did it in its own good time. The combat commander would transfer his airplane to the service group; and when the workers in the service group got through with it, they would transfer it back.

This same organization held during World War II. The service group was not under the combat commander, although the combat commander did command the base in Europe. When he wanted the service group to do the second-echelon maintenance on an airplane that was badly shot up, he would transfer it to the group, but he had no control over when the service group would finish with it. The service group didn't have the same urgency as the combat commander. This wasn't satisfactory to me or to other people, but as far as I know, nothing was ever done about it in England. Finally enough airplanes were sent over there that it didn't make much difference anyway.

In maintenance, the crew chief leads a crew of mechanics who work on a particular airplane and keep it in commission. Before the war we had enough trained engine mechanics, radio mechanics and airplane mechanics to make up the needed crews. However, after the war started, we would often have to fly an airplane that was out of commission because only the maintenance crew assigned to that airplane would work on it and the crews lacked the necessary skills to do a proper job. In India, because we didn't have enough trained mechanics to make the "crew system" work, I changed the system. I created a sort of assembly-line maintenance system on the base with one maintenance officer in charge of everything. The people who were qualified on radios, for instance, went right down the line checking the radios. With the proper people on it, the best we had, the job would get done right away. They could also train other people to do this kind of job quickly so that we could run a twenty-four-hour maintenance line. We had six bases around Calcutta when I started this up throughout the Twentieth Bomber Command. We didn't keep any airplanes sitting on the field at the advance bases in China unless it was one that just wouldn't fly. Then we would send a crew up to fix it so that we could get it back to India for the full maintenance that had to be done.

When I went over to the Marianas, I hadn't been on the ground for twenty-four hours before Possum Hansell's supply officer, Colonel C. S. "Bill" Irvine, came in to talk with me. I don't know to this day if he was pulling my leg or not, but he said he wanted to reorganize the maintenance routine. I asked him what he wanted to do and he outlined just about exactly what I had been doing down in India. I don't know if he had found out what I was doing or whether he figured that I was going to tell him to do that anyway. In any event, we had the same setup in the Marianas that we had in India—one supply center on the base. In the Marianas there were eventually five bombardment wings, not just one as we'd had in India, and so it was even more important to have everything centralized.

Having organized maintenance along these lines, I couldn't imagine putting a crew chief on each of the airplanes. First of all, we didn't have that many people who knew the airplane well enough to be crew chiefs. Then, the people we could assign to work under a crew chief weren't as well trained as the crew chief would be. I cannot picture all those untrained people crawling over an airplane trying to get it fixed when something broke. It wouldn't have worked at all. We would have been back to flying thirty hours a month like everybody else, and that wouldn't have gotten the job done.

The mechanics who had come into the Marianas had been through the mechanics school, but they had been formed into groups at a time when there were only a handful of B-29s to work on. The schools had finally gotten in some Wright Cyclone engines so that the engines could be torn down and looked at. So the mechanics had some training, but no experience. They had seen the airplane and worked on it, but they hadn't worked on it steadily, and they didn't know what was going to break next. A good, experienced mechanic would know about how long a part was going to last and where it was likely to give you trouble; and so when trouble came, he would look there first and not waste time finding it. That's experience.

With the centralized maintenance system we could use the few real experts we had more efficiently. Under their direction, we started a training program to get more work out of the less efficient people, and we had a twenty-four-hour operation going in no time. We increased efficiency and got more work done. The assembly-line technique cut engine-change time from three days to about four hours. There was no comparison. This system en-

abled us to get 120 hours a month out of all the airplanes. Bill
Irvine had set up a special supply line that bypassed the A-4
(supply) command in Hawaii. Irvine had been in the Air Materiel
Command during his service, and so he knew a lot of the people
who were running transport aircraft. One way or another he got
some Douglas C-54 transports and set up a private air service.
He kept in contact with the Air Materiel Command depot at
Sacramento by radio, and Air Materiel sent out the parts that we
needed. If Bill hadn't been able to do this, we would have had a
lot of airplanes sitting on the ground.

At five o'clock in the morning, we might have fifty Superforts
out of commission for lack of parts. At eight o'clock, Irvine's C-54s
would arrive, and at nine o'clock, those fifty B-29s would take off
on a mission. We ran it that close. We simply didn't have time to
wait the six weeks that it took for the Navy to bring in supplies by
ship. And it wasn't necessary to wait this long when the C-54s
could fly all the way from Sacramento to Guam (with stops in
Hawaii and Kwajalein) in only two days.

Irvine had perhaps a half a dozen C-54s flying in with as many
parts as he could get into them. I don't know exactly how he was
doing it, but I certainly wasn't going to ask any stupid questions
at the time. I had confidence in him getting things done in the
best possible way, and he did. I don't think anyone higher up
knew anything about this. It was the kind of initiative you don't
see much of now. It also violated all military principles. You got
that old dodge that supply originates from the rear and flows with
the continuity of command. That's all fine, but you come across
special situations. Nimitz probably didn't even notice what Irvine
was doing. His supply officer got suspicious and *did* find out about
it, but he was so busy doing other things that he didn't have time
to bother with us, and in the meantime, Bill Irvine's little airline
kept us going. He fully expected to be court-martialed at the end
of the war, but people kind of forgot about it.

I had faith in this system, Bill Irvine had faith in it, and when
the group commanders saw the way we were keeping their airplanes flying, they had faith in it too.

VII

Striking Back
at the Empire
January–July 1945

THE TASK AT HAND

I didn't waste any time getting down to business after I took over the Twenty-First Bomber Command. On January 21, 1945, the day after I relieved General Hansell, I had sent thirty B-29s on a training mission against Moen Airfield on Truk. There wasn't much there for us to destroy at Truk, but like Possum, I launched those missions to give the crews the feeling of flying over and bombing enemy territory, yet without the cost of an extra mission against Japan.

Two days later I sent the force up to Japan. Only twenty-eight Superforts were able to bomb the primary target—the Mitsubishi aircraft engine plant at Nagoya—but twenty-seven others hit secondary targets in the urban area of the city, while nine more bombed alternates and targets of opportunity. There were estimated to have been over six hundred interceptors thrown at us,

115

but only one B-29 was lost, while our gunners shot down thirty-two Japanese fighters.

As could have been predicted, our major problem was the lack of practical experience in the new crews that were coming in all the time. The situation was, however, somewhat better than it had been two years before in Europe. A lot of our pilots who went to England had gone right out of flying school into an airplane, without the proper training. For instance, the people I took to England had only 200 hours of flying time. Half of my class went with me to England, and the other half went into the Training Command, because we had to build it to teach the millions of people who were going to make up the huge air force we were planning for. Those who stayed in the Training Command, and later got into the B-29 program, had been flying airplanes and were in good shape, even though they hadn't had any combat training, particularly with the B-29. They flew the B-29 out to combat as soon as it came out of the factory instead of practicing with it.

I had several people in the Marianas who had flown in Europe or in the Southwest Pacific, but there weren't enough of them to make a major impact. So basically, we were having to make do with green crews.

As a result, those first B-29 missions that we flew out of the Marianas didn't go very well, and this led me to the conclusion that we couldn't do the job in the time we had, with the forces we had and were likely to get. Aside from the green crews, our major problem was that we had an airplane that still wasn't really ready for combat. We had a difficult time keeping the B-29s in commission, with the long maintenance periods that were required. We had crews that weren't trained, and we had outfits that weren't organized. Everything was wrong, and so I started some training procedures to try to whip the crews into shape so we would be more efficient when we did get up to Japan. In the end, the Twentieth Air Force probably flew more training missions than it did combat missions.

It took considerable skill for a bombardier to drop a bomb on the target. This is very exacting precision work, requiring a great deal of care even under the best circumstances, so it is a considerable problem when somebody is shooting at you. The difficulty was further exacerbated by the fact that many bombardiers had too little training and no maps—just photographs of the towns in which the targets were located.

Of course, we did have the Norden bombsight—the essential key to precision bombing—in the B-29, but, even with the Norden bombsight, the bombardier still had to see the target and identify it. He had to find the aiming point, and he had to do *that* far enough back so that he could level the bombsight. It had to be level. (If the plane was jigging around trying to duck flak or fighters, or if there was an error in leveling the bombsight, he wasn't going to hit anything.) Once the bombardier had gotten the bombsight level, it was good only for a short time. If the plane made even a *little* turn, the gyro precessed and the accuracy would go off. The bombardier needed a straight and level bomb run. To fly straight and level toward the target with the wind blowing the plane off course required heading upwind enough to compensate for it. The bombardier also needed to know the ballistic characteristics of the bomb, and to determine how high the plane was, using the barometric pressure and the altimeter. With that set, the bombardier would have to kill the ground speed drift by using the proper drop angle and getting that cross hair to stay on the target. When the plane was finally going straight toward the target at the proper time and the proper drop angle, the bombardier dropped the bombs. If all those things weren't done properly, the bombs didn't hit the target.

If the bombardier could see anything on the ground, and if he could *identify* it as a target, he'd try to make a bomb run on it. Sometimes it was harder at low altitudes, and sometimes not. In other words, the bombardier would try his best to get ready. He could always bomb more accurately with a Norden bombsight than he could with a radar bombsight, and so if he could see anything to hit, he would use the Norden bombsight. If not, he would use radar.

For the most part, we hadn't had radar bombsights in the B-17. A few came over to England in mid-1944, about the time I was leaving. Unfortunately, on the missions where we used them, they didn't do any good. The ones that we had on the B-29s in February 1945 were much better than the first, but still not really good enough for precision bombing.

The last wing I got—the 315th Bomb Wing, which arrived in

June 1945—had Superforts equipped with the more advanced AN/ APQ-7 Eagle radar. Instead of having a rotating antenna on the nose, these planes had a snub wing underneath the fuselage that gave much better definition. The antenna went back and forth instead of in a circular motion, and so you only saw a "V" out in front of you instead of a whole circle, but what it showed was much clearer and more well-defined. With it, we could identify oil refineries. These were the first targets that I assigned to the planes equipped with Eagle radar, and by using it we would get them every time.

Back in February 1945, though, we could only bomb coastal targets with radar because bombardiers needed the contrast between land and water to locate landmarks. I immediately started a radar school in addition to the lead crew school, and we rapidly got better. By the end of the war we were able to destroy an inland city in the middle of a thunderstorm by using radar.

A major part of planning those raids was simply knowing what the targets were. When the war started we had nothing in the way of real intelligence on Japan, and three years later in 1944 we still knew nothing. From that reconnaissance mission flown by Ralph Steakley over Japan on October 13, 1944, we got the best pictures we could have hoped for. There wasn't really another chance like that for the rest of the war. Those photographs were a godsend.

Steakley's photographs covered most of the ports and harbors and the towns surrounding them, as well as inland towns and any other collection of buildings that looked interesting. For instance, there was only one tetra-ethyl lead plant in Japan, and we received word what town it was in from Washington. Since we had a picture of that town, we were able to go up and get the plant.

For mission planning we would also get some intelligence reports from Washington, but these consisted mainly of information that such and such a plant was in such and such a town. Knowing what a plant might look like, we would then have to rely on road maps and our aerial photographs to determine the locations of specific industries and buildings where military outfits and government offices were located.

We really didn't know anything about Japan, because the Japanese had kept the place pretty well closed before the war. We didn't have any secret agents creeping around in Japan sending us information. Before the war, we really hadn't had any people whose sole duty had been to gather intelligence. We'd had air attaches, who were Air Corps officers, in certain foreign embassies around the world in the 1930s, but only a few. I don't think most of them knew they were supposed to gather intelligence!

They had an "intelligence" division in the State Department before the war, but the members of the division didn't do anything but balance teacups. Washington really didn't know very much either. General Arnold later recalled that "when we were talking in the Joint and Combined Chiefs of Staff meetings about possible landings on the island of Hokkaido, in Japan, the only information I could get from the G-2 [intelligence] section of the Army or the ONI [Office of Naval Intelligence] Section of the Navy, was a book dated 1858!"

As I noted before, the only way we could get *weather* information was literally to *go up and look*, and so we had individual weather airplanes flying up to Japan all the time. With that, the weather people would try to draw a weather map and make a forecast.

Things didn't line up so easily that we could fly a weather flight before each mission. We did try to fly a photographic *reconnaissance* mission to find out where the target was and what it looked like. After that, we had to make enough copies of that picture so that the crews who were going on the bombing mission could take a look at the target. Then we went up to Japan and destroyed it. Ideally we would go up on a postflight reconnaissance mission and take a picture of the target. After taking a look at it, we could say, "Yes, we destroyed the target, so you can check it off the list."

We tried to get in a postflight reconnaissance mission as soon after every mission as we could. The regular reconnaissance missions, however, were flown like strike missions—the weather determined when we could do it. If there was any possible chance of getting an airplane up to Japan, we would send one. If nothing else, the reconnaissance flight would report the weather, which would help our forecasters.

All these things, however, didn't occur with a nice, even continuity. Sometimes we went up there to do one thing and couldn't do it, but happened to see a lucky hole in the clouds and so were able to do something else that needed to be done.

When we sent a reconnaissance flight up, the number of planes that went depended upon the situation and how many reconnaissance planes we had *in commission*. The reconnaissance pilots had the same problems that the bomber squadron people had. Everyone talks about the fighter pilots and, although to a lesser degree, about bomber pilots, but nobody says anything about the reconnaissance pilot. He's the most important guy in the whole show because of the intelligence he provides. Because he goes up in advance and is very often alone, normally everybody in the enemy air force is after him—needless to say, the attrition rate is pretty high. But despite the danger, he has to get up there *first* so that the fighter and bomber guys can do their jobs.

How soon after a reconnaissance flight we would send up the bombers would depend on what the reconnaissance pictures showed, and whether there was a target there or not. If there *was* one, how soon we hit it depended on its priority on the target list, if it was even on the target list. It also depended on the weather and many other factors, but as I reviewed our situation in February 1945, the overall results of our high-altitude bombing weren't very satisfactory.

A RADICAL CHANGE

By the end of February 1945, most of the original design flaws of the B-29 were being addressed at the factory, and the changes I'd made in maintenance procedures in January were starting to be felt. Still, the trouble remained that we had untrained crews and, over Japan, the worst weather I had encountered to date. This was adding up to poor results. In spite of the fact that the force had increased due to the new airplanes that were coming in, it had now become apparent that as long as the weather situation kept up, we weren't going to be able to defeat Japan using high altitude precision bombing before the scheduled invasion was to begin. We had to do something really different. In other words, we had to use the tools we had in another way.

I made up my mind to make some major changes in the way we were using the B-29s because it was now clear that we couldn't possibly succeed by basing our strategy on our experience from Europe. That system wasn't working. It was a different war with different weather and a different airplane. It called for a different solution.

As I looked over the reconnaissance photos, I noticed that there wasn't any low altitude flak such as we'd encountered in Europe. It looked reasonable to me that we could fly a successful mission with less fuel and a larger bombload by going in low, particularly if we went in at night. After sizing up the situation and knowing that I had to do something radical, I finally arrived at the decision to use low level attacks against Japanese urban industrial areas using *incendiaries*. Even poorly trained radar operators could find cities that were on or near the coast, and going in at between 5000 and 8000 feet instead of 25,000 feet would ensure that all the bombs would fall in the target area. This method solved the weather problem because, instead of getting the force ready and then waiting for the right weather, we would go in *under* the weather when *we* were ready.

On the downside, the only question was that of the loss rate, but we calculated that the odds were in favor of successful low-level attacks without an increase in losses.

If there had been any serious planning before the war for the use of incendiaries, I hadn't heard anything about it, and I don't remember any mission that our group flew over Germany where we used them. I'm sure General Hansell knew as much about incendiaries as I did, but he hadn't used any in the attacks he made against Japan before I arrived in the Marianas. In March 1943, however, the USAAF had conducted a series of important secret tests with incendiaries at the Dugway Proving Ground in Utah. Antonin Raymond, a New York architect with eighteen pre-war years of experience in Japan, had been hired to design a town that would simulate, in precise detail, a typical Japanese city. Using materials that were brought in from as far away as Hawaii, the USAAF constructed a full scale Japanese town. It was exact down to the books on the shelves and the matting on the floor. Even a "fire brigade" was organized, equipped to simulate its typical counterpart in Japan. Attacks on this site, combined with the research efforts of DuPont, Standard Oil, and the National Research Defense Council, resulted in the new napalm-based M69 incendiary bomb that became available at the end of 1944.

In the meanwhile, the only major use of incendiaries against the Japanese in actual combat had been our December 18, 1944, attack on Hankow. All our estimating now indicated that we needed about 400 airplanes in order to put down enough bombs to get the concentration required for a good fire. We didn't, however, have 400 airplanes. We didn't have any time, either. We had to go *now*.

The first low-level incendiary attack was put on the schedule for the night of March 9–10, 1945. Tokyo would be our target—the primary target, the secondary target, and the *only* target. The raid would be a maximum effort of unprecedented scale. Except for the March 4 mission, in which 179 bombers (of the 192 launched) hit Tokyo, no B-29 raid had ever gone out with more than 150 bombers earmarked for a single target, but this raid would consist of over 300 Superforts.

The preflight briefing in the big quonset hut on Saipan was packed as no other. As we began to outline the plan, the aircrews were enthusiastic about the size of the attack, but low-level tactics gave it the pall of a suicide mission. Those with experience in Europe knew that a low-level formation like this would have been cut to ribbons by the Luftwaffe. The conventional wisdom among the crews held that this plan was impossible. However, we realized that the Japanese *also* considered it impossible and that they would not be expecting it. We knew that the Japanese early warning network was greatly inferior to that of the Germans, that the Japanese night-fighter threat was virtually nonexistent, and that the Japanese antiaircraft gunners had their shells fused to explode in the high altitude environment where they were used to finding the B-29s.

At 6:15 p.m. on March 9 the first B-29s of Rosey O'Donnell's Seventy-Third Bomb Wing began their takeoff roll on Saipan's Isley Field. They were joined by the 313th Bomb Wing launching from Tinian and the 314th from Guam, and by 7:17, there were 325 of the big silver bombers beginning the seven hours of monotony that would take them into the very heart of the Japanese Empire.

I had taken the best and most experienced radar operators in the Twenty-First Bomber Command and had put them in the lead, pathfinders designated to mark the targets. The rest of the huge force followed the pathfinders across Cape Nojima and north over Tokyo Bay into the city. Waiting at the command post, I received word of the first bombs being dropped at 1:21 a.m. on March 10.

The M69 incendiaries were set to burst at 2000-feet altitude, each in turn dividing into 38 separate submunitions covering a swath of Tokyo 500 feet by 2500 feet with burning gasoline. Wave upon wave of Superforts followed the pathfinders across Tokyo at altitudes staggered between 5000 and 8000 feet, dropping their M69s to the pattern set by the fires started by the pathfinders. With 8 tons of incendiaries crammed into the bomb bay of every Superfort, it didn't take long before there were small tongues of fire throughout the Tokyo urban area. Quickly these small fires spread and merged into larger fires, which in turn merged into a firestorm of incredible proportions.

The firestorm consumed so much oxygen that those who did not die by the flames simply suffocated. Huge updrafts from the fire tossed the Superforts like embers over a campfire.

For the B-29 crews, the night raid became almost as well lit as a daylight mission. For the populace of the city below, it was as though Tokyo had dropped through the floor of the world and into the mouth of hell.

When the conflagration finally burned out, 267,171 buildings had been destroyed and 83,000 people were dead—the highest death toll of any single day's action of the war, exceeding the number of deaths caused by the big Allied raids on Hamburg and Dresden, or the nuclear strike to come in August on Hiroshima. Millions of homeless found themselves facing an uncertain future with little or no food and clothing in the freezing cold.

I didn't like the idea of not being permitted to fly any combat missions to Japan. The Tokyo raid was a classic case where a commander should fly the mission. New and untried tactics and methods added to the normal tension and worry about the mission. The simple fact that a commander was *taking* his men to the target, rather than *sending* them, would have helped morale a lot. In this case, however, this commander had been briefed about the atomic bomb, and I was therefore grounded for the sake of security. I chose General Tommy Power of the 314th Bomb Wing, who I felt was my best wing commander, to lead the mission and to remain over Tokyo and observe the attack as it developed. He drew a series of sketches—every 10 minutes—as the fires spread, and this furnished invaluable information for planning future missions.

At first, we had decided to take out the guns and gunners to make up for the shortage of airplanes, because it would be another factor in helping increase the bombload. However, if the change to low altitude had been quite a step to take, then going in at low altitude with half a crew was *something else!* I find it impossible to describe the relationship that developed between crew members going into combat together. They were more than a team, they were like a family. If a crew member was sick, or for some reason could not go on a mission, the rest of the crew felt as though part of them was missing, and they would not do as well without him. So flying these missions with half a crew was quite an emotional experience for those who stayed as well as for those who went.

Tampering with crew morale was something I did not want to do, and so the gunners went back in, but only with ammunition for the bottom turrets, and with searchlights as the only targets for them to shoot at. I was much more worried about B-29s shooting at each other than I was about any fire we might receive from the ill-equipped and inexperienced Japanese night fighters.

The March 10, 1945, incendiary attack was easily the turning point in the air war against Japan and quite possibly of the entire war in the Pacific. I believe that it succeeded because we understood the tools we had. Our well-calculated gamble proved to be an important landmark in the history of modern aerial warfare.

The decisive effect of this and the raids that came during the following nights was due largely to our ability to send truly large masses of B-29s against the targets on a consistent basis. The 325 bombers launched on the Tokyo raid were nearly double the number that had been launched on the most ambitious raid before, and over seven times the average number on missions launched during January and February 1945. The capability of the Twenty-First Bomber Command to go from 50-plane raids to 300-plane raids in March was made possible by the revamping of the maintenance and supply systems.

We had stockpiled enough incendiaries to follow the Tokyo raid with four other maximum efforts in rapid succession. In a little more than a week, the Twenty-First Bomber Command firebombed just about all the major urban areas in Japan. The apprehensive mood of the crews was dramatically reversed in the wake of their success over Tokyo. Not only had they burned out 16.8 square miles of the enemy capital, but the mission most thought would be suicidal had suffered just a *4 percent* loss rate!

Our second incendiary raid was launched just 29 hours after the last B-29s returned from Tokyo. This time 285 bombers visited Nagoya, the heart of the Japanese aircraft industry. After the attack, the U.S. Navy reported that one of its submarines had surfaced 150 miles from the target to find visibility reduced to 1 mile by the heavy wood smoke.

On March 14, shortly after midnight, 274 Superforts began releasing their incendiaries on Osaka. The 8.1 square miles of Japan's second largest city incinerated that night by the Twenty-First Bomber Command included the 150 acre Osaka arsenal. The concussions from this exploding target were so powerful that some B-29s were batted out of the air. The appropriately named Superfortress *Topsy Turvy* was blown 5000 feet straight up by one of the shock waves. Turned upside down, the plane then fell 10,000 feet before the pilot got it under control.

On March 17, 307 bombers (out of 331 launched) hit Kobe with 4.7 million pounds of incendiaries—the largest bombload yet carried—and on March 19, 290 planes returned to Nagoya. In the space of 10 days, 1505 sorties had been launched against Japan, more than the total for the first five months of the Twenty-First Bomber Command's operations from the Marianas. For Japanese morale, it was the beginning of the end.

I was not happy, but neither was I particularly concerned, about civilian casualties on incendiary raids. I didn't let it influence any of my decisions because we knew how the Japanese had treated the Americans—both civilian and military—that they'd captured in places like the Philippines.

We had dropped some warning leaflets over Japan, which essentially told the civilian population that we weren't trying to kill them, but rather that we were trying to destroy their capability to make war. We were going to bomb their cities and burn them down. We suggested they leave for their own safety. I didn't think it did much good, but I did notice that the greatest number of casualties came on the first Tokyo attack. From then on, the number went down because of the evacuation of civilians and because the Japanese got somewhat better fire-fighting capability, although the latter never improved to a great extent.

Robert Nathans, vice president for the Safety Research Institute, who made an extensive study of the fires in Japan, said that the analysts who observed Japan after the war remarked that the strategic air offensive:

> would not have been possible without the bloody amphibious campaign of island-hopping that eventually provided the bases in the Marianas and Iwo Jima's emergency landing fields that saved hundreds of B-29s and their crews from watery graves. Nor would the Japanese Empire have fallen without the U.S. Navy's defeat of the Japanese fleet and clearance of the sea lanes. In the end, however, it must be underscored that *the strategic air offensive was the only battle of the Japanese home islands* (italics added).
>
> When General Hap Arnold came to the Marianas in June 1945 he told the men of the Twentieth Air Force that a continuation of their operations would enable U.S. Army infantrymen to walk ashore in Japan with their rifles slung. Other branches of the services expressed their doubts vividly and even the airmen were skeptical. When the advance guard of the U.S. Army Eleventh Airborne Division arrived at Atsugi, Japan, on August 30, 1945, history had borne out the General's prediction. While the first troops walked through the ashes and rubble of Yokohama with their guns at the ready, there were no "incidents." Fire had reduced the Japanese to a complete and abject surrender.

When we determined that we had the capability of flying 120 hours a month, I told Nimitz that we were going to do this and that he ought to beef up the supplies. His staff waved us away, saying, "Go away, don't bother us. You can't do *that* out here in the boondocks."

The Eighth Air Force in England flew only thirty hours a month. Nimitz had these figures and figured our best capacity from that. He would say, "How are you going to fly 120 hours out here?"

I told him, "We *can* do it. And we *will* do it." That didn't make much of an impression on the Navy, and so I finally got mad and said, "When we run out of supplies, *you* explain it to the Joint Chiefs of Staff. *That's your job—we'll go fishing.*"

Once we started the incendiary attacks, we wanted to fly as many as fast as we could. There was always the possibility that the Japanese would come up with a defense that would cause unexpected casualties, and we would then have to change the plan. We flew five missions in ten days before we ran out of incendiaries and had to go back to high explosive bombs.

It was April 13 before we had built up large enough stocks of incendiaries to support a full-scale mission, but we flew a lot of smaller-scale missions while we were waiting for more bombs. The Navy scurried around and got some ships, and in six weeks we had the bombs.

We never caught up from then on, though. We simply bypassed the bomb dumps, and with the help of the Seabees, some Marines that were supposedly in a rest camp, and anybody else that was around, we brought the bombs from the supply ships directly to the hardstands of the airplanes. Soon we were dropping over 3000 tons per mission, and that's a lot of tons to haul around. Of course, if we had been under attack, we wouldn't have dared to do that, but there wasn't any possibility of more attacks after the Marines took Iwo Jima. After the end of April we never used a bomb dump—the bombs went straight from the ships to the airplanes.

SUPPORTING THE NAVY

By March 1945, as our Twenty-First Bomber Command was showering the Japanese heartland with incendiary conflagration, the rest of the Allied war effort was tightening the noose on what was left of the once far-flung Japanese Empire. It was, by *now*, an empire which had—for all practical purposes—ceased to exist in the Pacific. In the course of three bloody years, the battlefront had been pushed from the doorstep of Australia to the doorstep of Japan. Since the summer of 1944 both the Marianas and the

Philippines had been liberated. Iwo Jima had been invaded only three weeks before the incendiary raids began, and yet there was already an emergency landing field on Iwo Jima that was available to B-29s returning from those raids.

Located halfway between Guam and Tokyo, Iwo Jima was a desolate volcanic island 5 miles long and nearly 3 miles wide that the Japanese had transformed into a truly formidable fortress. Because of its strategic location, the planners in Washington had long eyed it as a basing location for American tactical air attacks on Japan and as an emergency landing field for B-29s that had been shot up over Japan and couldn't make it back to the Marianas.

Three Marine divisions landed on the shores of the island in February 19, 1945, two years and a day after the death of Eddie Allen in the crash of the second XB-29 prototype. As they faced ferocious enemy fire, the Marines were backed up by heavy naval gunfire, carrier air power, and even by our B-29s from the Marianas. It took the Marines four weeks of the heaviest fighting in the Pacific war to finally defeat the Japanese defenders, and even then there were enemy holdouts fighting from crevices and caves.

The first B-29 to be saved because of Iwo Jima landed there not two weeks after the Marines had taken the airfield. The runway was yet to be widened, there were no facilities to support a B-29, and the island was still under constant fire from Japanese positions when a Superfort piloted by Lieutenant Raymond Malo came away from a mission over Japan badly shot up and with a malfunctioning fuel system. The transfer switch that should have given the plane access to its reserve tanks was shot out and there was only one alternative to ditching at sea—Iwo Jima.

The B-29s had yet to be cleared for landings on Iwo's barely functional runway, but Malo and his crew decided to take the chance. Malo managed to contact the jury-rigged entity that constituted the Iwo Jima control tower, and explained their desperate situation. "Okay *Monster*," the air traffic controller replied in reference to the huge plane's call sign. "You can land. Runway 4000 feet [the B-29s were used to 8500 feet]. Under mortar fire... steel craters on the left. Come on in. Good luck."

Malo would need that luck. He would be landing a damaged plane on a crude half-length runway that was under heavy mortar fire. The plane hit the runway hard, brakes and tire rubber steaming black smoke from the heat of friction, but it stopped. Safely.

Four hours later, the mortars had been silenced, and the big plane took off again for Tinian with its tanks full. Malo's *Monster* was only the first of 2400 Superfortresses that would live to fight another day, thanks to the invaluable field on Iwo Jima. Eventually the runway was lengthened, widened, and even paved. The Marines paid a heavy price for Iwo, but their sacrifice saved the lives of thousands of USAAF crewmen.

One major obstacle beyond Iwo Jima—and it was indeed a *major* obstacle—still lay between the increasingly powerful forces of the United States and the doorstep of the Japanese Empire. It was called Okinawa.

The largest island of the Ryukyu chain, Okinawa was a prefecture of Japan. Technically it was not a colony, but Japanese soil. As part of Japan proper, it was correctly predicted to be the most heavily defended territory that the Americans had yet landed upon. Even then, enemy strength was seriously underestimated. The overall plan for securing Okinawa included the naval and air bombardment of not only Okinawa itself but of the Japanese main island of Kyushu as well. The Imperial Japanese Navy had been largely destroyed during the great naval battles that had accompanied the American invasion of the Philippines, and so the most serious concern was that American forces would be under attack from land-based air power from the Japanese home islands for the first time.

In April 1945, as Halsey was conducting his naval campaign with the world's mightiest fleet against Japan, I received a message from Washington to support him and his mission. Halsey's plan was to run into Japanese home waters during the night, launch his airplanes, hit some targets, and continue working up the coastline. It was Halsey's operation, so I didn't offer anything; I just waited for him to ask. Finally, I received a message from him. He wanted me to support him by putting a maximum effort on the airfields in the vicinities of his strikes. If the weather was good and his planes flew two missions a day off the carriers, the planes could drop a maximum of 300 tons of bombs, but they actually averaged only 120 tons of bombs a day. By contrast, my maximum effort in those days was 3000 tons. Halsey wanted me to put those 3000 tons on the

Japanese airfields because he didn't want his carriers subjected to air attack. I sent him a reply saying, "This doesn't quite fit in with the Joint Chiefs of Staff directive on the mission of the Twentieth Air Force," and went on to suggest that I support him by hitting strategic targets in the area he was going to strike.

I heard nothing from Halsey, but he complained to Nimitz, and Nimitz spoke to Admiral King. King then went to the Joint Chiefs of Staff and said, "Maybe LeMay's not supporting us out there." I finally got a wire from Arnold that said, "Support Halsey in any way he asks."

I replied by saying, "Okay, I'll do it, but remember, I can't hit airfields by radar so I need to have the right weather for bombing in order to hit the airfields. When conditions are right for high-altitude bombing, I'll hit the airfields. If not, I'll hit strategic targets in Admiral Halsey's area." And that is what I did from April 17 until May 11. As it turned out, we never had visual bombing weather during the time that Halsey's fleet was carrying out its mission. In fact, as far as I know, the fleet was never attacked by Japanese aircraft during this mission, and meanwhile the B-29s *could* have been doing some good on strategic targets.

Another project to which the B-29s were diverted—and one which showed a greater degree of success—was mine laying. Beginning on March 27, 1945, the Tinian-based 313th Bomb Wing was assigned the task of mining Japanese waterways. The primary "target" for this operation—which continued for the rest of the war—was the Shimonoseki Strait, the waterway separating the main islands of Kyushu and Honshu. Other targets included ports on the west coast of Honshu, and the south coast of Korea. Because the Japanese had a vital dependency on these waterways for food and raw materials, the mining created extreme hardships in the empire's heartland.

The B-29 mine-laying operation succeeded in putting 8814 tons of mines into these waters. The mines sank or damaged over a million tons of enemy shipping, virtually isolating Japan from its Asian colonies. Monthly Japanese shipping tonnage went from 520,000 tons at the beginning of the operation to 8000 at the operation's conclusion in August 1945. In the end, the Japanese were so desperate for food that they were packing rice in wooden barrels in Korea and letting the current carry the barrels across to Japan!

BACK ON TARGET

The intensity of the maximum effort fire raids in early March was not repeated in April because of the lack of incendiaries and the diversion of B-29s in support of the Okinawa operations, but our May 14 raid on Nagoya marked the beginning of a pattern in which the big incendiary attacks now came several times a week.

By June it was finally possible for the Twenty-First Bomber Command to undertake a *sustained* strategic offensive against Japan. The March raids had wiped out our existing stockpile of incendiaries, but in June the flow of ordnance into the Marianas was such that 400-plane missions could be flown whenever the B-29s were ready, and the planes were ready. Our strength was constantly growing. It was behind schedule, but it *was* growing. There were new units and more airplanes coming out all the time. The units were of little immediate value because of their lack of experience when they arrived, but we put them through a training program and finally got them into combat. By June those 400-plane raids were becoming commonplace and routine. The Twentieth Air Force was a well-oiled machine.

During the nights of May 23–24 and 25–26 the Superfortresses went back to Tokyo. On the first night 520 out of 562 B-29s (the largest number of B-29s participating in a single mission during World War II) bombed Tokyo's urban-industrial area south of the Imperial Palace along the west side of the harbor. The following night 464 B-29s pounded urban areas near the Imperial Palace just north of what had been bombed the night before, including financial, commercial, and governmental districts, as well as factories and homes. There were 26 B-29s lost on the latter mission, the highest single-day loss.

On May 29, 454 B-29s bombed Yokohama and destroyed the main business district—a third of the city's area—along the waterfront. The burned-out area of Yokohama now amounted to almost 9 square miles. On June 1, 458 B-29s attacked the city of Osaka, and on June 5, 473 B-29s hit Kobe with incendiaries, burning over 4 square miles and damaging over half of the city. On June 7, 409 B-29s bombed Osaka again with incendiary and high-explosive bombs, hitting the section of the city that contained industrial and transportation targets as well as the Osaka Army Arsenal, which was the largest in Japan. Despite being forced to bomb by radar because of heavy undercast, the planes burned out over 2 square miles of the city, destroying over 55,000 buildings.

On June 9, two days after the second Osaka raid, 110 B-29s attacked aircraft factories at Nagoya and Akashi. The next day 280 B-29s bombed aircraft plants at Tomioka, Chiba, and Ogikubo; the seaplane base at Kasumigaura; Tachikawa Army Air Arsenal; and engineering works at Hitachi.

I had a directive which was never changed and was approved by the Joint Chiefs, a list of targets ranked by priority. When we were ready to run a mission, we would get the airplanes loaded with fuel and bombs, and the crews would be briefed and prepared. If the weather was good we'd hit a precision target that had a high priority on the target list. If the weather wasn't good, I would pick a target out of what was left of the good incendiary targets. We always assigned secondary targets in case the bombers didn't have a chance at the primary because of the weather, but I don't remember what they were. Usually if the weather was bad over the primary target it was bad over the secondary target too, in which case the B-29s would scatter their bombs all over the place by radar. They didn't do very well from high altitude with radar. We would hit one of the areas that had a low priority on the target list and burn down a dozen targets in addition to the whole damn town. By June 1945, however, we were hitting the high-priority industrial areas just as fast as we could, bombing both at night (low-flying incendiary missions) and in the daytime (high-altitude precision bombing). When the war ended, our score was more than sixty-five cities completely burned down.

At night we couldn't hit precision targets that were high on the target list, such as airplane plants, because we couldn't see them. These were the targets that we had to see in order to bomb accurately. At night or in bad weather, though, we could hit a big industrial area, or a section of a city that we could identify. At night we could identify a city without identifying *anything in it*.

We would then try to get our best radar operators in there first to put down some incendiaries. That would get a fire started that would show up the target and orient the rest of the bombers as they came in. We could get an area, like the south side of a city for instance, or the whole town when we had enough airplanes. We wouldn't hit an oil refinery or a shipyard during the night until the 315th arrived in June with the AN/APQ-7 Eagle radar. From that point, we could bomb as many as four precision targets nightly.

I don't know whether we flew an equal number of daylight versus nighttime missions, because I never kept track, but I would say there were probably more night missions than day missions, because there was more bad weather than good weather.

War is not a nice, clean-cut affair where you look at the facts and say, "Okay, we do this." It's never like that. You never have all the facts, and some of the "facts" are incorrect. As you're trying to line them up, your decisions are liable to come out of a feeling derived from all the things that you have done.

We got a report at five o'clock every morning on the number of airplanes in commission and which squadrons had them. We would ask the combat-ready groups how many airplanes they could get into commission, and then we'd check on the weather over Japan to see if it would permit a high-altitude mission. As we got enough airplanes into commission, we'd pick either the high-altitude or the incendiary mission. I would then have meetings with the weather officer, the intelligence officer, and the operations officer, to get the information I needed to brief the crews.

These meetings would take place at 5 a.m. in the headquarters building as soon as we received the status reports. We'd look to see what we had and where we could go, and what was possible on a given day. It was important to know where we would be going because it took a lot of time to load the bombs for either a high-altitude precision target or a low-altitude incendiary target. Once we had the bombs loaded, we'd leave them loaded until we took off or until we told the aircrews that the bombers were going to fly another kind of mission. Then the ground crews would scramble to unload the bombs on board and load the others.

It was then a matter of getting the crews ready and briefed while at the same time getting the airplanes ready and gassed.

Everybody who was going on the mission would be briefed at once, and after that we usually had a special briefing for navigators and bombardiers with more detailed information—if we had the information. The exact time that these briefings took place would depend upon when we were going to run the mission— whether it was going to be a daylight or a nighttime mission. We would try to run a briefing about four hours before takeoff. We never knew what we were going to do until we looked at the conditions. There was no set procedure for doing anything. In wartime it's hard to have a neat, crisp schedule for everything. There was nobody to say, "This is going to happen to you at four o'clock this afternoon," and so on.

We hadn't had a schedule in England either, except that we generally knew we were going to fly in the daylight (the Royal Air Force Bomber Command flew the night missions); and so if we wanted to get back before dark, we had to take off by a particular time. From that standpoint you could tell about when you were going to have a field order and when you probably weren't going to have a field order.

Most of the time I didn't know when my day started and when it ended. When you have things to do, you do them, and you lose track of time and days.

By July we were able to launch B-29 missions continuously, but they were still the longest, toughest bombing missions in history. A typical mission—if there was such a thing—might begin about twelve hours ahead of takeoff in the war room on Guam with our staff receiving a report on the next day's weather over Japan. Nagoya might have clouds above 8000 feet, while in the east—in the Tokyo area—the clouds might be at 22,000, closing up solid after about eleven o'clock. Meanwhile, Osaka and everything west might be reported as completely socked in. With our B-29s up against a blank wall except for a possible opening around Tokyo, we would have to consider all the vital factors and make the decision about how many wings would go in under that weather at 12,000 feet to strike Tokyo at ten o'clock before the clouds blocked out everything.

If intelligence showed that the first priority in the Tokyo area was already mostly destroyed and the next on the list was still untouched, the lower-priority site would become more important.

We would ask the operations staff to check the technical plans for the latter and make the required changes. In the resulting plan folder would be a mountain of preparation by special sections of intelligence and operations—a thousand hours of research, collated facts, and figures were distilled into one day's mission. Smoke markers would be planned at one-minute intervals to be dropped by lead B-29s to expedite departure from the assembly point. One squadron in each bombardment wing might carry incendiary clusters, while the balance of the squadrons might be armed with 500-pound and 1000-pound high-explosive bombs. A calibrated airspeed of 210 mph would typically be flown by all aircraft on bombing runs.

The Navy would be requested to furnish facilities for air-sea rescue purposes. These would include surface vessels, submarines assigned to lifeguard duties at another position, and "Dumbos" (PBY Catalina air-sea rescue planes) to fly in orbit around a station off the Japanese coast.

Our staff would also assign B-29s from the Twenty-First Bomber Command to function as "Super Dumbos" at selected positions. As Super Dumbos, the big bombers could not land to pick up downed crews like a PBY could, but with their great range, they could search farther and remain over a downed crew for a longer time, dropping lifeboats and vectoring ships or seaplanes in for the rescue.

Admiral Nimitz, as the theater commander, had control over the air-sea rescue operations. The crews weren't doing very well when we first got out there, but after raising a little hell, and inviting the air-sea rescue crews over to play poker, we got it squared away. They got pretty good, particularly toward the end of the war. The submarines didn't have too much to do by that time, and so we had more of them available for air-sea rescue. Some of the submarines picked up downed B-29 crewmen within sight of the Japanese-held islands. As a matter of fact, one B-29 got shot up over the target and came down near the submarine that was on the surface about a mile offshore. The crew climbed out of their B-29, and they were only in the water for about 10 minutes before the submarine picked them up.

To supervise certain aspects of planning, I brought Lieutenant Colonel Jack J. Catton, a former lead group pilot, over to my staff as project officer. His extensive combat experience was an invaluable aid in ironing out operational kinks, and he would often accompany a mission to observe the smoke signals at assembly points. Each section of the plan would be double-checked and a field order would be dispatched to the wings. Takeoff time would be flashed to the flight controller, who coordinated the vast network of communication gathered there at the heart and nerve center of the command.

In this control room, status panels and the mission board were maintained to show the countless up-to-the minute details of all daily operations. Before takeoff, each mission would be set up on the board to afford a visual view of the flight's progress from takeoff to target and return. Colored yarns, one for each wing, were laid out to indicate the flight lines which pass close to Iwo Jima, the halfway point, and which led, as specified in the field order, to the proper target. Other symbols were used to mark air-sea rescue positions, and a timetable of statistics for each wing would be planned and marked as recorded in hourly reports from the status panel, beginning with takeoff time.

By July 1945, the missions involved at least 100 B-29s from *each wing,* and so planes were launched simultaneously from Guam, Tinian, and Saipan. When the last B-29 was airborne, the tower at Saipan (the tower farthest north) relayed this information to the controller back at Guam. The first and last takeoff times of each wing were then recorded at the operations center where the staff began to make up the first of a series of tabulated mission reports. Copies of the completed reports would be dispatched to USAAF headquarters in Washington as well as being posted on the control room report board.

During the first hour of a typical mission, the B-29s settled down to the big grind, cruising at 1000 feet to save precious fuel. The navigators set the course, logging in at the checkpoints as the bombers climbed past the northern Marianas (Pagan, Asuncion, and Maug) and the Bonins. After about four hours the bombers would pass close to Iwo Jima and begin pushing up to the designated 12,000-foot altitude. As the bombers arrived close to the assembly point, oxygen masks would be adjusted and readied for instant use. The central fire control system would be warmed up, and each gunner would flex his sights and try the coordinated fire control with a few short bursts to clear his guns.

As the lead bombers reached the assembly area, they would begin to circle, dropping their parachute flare markers for assembly. From various zone positions the groups would separate and form up behind their lead planes in nine- or eleven-plane waves and head for an initial point chosen to afford a good land-water contrast check. Landfall was usually picked up along with the first antiaircraft fire from enemy coastal batteries, which would become heavier and more accurate as the B-29s closed on their targets. From the turn at the initial point, the bomber waves would move steadily toward the target.

After the bomb run, the bombers would turn downwind across the burned acres of Tokyo, across the bay down the Chiba peninsula, and out across the Pacific, toward emergency landings on Iwo Jima if necessary, or on to the Marianas and home sweet home.

A MOMENT OF HEROISM

If bombing runs over Japan were serious business, the dropping of parachute flares as assembly markers was in itself not without a certain inherent danger. At no time was this more clearly demonstrated than on April 12, 1945, the day that bore witness to the heroism of the only Twentieth Air Force crewman to win the Congressional Medal of Honor. The B-29 *City of Los Angeles* was 55 miles south of Tokyo leading the attack on a chemical plant at Koriyama with Captain Anthony Simeral in the pilot's seat and Lieutenant Colonel Eugene Strouse—commander of the Fifty-Second Bomb Squadron—aboard as an observer. As the *City of Los Angeles* reached the assembly point, Tony Simeral gave the high sign, and Sergeant Red Erwin began the routine task of dropping the phosphorous flares into a release tube.

Suddenly, things were no longer routine. One of the flares jammed in the tube. Timed to a six-second delay from the time Erwin released it, the flare exploded in the tube and was propelled straight up! Burning at 1300° F, the white-hot object struck

Red Erwin in the face, searing away part of his nose and ear, and bounced onto the floor of the flight deck where it started burning through the floor boards toward the several tons of incendiaries in the bomb bay below. Blinded momentarily by the flash of the phosphorous and the acrid black smoke, Tony Simeral lost control of the big plane and did not regain it until the B-29 had fallen to an altitude of barely 700 feet.

In those few moments the situation had become desperate. Within a few seconds the flare could burn through the floor.

Badly burned, Red Erwin staggered to his feet and *picked up* the flare, which was so hot and bright it could sear the retina of someone just *looking* at it. Somehow Erwin summoned the fortitude to carry this piece of the sun itself across the flight deck and push it out the cockpit window. Erwin then collapsed on the floor, a ball of fire. The skin on his right hand had literally melted away. Simeral immediately turned the *City of Los Angeles* back to Iwo Jima to get medical attention for the wounded sergeant, while his comrades pumped Erwin full of morphine and plasma.

Ironically, the B-29 arrived while the safe haven of Iwo Jima was under Japanese mortar attack! Simeral set the plane down anyway, and Red Erwin was rushed to waiting doctors. Four days later, he was evacuated to Guam, where, in June 1945, he was awarded the Congressional Medal of Honor. In awarding the medal personally, Hap Arnold said that even "the country's highest honor will still be inadequate in recognition of the inspiring heroism of this man."

Red Erwin responded simply by saying that "they made a fuss about my being a hero. It didn't occur to me at the time. I knew the flare was burning, and I just had to get it out of there!"

FIGHTERS: FRIEND AND FOE

In the daylight runs, even during the last three months of the war, Japanese fighters would bother us occasionally—diving into the formation, dropping phosphorous bombs, or trying to ram the B-29s—but we'd bother them back. On the May 7 mission, for example, our gunners shot down a hell of a lot of fighters—thirty-four to be exact. We positioned our own fighter escorts out in front and made them stay there. This forced the Japanese fighters to attack from the rear, where the compensating gunsights of the B-29s would handle them. It didn't make the Japanese very happy.

On the B-17 we had to aim the 50-caliber machine guns manually like you'd aim a shotgun or a rifle. We were supposed to be a nation of riflemen, but the bulk of our gunners had never, before the war, picked up a firearm in their lives. Furthermore, their basic training was so poor that when they came up against the Germans, they got killed. I remember that the USAAF group commanders in England complained about the poor training so much that they sent the gunnery school commandants over to England to observe actual operations. There were seven of them, two of whom had been classmates of mine at flying school. We sent them out with some B-17 crews, and four of them got shot down on the first mission, so the others didn't go on any more. I do remember that by the time the survivors of this group went home, we had definitely gotten their attention.

The gunnery was better on the B-29 because of the computing gunsight, which could put the lead on an interceptor if you operated it properly. The first ones required a lot of dexterity and our gunnery was still lousy, but later computing gunsights were better, and the gunners got better as well.

The Japanese pilots that the B-29s faced weren't on the same level as the Luftwaffe interceptor pilots over Germany, nor did we get hit by the same quality of Japanese pilot encountered earlier in the Pacific war. This was because the best Japanese aviators had been lost between 1942 and 1944. The people *we* faced in 1945 were, for the most part, poorly trained and had more of a gunnery problem than we had.

The Japanese did have a few night fighters, but they didn't give us any trouble. We never lost a B-29 in any attack that could be attributed to one. Nobody came back with a story that convinced me that's what it was, although some of the men *may* have seen a night fighter. As I've said, one of the reasons I took the guns out of the night bombers in early March was that I was more worried about our guys shooting each other than I was about the night fighters.

In Germany the night-fighter threat, like that of the daylight interceptors, had been a different story, and it warranted carrying defensive armament. The Luftwaffe simply had better airplanes, the pilots were well trained, and they had a good radar network. Most people don't know it, but for a while the RAF Bomber Command was very worried that its forces couldn't stand the attrition that the night fighters were causing them.

Most of the bombers we lost in the Pacific came down due to mechanical malfunctions, but of all the things that the Japanese threw at us, I was probably more concerned about antiaircraft fire than interceptors.

Eventually, the Twentieth Air Force also took control of our own *fighter* command. Originally activated in Hawaii in February 1942 as the Seventh Interceptor Command of the Seventh Air Force, it soon became the Seventh Fighter Command, and in August 1944, it moved to Saipan to provide air cover for the B-24 operations from the same bases that would ultimately be the home of the Twentieth Air Force. In March 1945, the Seventh Fighter Command was equipped with P-51D Mustang long-range fighters, and moved to bases on recently captured Iwo Jima. After April 16 it began to send Mustangs to escort the B-29s on their missions.

We could have eventually based B-29s on Iwo Jima, and it would have saved us time and fuel because it was so much closer to Japan. However, there just wasn't enough room on Iwo Jima to have both fighters and bombers. In retrospect, it probably would not have been a bad idea to cut down on the fighters and put the B-29s in there. Iwo Jima did, of course, serve as an emergency landing site for B-29s that were short on gas or had been shot up over Japan, many of which would have been lost otherwise.

In Europe the fighters had been under the Eighth Fighter Command, and they furnished the cover as they saw fit. The Eighth Air Force didn't get too much good out of the fighters to start with, but things got better later on when the fighter command got a new commander. After May 25, I took control of the fighters of the Seventh Fighter Command, and I used them to defend the bombers *my* way and not the way the fighters would have done it. When a bomber commander asked for fighter support, he wanted enough to protect his bombers, not simply what the fighter commander wanted to give him.

I would disperse the fighters ahead of a bomber squadron, and this caused the Japanese fighters to come in from the rear. That's how I wanted them to come in, because the closure rate would be small from back there. Even the least skillful gunner could handle it, and the compensating gunsight put the proper lead on the enemy interceptor. The result was that we shot down a lot of fighters. I'm sure that we reported more than we actually got, but I have no doubt that we shot down more of them than did the Seventh Fighter Command's P-51s.

If the Mustangs were helpful at times, they were also very dependent on us because of the weather. There were always a couple of weather fronts lying between us and Japan—usually north of Iwo Jima. Once the Seventh Fighter Command was based up there and escorting us on missions, we had to do a little cogitating, because fighters could fly through a front on instruments, but they couldn't fly *formation* on instruments. Thus, if there was a front, we would have to spread them out. If they hit some bad weather, the fighters could close up on the B-29s that we designated navigator airplanes and open up their formation when they went into it. They'd fly through at the same course, and when they came out, they could, theoretically, look for either a B-29 or another fighter, and get their formation back together. Normally, when flying through a little front, this worked fine. On June 1, 1945, however, we hit a bad storm, and we lost twenty-seven fighters. They just disappeared.

The fighters had B-29s acting as navigator ships to carry them up there, and when they got to Japan, we'd turn them loose, move down the coast, and pick them up at another point coming out to take them home. We had only about a five-minute leeway to hook on because everybody was short of gas, and there was no waiting around for stragglers. One time a P-51 arrived late at the assembly point, and everyone else was gone. The pilot started off in what he hoped was the right direction, screaming for help all the way. Finally about 300 miles out he picked up one of the B-29s on his radio. The B-29 asked where he'd come out of his altitude, his indicated airspeed, and his heading, and worked out a dead reckoning position on him. The B-29 then gave him a course correction for Iwo Jima, which was about a 30° to 40° correction. The pilot didn't feel comfortable making that big a change in course, but he did it and came out over Iwo.

After about the first of June 1945 it was almost safer to fly a B-29 combat mission over Japan than it had been a year or so earlier to fly a B-29 training mission in the United States, because the casualty rate was lower. Once in a while there would be an attack, but very little effort was made to intercept B-29s after May. We lost eighty-eight B-29s in combat during May 1945, our worst month of the war, but in June, despite the greatly increased number of missions being flown, losses were cut in half. In the six weeks from the end of June through the end of the war, we lost only thirty-three Superfortresses in combat.

THE END IN SIGHT

General Hap Arnold came out to visit us in the Marianas on June 13, 1945, a couple of months after I had decided that we had the capability to fly up to 120 hours a month. We gave him a briefing on what we had done to date, what we were doing, and what we planned to do. We also gave him a list of targets that we were going to hit. My staff and I were convinced, when we came up with this plan, that this was the best that could be done at the time, and that we had a good chance of defeating Japan before the invasion. I believe that General Arnold always thought air power could do the job, but he was more convinced than ever after we gave our briefing.

The decision to go ahead with the amphibious invasion of Japan had already been made on May 25, and I think Arnold realized, when he visited us, that our strategic air offensive might be the one chance of stopping it. I imagine that he wanted to make one more effort to delay the invasion—or to stop it entirely to prevent the American bloodshed we knew would come with the invasion—and so he sent me and two of the staff back to Washington to make a presentation to the Joint Chiefs, while he continued his visit of the Pacific. "Go now," he said.

On June 15, as Arnold flew over to West Field on Tinian to greet the troops on the first anniversary of the Yawata raid, I took a B-29 from General Power's North Field on Guam, flew 3780 miles nonstop to Honolulu, refueled, and took off again. We tried to get clearance to go nonstop to Washington, but the air controllers wouldn't let us past San Francisco. They tried to get us a clearance, but by the time they came back to the radio, we had gone out of communication range. We never did get that clearance. When we flew into Washington National Airport in a B-29 just before midnight on June 16, we created quite a sensation!

The next morning we drove over to the Pentagon and presented our plan to the Joint Chiefs of Staff and their staff officers. Throughout the briefing, each of them had completely blank expressions on their faces. They paid absolutely no attention to us. Marshall was sleeping or dozing through most of it. Admiral Ernest King, the chief of Naval Operations, reacted with disbelief and a complete lack of interest, just as the Navy brass always had. General Arnold, the other member of the Joint Chiefs, wasn't there, of course. I don't blame Marshall for dozing off, though. He was probably whipped down to a nub by then, and needed the sleep. In any case, they had already approved the decision to go ahead with an invasion.

We got the same treatment from the Joint Chiefs of Staff as we had gotten ever since I had been in the USAAF. The conventional wisdom was *still* that you can't do anything with strategic air power and that was that. Nevertheless, we went back to the Marianas and we *did* the job.

We were in Washington barely long enough to get a night's sleep. The two guys on the staff, who had wives in the area, did manage to let them know, so that they could meet us at the field. I gave them one night, and then we flew back.

While we had been giving him our briefing on Guam, General Arnold had asked me when the war was going to end. I didn't have an answer. I told him I was too busy fighting it to figure that out. I said, "Give me thirty minutes and we'll give you an answer." So I consulted with Monty Montgomery in operations to determine how many cities we had left on the target list and how long it would take us to hit them. I then multiplied by 2 and subtracted 3, or something. I took a look, and I guessed at it.

I told General Arnold that with those targets gone, there

wouldn't be any targets left. I could then start to work over the Japanese rail network, but that wouldn't take long. Finally I picked a date six months after the initial Tokyo incendiary attack and three months after we began the routine 400-plane raids. I gave him the date of September 1 for the war's end. I was off by just a few days.

TOP: A furious pillar of smoke billows up from Kobe, Japan, during an incendiary raid by Twentieth Air Force B-29s in June 1945. (*USAF photo*)

BOTTOM: In a setting of cathedral-like majesty, this B-29 from the 314th Bomb Wing is about to go down near Kobe, Japan, June 5, 1945. (*USAF photo*)

Ground crewmen of General Hansell's Twenty-First Bomber Command stand by as the first B-29s to bomb Tokyo are launched from Saipan's Isley Field on November 24, 1944. (*USAF photo*)

Japan's most visible landmark, snow-capped Fujiyama, was used by Twentieth Air Force crews to mark the initial point of their bomb runs against targets in the sprawling Tokyo/Yokohama metropolitan area. (*USAF photo*)

Four Twentieth Air Force B-29s begin their bomb run against the Kure Naval Arsenal in Japan during a mission in June 1945. (*USAF photo*)

After World War II, Boeing developed a *super* Superfortress, designated B-50, which first flew in June 1947. Very similar to the Superfortress, the B-50 differed from the B-29 in having huge airscoops beneath the four Wasp Major engines and a tail 3 feet taller than the B-29's. Boeing's Renton factory, having concluded B-29 production, went on to build 79 B-50As, 45 B-50Bs and 222 B-50Ds. The B-50C was designed with a 10-foot increase in wingspan and a longer fuselage, and was specified for 4500-horsepower Pratt & Whitney R-4360-51 compound engines. The B-50s reached a peak number of 263 (including 39 RB-50 reconnaissance conversions) in SAC's inventory in 1952. (*USAF photo*)

On June 15, 1945, General "Hap" Arnold, Commanding General of the USAAF, flew into the Marianas to take a firsthand look at B-29 operations as the strategic air offensive against Japan reached its climax. He is seen here, during his inspection tour of Guam's North Field, chatting with 314th Bomb Wing crew chief Sergeant Leo Fliess. General LeMay is behind General Arnold's right shoulder, while behind General Arnold's left, partially obscured by Sergeant Fliess, is General Carl "Tooey" Spaatz. General Spaatz had just arrived to command the U.S. Army Strategic Air Forces in the Pacific (USASTAF), a yet-to-be-assembled strategic air armada that would include both the Twentieth Air Force and the Eighth Air Force. The war would end, however, before the USASTAF was activated. General Spaatz went on to succeed General Arnold as chief of the USAAF. (*USAF photo*)

TOP: B-29s assigned to the U.S. Air Force Far East Air Forces on the ground at Yokota Air Base, Japan. This photo, released to the news media during the Korean war, carried a caption that read: "In their role of the 'big stick' in the Korean war, high-flying 'Superforts' make nightly attacks against key military targets in North Korea and along the enemy's frontlines." (*USAF photo*)

BOTTOM: A USAF Far East Air Force B-29 touches down in Okinawa after completing its sixteenth bombing mission against enemy targets in North Korea. (*USAF photo*)

TOP: An armada of USAF Strategic Air Command B-29s on a bombing run over North Korea in 1951. (*USAF photo*)

BOTTOM: A B-50 is refueled by a KB-29P, one of 116 Superfortresses modified as aerial refueling tankers (after 1950) with a Boeing-designed, gravity boom-type aerial refueling apparatus that has since become standard on all USAF aerial refueling aircraft. (*Boeing photo*)

VIII

Coup de Grace
August 1945

The decision to develop nuclear weapons had been a hard one for President Franklin D. Roosevelt, but no more difficult than the decision President Harry Truman faced when the bombs actually became available for use. There was no difficulty, however, in determining which aircraft should be modified to carry the bombs. There was little doubt that it should be the B-29. The task of developing nuclear weapons had gone to the Army Corps of Engineers—specifically the Manhattan Engineering District under Major General Leslie R. Groves, while the task of preparing the men and machines to deliver them went to the USAAF—specifically the Second Air Force under General Uzal G. Ent.

The process of building the bomb began in December 1942 with the first self-sustaining nuclear chain reaction in a converted squash court under the bleachers at the University of Chicago's Stagg Field, and with Roosevelt's commitment to building a bomb. From that point forward, the Manhattan Project took on a life of its own as one of the most secret and most expensive weapons-development programs of the war. As dozens of the brightest physicists and engineers in the country were brought into Los Alamos,

New Mexico, to work on the project, there was still a good deal of doubt about how the bomb would work and indeed about *whether* the bomb would work.

It was generally accepted by the Manhattan District staff—as well as by those within the War Department who knew of the secret project—that a weapon with explosive power on the magnitude of an atomic bomb had the ability not only to defeat the Axis power, but to shorten the war and save tens of thousands of lives. For this reason, the Manhattan District, and its engineers in turn, felt tremendous pressure to figure out how to make a workable bomb as soon as possible. By September 1944, the Manhattan Project scientists at Los Alamos, New Mexico, had already invested two years toward that end when the USAAF began putting together the aircrews who would carry the weapons—should they be successfully developed—to the enemy.

The USAAF's road to Hiroshima actually began a couple of hours' air time north of Los Alamos in General Ent's office at Colorado Springs. At 10 a.m. on September 1, 1944, the fifth anniversary of the German invasion of Poland that had triggered the war, Ent met for the first time with Colonel Paul Warfield Tibbets, the man selected to command the world's first nuclear strike force.

Colonel Tibbets had a distinguished record as a B-17 commander with the Ninety-Seventh Bombardment Group in Europe and North Africa. His combat career had begun on August 17, 1942, in the first American heavy bomber attack against Nazi-occupied Europe. When the bomb-bay doors of Tibbets's Flying Fortress *Butcher Shop* slammed open over Rouen, France, at 5 p.m. that afternoon, it was only the beginning of a career that took him over targets throughout two continents. That career also included flying General Mark Clark to his secret rendezvous with the French in North Africa and piloting Dwight Eisenhower to Gibraltar to initiate the Operation Torch invasion of North Africa in November 1942.

Tibbets developed a reputation as a fearless combat commander, but also as a man prone to be brash and outspoken. He was particularly critical of officers who reached the higher levels of the USAAF through administrative, rather than flying, jobs. A disagreement with General Lauris Norstad over tactics to be used in the Mediterranean turned into a feud in which Norstad refused to accept the recommendation of a junior officer and Tibbets was scornful of a nonflying general, who Tibbets felt did not understand the tactical situation. Once, upon his return to the United States in February 1944, Tibbets pulled a .45 caliber automatic on a customs officer who he felt was trying to unjustly "confiscate" $1600 from him. Having taken the matter into his own hands, Tibbets cleared customs with his $1600, and a subsequent investigation of the incident uncovered a considerable stash of contraband in the possession of the customs officer.

After being briefed on the B-29 in the spring of 1944, Tibbets was assigned as a B-29 crew instructor at Grand Island, Nebraska, but was soon reassigned to advanced B-29 operational testing at Alamogordo, New Mexico. It was during this phase of operational tests that Tibbets discovered during a training exercise with a P-47 fighter—almost accidentally—that if a B-29 was stripped of its turrets and armor, it could outmaneuver the smaller high-performance aircraft at 30,000 feet.

In September 1944 Tibbets was introduced to General Ent and to Navy Captain William "Deak" Parsons, the Manhattan Project ballistics engineer with whose career Tibbets's own would be intertwined so closely over the next eleven months. When Tibbets piloted the first nuclear-armed bomber in August 1945, Parsons would be sitting in the bomb bay arming the first operational atomic bomb.

The 29-year-old Tibbets was assigned a "private air force" consisting of 15 B-29s, along with 1800 personnel including flight crews drawn from the 393rd Bomb Squadron. Tibbets and his group set up shop a week later on September 8 at a base called Wendover Army Airfield, in the isolated northwest corner of Utah. The base was located in a lonesome—almost loathsome—backwater that comedian Bob Hope called "Leftover Field" when he came through that winter to entertain the troops.

The new unit was officially activated as the 509th Composite Group on December 17, 1944. It was theoretically part of the organizational structure of General Frank Armstrong's 315th Bomb Wing, although Armstrong was not officially let in on the secret of the mission until after the first atomic bomb was dropped. The

509th Group operated with the autonomy usually reserved for wings, an administrative unit that usually contained four groups. (The 509th was not finally elevated to wing status until July 1946.)

The first task faced by the 509th after the men adjusted to the cold wintry isolation of Wendover was to figure out how to drop nuclear bombs. It was no simple matter. Deak Parsons had calculated that the shock wave from the atomic blast could knock a B-29 out of the sky at a distance of 8 miles. Tibbets, meanwhile, knew that the size of the bomb, the fuel capacity of the B-29, and, finally, the distance to be flown, all dictated that the bomb could be dropped from an altitude of no more than 30,000 feet, or just less than 6 miles. The obvious problem was how to extend this distance by 2 miles. The odds could be improved somewhat by stripping the B-29 and reducing its weight, but the problem was ultimately solved by a change of tactics.

Because a bomb, when dropped from a moving aircraft, has a forward as well as a downward velocity, Tibbets realized that a sharp, 155° turn immediately after the bomb was released would take the bomber in nearly the opposite direction of the bomb's forward velocity. This meant that, at full throttle, the B-29 could be 5 miles from the release point when the bomb exploded. In turn, the diagonal line from the B-29 to the exploding bomb would be the requisite 8 *miles*.

The 509th Composite Group was supplied with roughly 200 dummy bombs that simulated the size, weight, and bulbous shape of the plutonium bomb that the crews would be expected to drop, although nobody but Tibbets realized that this rare metal would be part of the awesome punch. Indeed few of the men in the 509th had probably even heard of plutonium. Because of their shape, which was identical to that of the planned plutonium bomb, the nonnuclear practice bombs were dubbed "pumpkins." Assumed to be simply harbingers of some conventional new explosive device, they were dropped by the 509th crews throughout the Utah deserts until the 155° getaway maneuver became second nature.

By the late spring of 1945, Germany was out of the war, our B-29 strategic offensive against Japan was gaining in intensity, and the scientists at Los Alamos were in the final stages of the parallel development of both plutonium and uranium-235 nuclear bombs. Unbeknownst to Paul Tibbets there was a growing disagreement at Los Alamos about whether the bomb should actually be used. Many of the scientists were refugees from a Nazi-dominated Europe, and for them, Germany was a mortal enemy. They had set aside their inherent pacifism to develop a weapon to destroy Hitler—but now Hitler was dead. Despite Japan's ruthless attack on Pearl Harbor and brutal enslavement of the Philippines, there was now some hesitation among the Manhattan Project engineers in the New Mexico desert.

For the 509th, however, it was business as usual, and this meant the long-awaited deployment to the Pacific. Tibbets arrived at North Field on Tinian with the advanced air echelon on May 18, reported in, and awaited the arrival, eleven days later, of the 509th's ground echelon. On June 11, the specially modified B-29s, which now numbered eighteen, began to arrive.

During this period, Tibbets made three round trips back to the United States, which included high-level target selection conferences at the Pentagon. One major caveat in the selection of a target was that, in order to measure the bomb's effect precisely, it should be a city that was relatively undamaged by earlier, conventional raids. General Groves favored Kyoto, which was—after Tokyo, Osaka, and Nagoya—Japan's fourth largest city. With a population of 1,089,726 in the 1940 census, it was, by far, the largest city in Japan that had not yet been the target for attacks by B-29s. Secretary of War Stimson, however, removed Kyoto from the target list because of its importance to the cultural history and artistic heritage of the Far East. The remaining targets on the list—Hiroshima, Yokohama, and Kokura—were all of military and industrial importance. The actual mission was provisionally scheduled for the first week of August.

I had first learned about the atomic bomb from an engineer colonel from the Manhattan District staff who came out to Guam around the end of May. I got only the information I needed to prepare for, and operate, the 509th Group. My degree in civil engineering had not exposed me to nuclear physics. I knew the bomb would deliver a big bang, but I did not realize it would be so big, and I really don't think the Manhattan Project people did either.

On June 30, the 509th began an intensive series of training missions. For most crews, this meant five or six navigation flights to American-held Iwo Jima with a bomb run against Rota in the Marianas on the return flight, as well as shorter bombing missions against Rota. These were followed by two long-range bombing missions against Truk and Marcus Island. Each of these missions was flown by a detachment of between two and nine aircraft. These series of missions were followed by another series of twelve precision bombing raids over Japan itself, dropping "pumpkins" armed with high explosives on targets that had been previously bombed, but which were in the general area of the targets earmarked for nuclear strikes. The B-29s went up in groups of between two and six for the purpose of getting Japanese plane spotters used to seeing small formations of B-29s at high altitude, because the nuclear attacks would be flown by a single bomber accompanied by a couple of reconnaissance B-29s configured to observe and record the attack and its effects.

The missions flown by the 509th Composite Group over Japan began on July 20, four days after the still-secret successful first test of a plutonium atomic bomb at a site code-named Trinity, which was—coincidentally—adjacent to Alamogordo Army Air Field where Colonel Tibbets had been stationed a year before.

On July 26, the cruiser *USS Indianapolis* arrived off Tinian with the first atomic bomb, not a plutonium pumpkin but a uranium-235 weapon of more conventional cylindrical shape. I was told about it because of the preparations that had to be made on Tinian for it. The only way to load the bomb was to put it into a hole in the ground, taxi the airplane over the top of the bomb, and then jack it up into the airplane. We also had to have some special security measures in place, and there were a few other odds and ends that I had to know beforehand. Of course the bomb was so secret that almost no one else in the Marianas knew it was there. Even most of the people in the 509th Composite Group who were supposed to drop it didn't know what was going on. They knew they were going to drop a special bomb, but that's about all.

The arrival of the atomic bomb in the Marianas didn't cause a ripple in the Twentieth Air Force operations. We went along the same as we were, but it wouldn't have gone on very long. The Japanese were trying to get out of the war because our 400-plane raids were destroying more cities and oil refineries nearly every night. When we were out of oil refineries, we would have put the 315th Bomb Group with the new Eagle radar sets on more precision targets.

When the bomb arrived, I made no change in the course of operations because I didn't know what this thing was going to do, or what it was supposed to do. The Twentieth Air Force really didn't make any plans for the atomic bomb, because it was the Engineer Corps' baby all along. Even when it was ready to use, the Engineer Corps wouldn't let go of the thing and give it to the operating units to use.

The men of the 509th—according to the 509th—were something special. They were the second coming of Christ, and they thought that they were supposed to have everything. Not so— when they arrived on Tinian, they were just like anybody else. We knew that they had a special bomb and that they were going to drop it individually, and so we gave them special training and let them drop individual bombs. All the rest of the support and combat training that they got was the same as anybody else got.

On Sunday, August 5, the weather over Japan cleared and the nuclear mission was given a "go" for the following day. The primary target was the port city of Hiroshima on the main Japanese island of Honshu. The secondary target was Kokura.

The plane designated for the mission, to be flown by Tibbets himself, was named *Enola Gay* after Tibbets's mother. The uranium-235 bomb, which took crews much of Sunday afternoon to load aboard the B-29, belied its nickname. Called *Little Boy*, it was 12 feet long and weighed 9000 pounds. Tibbets later noted his own disbelief that this "ugly monster," as he called it, could possess the explosive force of 200,000 of the type of bombs he had dropped on German targets.

Tibbets's *Enola Gay* would be accompanied by Major Charles W. "Chuck" Sweeney's B-29, *The Great Artiste*, which would drop instruments by parachute to record the blast and measure the radioactivity. A third B-29, *No. 91*, flown by George Marquardt, would photograph the event from a distance. Three B-29 weather planes would precede them by an hour and fly over the primary and secondary targets, as well as over Nagasaki, the tertiary target, to report on visual bombing conditions.

The weather planes, *Straight Flush, Full House*, and *Jabbitt*

III, took off at 1:37 a.m. on August 6, followed by *Enola Gay* at 2:45 and then *The Great Artiste* and *No. 91.* At 6:07 the *Enola Gay* passed over Iwo Jima, and by 7:30 a.m. Deak Parsons reported to Tibbets that he had finished arming the fuse on *Little Boy.* An hour later the *Enola Gay* crossed the Japanese coastline and heard from *Straight Flush* that the weather over Hiroshima would permit a visual run on the target.

Originally the Manhattan Project people had wanted to take the *Enola Gay,* surround it with every airplane I owned in the Marianas, and fly them up to Japan in formation to make sure the atomic bomb got there. This scheme never came to my attention, but the Air Staff convinced them that wasn't the way to do it. The Air Staff told them that the plane carrying the bomb should go up there alone—or with just one or two others as observers—like a reconnaissance airplane or a weather airplane, drop the bomb, and come home—which is exactly what it did.

I'd had a talk with Colonel Tibbets when he got to the Marianas, and I had a talk with him again when we got close to the time of his mission. We discussed whether he thought the crewmen were ready or not. I thought they were ready to go, and so did he. The only thing I told him was that while a commander normally will go on the first mission, this was a special mission. Although I didn't know how special, I wanted to give Tibbets a little leeway. As I have noted, there is no commander worth his salt who would send his troops on their first mission into combat without leading them, but I thought Tibbets should put his best crew on that first mission and that he didn't necessarily have to be one of them. He made the decision that he would fly, and I didn't quarrel with his judgment.

At 9:15:17 (8:15:17 Hiroshima local time), only seventeen seconds past schedule, the *Little Boy* was released, and Tibbets wrenched the *Enola Gay* into the 155° right turn that the crews had practiced so often. Just forty-three seconds later the bomb exploded over the Aioi Bridge at the center of Hiroshima. Tibbets estimated that he was 9 miles from the explosion when the shock wave slammed the B-29.

As everyone in the three Superforts stared on in awe, a huge purple mushroom cloud rose up out of that patch of earth that had, until recently, been Hiroshima. It rose to 45,000 feet, and

Bob Caron, the *Enola Gay* tail gunner, reported that he could still see it 400 miles away from the target. On the ground below the mushroom cloud, roughly forty people died for each person that had been killed at Pearl Harbor.

President Truman got the news of the world's first nuclear strike aboard the *USS Augusta* en route home from the Potsdam Conference, and General Arnold received word even before the *Enola Gay* returned to Tinian, over the private wire that connected his Fort Meyer, Virginia, home with the White House. Most of the people in the United States heard about it over the radio, in the same way they had first heard about the Pearl Harbor attack. This time, however, the news was hopeful—the war would soon be over.

The Japanese authorities quickly realized what had happened. They knew what nuclear weapons were because they had tried unsuccessfully to build their own. They did not, however, announce these specifics over their own radio network. The dawning of nuclear warfare was reported as though it were just another incendiary attack.

Publicly complacent, privately the Imperial Japanese hierarchy was in a state of panic. The Potsdam Declaration issued by the Allied leaders on July 26 had demanded that Japan surrender unconditionally or face "total destruction." It was now clear that this was no idle threat. The Japanese had been secretly attempting, since the winter, to get the Russians to help negotiate a cease-fire that would be something less than unconditional surrender, but the incendiary raids and now a nuclear attack made it seem impossible that anything short of acceptance of the Allied demands could avert total destruction. Furthermore, since the Soviet Union had been a signatory of the Potsdam Declaration, it was more likely that the Soviets would themselves go to war with Japan than help negotiate a cease-fire.

While the Japanese were trying to make up their minds about what to do, the Twentieth Air Force kept up the pressure. The day after Hiroshima was bombed, 153 B-29s went to Japan, and the day after that 375 Superforts were launched, including a 224-plane incendiary effort against Yawata. Ironically, Yawata had been the first Japanese city to be attacked by B-29s when the strategic air offensive was initiated in June 1944.

The third day after the uranium-235 attack was earmarked for the second nuclear strike, this time with the plutonium pumpkin nicknamed *Fat Man*. The theory behind launching the second strike so soon after the first involved convincing the Japanese that the United States had a sufficient stock of nuclear weapons to be able to use them—almost casually—every few days, or whenever we wished. This, of course, was untrue. *Fat Man* was the third and the last atomic bomb. However, the Trinity detonation three weeks before had already proved that the technology for building plutonium bombs worked, and if *Fat Man* confirmed this, it would be relatively easy to get more atomic bombs into the pipeline. (This *ease* would, of course, be relative to the massive effort that had already gone into the Manhattan Project.)

To fly the second nuclear strike, Tibbets picked Major Chuck Sweeney, who had flown his instrument-laden B-29, *The Great Artiste* over Hiroshima on Tibbets's heels three days before. Because *The Great Artiste* was configured as an observation plane, Sweeney traded B-29s with Captain Fred Bock, and flew *Fat Man* to Japan in Bock's B-29, which was aptly nicknamed *Bock's Car*, while Bock followed him in *The Great Artiste*. Because of this switch, it was later erroneously reported that *The Great Artiste* had dropped the second atomic bomb.

If the *Enola Gay*'s mission to Hiroshima had been an example of textbook perfection, *Bock's Car*'s trip to the Chrysanthemum Empire was anything but. A fuel pump malfunction rendered 600 gallons in the *Bock's Car* bomb-bay tanks unreachable, and to make matters worse, forty-five minutes were lost at the rendezvous point south of Kyushu. *Bock's Car* then arrived over Kokura—the primary target—only to find it buried under cloud cover. Sweeney made three bomb runs over the city before deciding to break off and dash for Nagasaki, the secondary target. This time there was a hole in the overcast, and *Bock's Car* went into it and dropped the bomb. Desperately short of fuel, Sweeney barely made it back to Okinawa where he set *Bock's Car* down for an emergency refueling stop. He returned to Tinian after twenty hours to find that the Soviet Union was now at war with Japan.

The following day the Japanese advised the Americans that they would accept the Potsdam Declaration if they could keep their emperor. The Truman administration responded that, in effect, this was a "condition" and that the Potsdam Declaration called for *unconditional* surrender. It was added that Japan should ultimately be ruled by a form of government freely selected by its people. On August 15, Emperor Hirohito made an unprecedented radio address to his subjects in which he submitted the monarchy to the conditions of the Potsdam Declaration. Opposition within the military government quickly collapsed, and the war was over.

The Soviet people were told by their government that it was their entry into the war that caused Japan's surrender—a ludicrous notion given the millions of men the Japanese still had under arms in Manchuria and Korea to defend against the Soviets, coupled with the fact that the Soviets had neither the equipment nor the expertise to conduct an amphibious invasion of Japan. Throughout the rest of the world it was clear that the nuclear strikes were the straw that broke the camel's back. They were, however, merely straws among straws. They were part of the mix of ordnance—high explosive, incendiary, mines, *and* nuclear—that together proved to be Japan's undoing, all of which was delivered onto Japan *from the air* by the B-29s of the U.S. Twentieth Air Force.

In his analysis of the effects of the bombing on Japan, Robert Nathans states that the atomic bomb:

> had a tremendous impact physiologically and psychologically on the Japanese people, but there is a tendency to overestimate the physical damage in relation to the entire sum of the destruction. The Japanese had begun to sue for peace before the bomb fell on Hiroshima. Japanese spokesmen have admitted that their fight was lost before the atomic bomb fell. [I have] no doubt that the atomic bomb precipitated unconditional surrender and in so doing saved American lives.

Even given that strategic bombing could have ended the war without the atomic bomb, I think it was a wise decision to drop the bomb because this action *did* hasten the surrender process already underway. We were losing people and expending resources every day that the war went on. The Japanese were also losing people. What guided me in all my thinking, and guided all our efforts—the reason the Twenty-First Bomber Command worked like no other command during the war and the thing that kept us going—was the million men we were going to lose if we had to invade Japan. That says nothing of the Japanese losses, although we didn't give a damn about them at the time. We were worried primarily about our own people.

When the people from the U.S. Strategic Bombing Survey went into Japan after the war, they wanted to find out not only what happened to the targets, but also what kind of thinking had gone on at the top Japanese military staff level at the time. They discovered that the Japanese militarists had been battling the civilian element of the government, and that even the emperor himself had wanted to get out of the war long before they did. It turned out that these were the people who really controlled the government in the final years of the war, and who were responsible for the doctrine of fighting to the last man at home, just as they had on every island that we had captured in the Pacific war.

That philosophy had cost the United States a casualty for every man the Japanese had on each island. In spite of our superiority in weapons, men, and equipment, we'd had to kill nearly every Japanese soldier defending every Pacific island that we'd captured, and the same would have been true on the Japanese home islands. On the mainland the fighting would have been at least as bad. It probably would have been much worse fighting them for their homeland than it had been on any other island, even the likes of Iwo Jima and Okinawa, which were gruesome beyond anything we can imagine today.

On top of that, the militarists were arming the entire civilian population. If we'd invaded Japan, we wouldn't have known which civilians were or were not part of the fighting force. Even the children were armed. You wouldn't have been able to tell who was in the army, who was a civilian, and who was just a kid. What that meant is that we would have had to kill practically every man, woman, and child that we saw. That would have been an awful slaughter. The atomic bomb probably saved 3 million Japanese, and perhaps a million American casualties.

The Twentieth Air Force got the job done before the Allied armies had to do it, but it was touch and go. We never would have made it without the command structure that had been set up, and we never would have made it without the B-29.

IX

Postscript to Victory

By July 1945, the strategic targets in Japan had been almost totally destroyed by the B-29s of the Twentieth Air Force, the type of massive strategic strike force that airmen had to beg for just a few years earlier. In anticipation of Operation Olympic, the invasion of the Japanese main island of Kyushu, which was set for November 1, 1945, plans had been laid to supplement the B-29s of the Twentieth Air Force with the striking power of the strategic air forces that had been brought to bear on Germany.

The plan called for the creation of U.S. Army Strategic Air Forces in the Pacific (USASTAF) along the lines of the U.S. Strategic Air Forces in Europe (USSAFE) that had been set up to coordinate the activities of the Eighth and Fifteenth Air Forces in Europe. General Carl "Tooey" Spaatz, who had commanded the Eighth Air Force, and later the USSAFE, was assigned to command the USASTAF.

July 16 was the beginning of the final chapter of World War II. In Potsdam, a suburb of the defeated Germany's battered capital city, the leaders of the Grand Alliance—Truman, Churchill, and Stalin—sat down to draw up the surrender terms that would be imposed upon Japan. At that same moment, across the world in the New Mexico desert at the place called Trinity, the Manhattan Project crew had detonated the first atomic bomb.

July 16 was also, coincidentally, the date that the bomber components and headquarters of the Eighth Air Force, the strategic air force that had helped to defeat Germany, were moved from Charleroi, Belgium, to Okinawa, where, two days later, they were officially integrated into the USASTAF.

At this time, there were 3692 B-17s in the USAAF, most of which had been assigned to the USSAFE and which would now be deployed to Okinawa via the Eighth Air Force. There were also 4986 B-24s in the USAAF. These were divided among the USSAFE, the Eleventh Air Force, which was attacking the Kuril Islands north of Japan from bases in the Aleutians, and the Far East Air Forces (FEAF) that were already flying raids against southern Japan from Okinawa. General Hap Arnold had been to Okinawa in June and now was impatient to see a *thousand* B-17s there as soon as possible!

General Jimmy Doolittle, who had led the first raid on Tokyo in April 1942, had gone on to lead the Eighth Air Force against the Germans. Now he was being assigned to lead the "Mighty Eighth" against the Japanese. He had left the Eighth Air Force on May 10, 1945, to go back to headquarters in Washington, and he was there on May 25 when the Joint Chiefs of Staff approved Operation Olympic. In the meantime, there were 1056 B-29s in service, and more than enough in production to bring the total to almost 2500 by November. Boeing's Seattle factory was also about ready to come on line as a fifth production facility with an order in place for 5000 B-29Cs.

Britain's Royal Air Force was also assembling the Tiger Force, a flotilla of Lancaster VII heavy bombers scheduled to join the USAAF heavy and very heavy bombers converging on Okinawa in anticipation of Operation Olympic. Prime Minister Winston Churchill had discussed the participation by the British in the final assault on Japan with Hap Arnold as early as September 1944, during the Octagon Conference in Quebec. Though the British were at that time fully committed in Europe and southern Asia, Churchill was keen to have the Union Jack flying alongside the Stars and Stripes when the Rising Sun finally set.

Arnold recalled that during Octagon,

> As the days passed, it became more and more apparent that the Prime Minister desired, for political reasons, to see Britain in on the final conquest of Japan. He wanted to be there with his main [Royal Navy] fleet; he wanted to be there with some 500 to 1,000 [Royal Air Force] heavy bombers; and there was no doubt that the President [Roosevelt] would [have liked] very much to have it arranged along that line. The Prime Minister said the British would not be able to hold up their heads if they were denied this opportunity to cooperate. Then he turned to me and said, "with all your wealth of airdromes, you would not deny me the mere pittance of a few for my heavy bombers, would you?"

Arnold told Churchill that it would be a matter for the Combined Chiefs of Staff to decide, but added that the FEAF and the Twentieth Air Force planned to be using every available airfield on Guam, Saipan, Tinian, and Iwo Jima. Arnold went on to cynically recall, however, that had the Combined Chiefs of Staff actually gone along with Churchill and "decided to replace B-29s with Lancasters, it was all right with me."

Admiral King, for his part, simply refused to go along with Churchill's idea for joint naval operations, noting—as Arnold remembers—that "The American Navy had carried the war all the way from Honolulu to the west and it would carry it to Japan!"

As for the question of heavy bombers, the Lancaster VII modification program was proceeding when the end of the war rendered the issue moot. The key to any strategic bombing effort against the heart of Japan using airplanes other than B-29s, however, was air bases on Okinawa, and these would probably not have been ready to sustain such an effort until at least September.

By including the Tiger Force, there could have been as many as *10,000* strategic bombers available to support Operation Olympic, and as many as half again more on hand for Operation Coronet, the final assault on the Kanto Plain surrounding Tokyo, which was scheduled for March 1946. As Hap Arnold later articulated, the coordinated air plan called for B-29s to drop 200,000 tons of bombs per month on the invasion area alone, to be followed by 80,000 tons in the twenty-four hours preceding the landings. This compared with a monthly average of 34,402 tons that we dropped on Japan between May 1 and August 15, 1945.

It was ironic that the Allied leaders had *finally* gotten around to creating this type of strategic bomber armada after the strategic targets in Japan had already been wiped out and Japan itself already defeated.

On September 3, 1945, when the Japanese warlords politely shuffled aboard the *USS Missouri* to sign the instruments of surrender that ended mankind's most deadly war, they were treated to a thundering overflight by no fewer than 435 mighty B-29s. In just five years, Boeing, the USAAF, and the American people had created the most awesome warplane ever put into service, a warplane that had become the single most important weapon contributing to the destruction of the war machine that had ravished Pearl Harbor and so much of the Far East.

I went up briefly to Japan from my headquarters on Guam for the September 3 surrender exercise in a C-54 and landed near Yokohama. A B-29 couldn't land there because the runway couldn't take the weight. Driving into Yokohama from the airfield we went through a big area where tall weeds had grown up. For a long way that's all we saw, but in places where they weren't so thick, we would see a drill press or some other machinery, marking the site of one of those little family factories that had been set up to make just one part to send to a main factory. There weren't as many chimneys left standing as we had seen in the German cities we'd bombed, and there were walls only where there had been a masonry building. Occasionally there would be a building left standing, but it was usually gutted. In Germany there was more rubble than we saw in Japan, but neither of them was a very pleasant sight.

On the flight back to Guam after the surrender ceremony, General Doolittle and I decided to take a look at whatever targets we could see and still have enough gasoline to get back to Iwo Jima (there was no fuel available at Yokohama at that time). Those cities we observed, including Tokyo and Yokohama, were completely flattened. I knew what I was going to see, because I had been looking at reconnaissance photos of these cities for six months, so I never did spend very much time examining the bomb damage done in Japan, except from the photographs. There was no particular reason for me to do it. Experts were doing that. Bombed cities looked mostly the same. We knew what was there, or more importantly, what wasn't there. We knew that we'd done the job.

After looking at the damage done by a relatively few B-29s, I could visualize what could have been done by the new USASTAF, which would have 2000 B-29s in the Twentieth Air Force and at least 2000 B-17s in the Eighth Air Force, not to mention what the RAF would have added. The devastation that could have been wrought by such a force is beyond imagination. I thought to myself that if we'd had such a force in place on December 7, 1941, there probably wouldn't have been an attack on Pearl Harbor.

From that moment forward, I believed that it would be possible to maintain peace through strength. If we could build and maintain a force that was so well trained and dedicated to that cause, no one would ever again choose to attack the United States.

I had the opportunity to participate in building such a force—the Strategic Air Command—and it *did* maintain the peace in the 1950s, but that is another story.

EPILOGUE

by Bill Yenne

With the defeat of Germany and Japan, the war against tyranny seemed forever won, and the American people, who had rallied together to build the grandest military force in history, were only too willing to beat their swords into plowshares and their B-29s into 1946 Buicks. The Superfortress had become a symbol of that victory, and for a time it stood as a major tool in the keeping of the hard-won peace.

When the war officially ended in September 1945, there were 2242 B-29s of all varieties in the inventory of the USAAF, compared with 647 a year earlier. Over the course of the next few months, roughly eighty of these airplanes were written off, and most of the remainder were stripped of their guns and flown back to the United States to be placed in permanent storage. At a time when most of the USAAF inventory was being sold off as scrap, the Superforts were considered worth preserving. Perhaps this was because they were seen as potentially useful, should the United States become embroiled in another war, and perhaps it was because they each had an assessed value of $509,465.

While the surplus airplanes retained by the USAAF after the war were scattered over roughly thirty-five Army air fields around the United States, the B-29s were largely concentrated at Warner-Robins Field, Georgia; Victorville Field, California; and Pyote

Field, Texas, with the largest concentration being flown immediately to Davis-Monthan Field outside Tucson, Arizona, where the warm, dry climate was determined to be particularly conducive to the long-term preservation of aircraft. Within a year, more than 200 of the other B-29s were moved to Davis-Monthan Field, which eventually became the sole long-term storage site.

In 1947, the USAAF Air Technical Services Command (successor to the Air Corps Materiel Division and predecessor to today's U.S. Air Force Logistics Command) contracted with the Fort Pitt Packaging Company to begin "cocooning" 486 of the 619 B-29s at Davis-Monthan, so that they could remain in storage for up to ten years without deterioration. The process, which began in July and lasted for ten months, involved two layers of gilsonite plastic to be sprayed over the surface of the airplane, followed by a layer of black, tarlike insulmastic and a layer of aluminum paint to reflect the bright Sonora Desert sun and prevent heat damage to the cocooned B-29s.

On March 21, 1946, the USAAF reorganized its dwindling handful of combat aircraft into three major operational commands: the Air Defense Command (ADC), the Tactical Air Command (TAC), and the Strategic Air Command (SAC). The latter was, in the words of General Carl "Tooey" Spaatz, who had succeeded Hap Arnold as USAAF command general, charged with being:

> prepared to conduct long-range offensive operations in any part of the world either independently or in cooperation with land and Naval forces; to conduct maximum range reconnaissance over land or sea either independently or in cooperation with land and Naval forces; to provide combat units capable of intense and sustained combat operations employing the latest and most advanced weapons; to train units and personnel for the maintenance of the Strategic Forces in all parts of the world; to perform such special missions as the Commanding General, Army Air Forces [Spaatz himself] may direct.

It was a tall order for an organization that had almost no weapons with which to carry out the task. The B-29 was still the best strategic bomber in the world, and the USAAF still had 2174 of them. Most of these, however, were parked in the deserts of the southwestern United States and were far from being in flyable condition. By the end of the year, SAC had nine Very Heavy Bomb Groups, but only 148 B-29s, so few that three of the nine groups existed only on paper!

It was incredible that SAC had been assigned such a formidable task, yet was able to scrape together *fewer than a third* of the number of B-29s that the Twentieth Air Force would launch on a typical *single day* just the year before.

On March 31 and June 7, 1947, the former components of the USSAFE — the Fifteenth and Eighth Air Forces — were assigned to the newly formed SAC. In turn, the major component of the latter was the Fifty-Eighth Bombardment Wing (Very Heavy) under Brigadier General Roger Ramey. Formerly a part of the Twentieth Air Force, the Fifty-Eighth was the original B-29 wing and the only wing to have been part of both the Twentieth and Twenty-First Bomber Commands. The Twentieth itself was now redeployed in greatly depleted form to Okinawa as part of the Far East Air Forces Command.

Within this organization, the only unit that was capable in 1946 of conducting offensive operations with *nuclear* weapons, should the need arise, was still the 509th Composite Group, which was now assigned to SAC. In July 1946, the B-29s of the 509th took part in Operation Crossroads at Bikini Atoll in the mid-Pacific, the first postwar exercise involving live nuclear weapons. At 9 a.m. on July 1, the B-29 *Dave's Dream,* under the command of Major Woodrow "Woody" Swancutt, became the third 509th Composite Group B-29 — and the third airplane of any kind — to drop a live atomic bomb.

On September 18 of the following year, the U.S. Army Air Forces became the completely independent U.S. Air Force, and by the end of the year, SAC had 19 Very Heavy Bomb Groups with 319 B-29s. Also, during 1947, one of the few B-29s assigned to the Air Research & Development Command achieved notoriety on October 14 by being the "mothership" that carried Captain Chuck Yeager and the Bell X-1 aloft on the first leg of their historic rendezvous with the sound barrier.

Among the Superforts that were being disposed of at the war's end were eighty-eight B-29As and one B-29 that were delivered to the Royal Air Force under the designation *Washington B Mk 1.*

Technically the Washingtons were intended to replace the Lancaster as the RAF Bomber Command's first line long-range bomber, a role it would continue to fulfill until the British built V-series jet bombers became operational in the early 1950s. Politically, however, it was a goodwill gesture of the highest order for the United States to share the world's largest and most advanced bomber *exclusively* with our closest wartime ally.

In the meantime, however, aircraft that appeared to be B-29s had turned up unexpectedly in the Soviet Union in 1947 in what turned out to be one of the most peculiar footnotes in the Superfortress saga.

The Soviet Union was ostensibly an ally of the United States and Britain during World War II — Stalin willingly attended conferences with Allied leaders and gladly accepted American aid — but his perception of the war was quite different from that of Churchill and Roosevelt. The Soviet Union saw itself not as part of a global conflict, but solely as the principal combatant in the effort to destroy Nazism. The fact that Britain and the United States were also at war with Germany was convenient but perceived as coincidental, while the fact that Britain and the United States considered their fight against Japan as part of the *same* war was irrelevant to Stalin. The Soviets ultimately did declare war on Japan, but not until the day before the second nuclear bomb had been dropped on Nagasaki.

Throughout the war, the Soviets had refused to cooperate with Britain and the United States in the war against Japan. The big Soviet Far Eastern base complex at Vladivostok was closer to Tokyo than Iwo Jima, and yet requests to use its airfields as a B-29 base — or even as an emergency landing site — were repeatedly denied. The Soviets, in the meanwhile, gave only grudging approval for limited use of their airfields in the west for American bombers attacking the common enemy, Germany!

Despite this lack of cooperation, thousands of American-built aircraft had been delivered to Stalin under the lend-lease program. Several times in his requests for materiel aid, the Soviet leader had added that he'd also like to obtain B-29s! Because the Superfortress represented the leading edge of American technology and because every one of them was a vital necessity in the USAAF effort, the United States did not include its biggest strategic bomber among the assortment of aircraft that left American factories marked with red stars.

Premier Stalin's wishes, however, were unexpectedly answered on July 29, 1944, after a Twentieth Bomber Command attack on Anshan, Manchuria. Having run low on fuel, a B-29 made an emergency landing at Vladivostok, which was barely 30 miles from Anshan. During November 1944, two more B-29s landed—intact— at Vladivostok. One of these, ironically, was the *General H. H. Arnold Special*, a Superfortress singled out and autographed by General Arnold a half year earlier in Wichita, Kansas.

The treatment received by the crews was hardly in keeping with the notion of an airplane making an emergency landing in an allied nation. Fired at by Soviet anti-aircraft batteries despite their planes being clearly marked, the crews were greeted with extensive interrogation and interned at Tashkent for more than a month before being turned over to American authorities on the Iranian border on January 29, 1945.

The crews never saw their B-29s again, but when several aircraft identified as B-29s were observed at the 1947 Soviet Aviation Day flyby, the story of what had happened began to unfold. In January 1945, the design bureau headed by Andrei Nikolayevich Tupolev was assigned the task of copying the design of the "interned" B-29s as closely and quickly as possible, to be followed by the delivery of twenty heavy bombers which would be designated Tu-4. At the same time, Tupolev undertook development of a single transport aircraft which differed from the Tu-4 and the B-29 in that it had a much simpler fuselage and no bomb bay. Designated Tu-70, this aircraft reportedly utilized American-made components such as the tail, engines, and landing gear taken *directly* from one of the three American B-29s that landed at Vladivostok. The "shortcut" Tu-70 with its simplified fuselage, first flew on November 27, 1946, and the first Tu-4 flew on July 3, 1947.

Unlike the Tu-70, the Tu-4 was outwardly identical to a B-29 down to the apparently faithful copies of Wright Cyclone engines. These bootlegged Cyclones were in fact, *so* faithful to the originals that the Soviets had many of the same technical problems that the USAAF faced with the originals early in the B-29 program. Other problems—including creating distortion-free plexiglass panels for the cockpit—delayed completion of the first twenty

Tu-4s until 1949. By that time, however, western observers had seen the Tu-70 and enough of the Tu-4s to realize what had happened. Code-named "Bull" by NATO, the Tu-4 went into full-scale production, with about 400 having been delivered through 1954.

If imitation really *is* the sincerest form of flattery, then the bootlegged Tu-4 was among the highest tributes that would be paid to the Superfortress in the postwar years.

In the U.S. Air Force, however, the great Superfortress had begun to slip past its prime. By 1948, SAC was taking delivery of the long-awaited Convair B-36 Peacemaker, the huge six-engine bomber that had originally been conceived as part of the AWPD-1 in 1941 as being necessary to reach Germany from the Western Hemisphere, if bases in England became untenable. Postponed until after the war, when Germany did not defeat Great Britain, the B-36 made its first flight in August 1946. An enormous bomber, the B-36 dwarfed the B-29, the way the B-29 had dwarfed the B-17. The new groups to which the B-36 was assigned were to be designated Heavy Bombardment Groups, and so the B-29 groups, heretofore known as Very Heavy Bombardment Groups, were redesignated as *Medium* Bombardment Groups!

On October 19, 1948, General LeMay took over as commander in chief of the Strategic Air Command, and in the course of the next nine years—first with B-36s and then with Boeing B-52 Superfortresses—he transformed SAC from a paper tiger into a tiger in fact. By applying the same strict guidelines for maintenance and crew readiness that he'd used in the Twentieth Air Force four years earlier, General LeMay created a powerful and efficient deterrent force that played an important role in preserving peace in the troubled world of the 1950s. However, as the general has said, this is another story.

On June 27, 1950, two days after North Korea invaded South Korea, touching off the bloody Korean war, President Harry Truman ordered American forces under General Douglas MacArthur—including available units of the U.S. Air Force—to come to South Korea's aid. The U.S. Air Force component most directly and immediately affected was the Far East Air Forces (FEAF) Command under General George E. Stratemeyer. The centerpiece of General Stratemeyer's FEAF was the Fifth Air Force, now based in Japan, but the FEAF also included the Twentieth Air Force. Barely a ghost of its former self, the Twentieth Air Force had only twenty-two B-29s remaining in a fleet that had numbered in the hundreds just five years before. Nevertheless, four Superforts were available for strikes against North Korea on June 28.

On July 8, General Stratemeyer established a FEAF Bomber Command, naming Major General Emmett "Rosey" O'Donnell as its commander. As the wartime commander of the first B-29 wing activated in the Marianas, Rosey O'Donnell was a respected choice. The strength of the FEAF Bomber Command eventually grew to nearly a hundred B-29s, thanks to aircraft loaned by General LeMay at SAC.

MacArthur's planners had earmarked the Superfortresses for use against tactical targets, but by July 30 at General Stratemeyer's urging, O'Donnell's B-29s were released to begin a systematic strategic offensive against North Korea's ports, industrial centers, and rail network. So complete and thorough was this campaign that the FEAF Bomber Command simply disposed of all the targets within three months and was formally disbanded on October 27, 1950.

The unified United Nations command which had been set up under General MacArthur was on the verge of complete victory by this time, and the Korean war was considered all but over. However, the complexion of the conflict changed entirely just a few days later with the massive intervention by Chinese troops. The FEAF Bomber Command was hastily reformed, but it was no longer the same war.

From the days of Billy Mitchell, the concept of strategic air power has always been to fly over the front lines to strike the enemy's heartland, and to destroy his ability and his will to wage war. This concept had worked against Japan in 1945 and against North Korea in 1950. After November 1950, however, the enemy heartland was no longer in North Korea, but in China. General MacArthur favored using the FEAF Bomber Command against targets in China and especially against the bridges across the Yalu River which formed the only access to the Korean peninsula for Chinese troops and materiel.

Political considerations suddenly came into play. In Washington, the Truman administration had become fearful of widening the conflict beyond Korea itself and running the risk of having the Soviet Union (a nuclear power since 1949) enter the fray. The directive came down to the troops in the field that not only were they forbidden to attack targets within China, but that the B-29s were restricted from bombing the *north* end of the Yalu River bridges. Like a prize-fighter with one hand tied behind his back, the Superfortresses attacked the southern spans of the Yalu bridges on November 8 and November 25, 1950. Thus restricted, the B-29s were forced to carry bombs that were too small to do the job properly. The bomb runs themselves were made more diffi- cult—and fatally costly—by the ban on intrusion into Chinese air space, because enemy anti-aircraft guns on the north shore of the Yalu were now immune from American attack.

Though the B-29s continued to be used until the end of the Korean war, the entry of the Chinese into the hostilities truly marked the beginning of the end for the great bomber. Politics kept them away from true strategic targets at a critical juncture and then went on to create a safe haven where the enemy could base fighters without fear of attack. By 1951 the enemy fighters were Soviet-built MiG-15 jets, much more sophisticated than any- thing the Superforts had faced over Japan six years before. This meant that the FEAF Bomber Command found American fighter escorts much more of a necessity than the Twenty-First Bomber Command had in World War II.

In June 1952, Superfortresses played an important part in de- stroying North Korea's hydroelectric power system, but aside from that, their importance declined acutely from the October 1950 turning point. Nevertheless, the FEAF B-29s dropped 167,000 tons of bombs on North Korea between 1950 and 1953, compared with 169,676 tons dropped on Japan by the Twentieth Air Force in 1944 and 1945. The last B-29 combat mission was an armed reconnaissance mission flown by the Ninety-First Strategic Re- connaissance Squadron on July 27, 1953, the same day that the armistice was signed ending the Korean war.

In the meantime, Boeing had undertaken the development of a *super* Model 345, a *super* Superfortress. In July 1944, the USAAF had ordered a B-29A retrofitted with four Pratt & Whitney R-4360 Wasp Major engines which delivered 3000 horsepower, compared with the 2200 horsepower of the conventional Wright R-3350s. The re-engined Superfort made its first flight in May 1945 under the designation XB-44. The idea at the time was to use the XB-44 as a prototype for a series of improved bombers that could go into production at Renton, Washington, under the designation B-29D. In the course of the design of the B-29D and the testing of the XB-44, so many changes were made that the USAAF redesignated the production version of the project as B-50. In 1946 General George Kenney, wartime commander of the FEAF, and General LeMay's predecessor at SAC, actually considered developing the B-50 for SAC instead of the larger and more expensive B-36.

The B-50A, first flown on June 25, 1947, differed from the B-29 configuration by the huge air scoops beneath the four Wasp Majors, and by its tail, which was 3 feet taller than that of the B-29. Boeing's Renton factory, having concluded B-29 production, went on to build 79 B-50As, 45 B-50Bs and 222 B-50Ds. The B-50C was designed with a 10-foot increase in wingspan and a longer fuselage, and was specified for 4500 horsepower Pratt & Whitney R-4360-51 compound engines. Redesignated as B-54A in May 1948, these *super,* super Superfortresses were canceled by the Air Force on April 5, 1949, in favor of building more Consolidated B-36s.

The B-50s, meanwhile, reached a peak number of 263 (including 39 RB-50 reconnaissance conversions) in SAC's inventory in 1952. The bomber version was finally retired in 1955, and the reconnaissance version disappeared from SAC's active roster the following year. There were at least thirty-three B-50s converted to aerial refueling tankers under the designations KB-50D, KB-50J, and KB-50K. These remained in service with the Air Force's Tactical Air Command until 1965.

As for the B-29 itself, it reached a postwar peak of 425 (including 18 RB-29s) in SAC's inventory in 1952, and was dropped from the official SAC roster the following year after the end of the Korean war. In the meantime, work had begun toward the conversion of B-29s and B-29As into aerial refueling tankers. The first of these was delivered to SAC's Forty-Third and 509th Air Refueling Squadrons (attached to the Forty-Third and 509th Bomb Groups) on June 18, 1948. Designated KB-29M, the tankers uti-

171

lized the British-developed aerial refueling technique using trailing hoses and grapnel hooks. In July 1948, a month after the KB-29Ms became operational, they supported a round-the-world flight by B-29s of the Forty-Third Bomb Group. In July 1951, during operations over Korea, KB-29Ms of the Forty-Third Aerial Refueling Squadron would be the first aircraft to conduct aerial refueling in combat. On September 1, 1950, SAC took delivery of the first KB-29P, a B-29 tanker conversion with the Boeing-designed gravity boom-type aerial refueling apparatus that has since become standard on all U.S. Air Force aerial refueling aircraft.

In all, 92 B-29s were converted as KB-29Ms, and 116 were converted as KB-29Ps. While SAC was not the only user of these tankers, it *was* by far the largest. They reached an aggregate peak total of 179 within SAC in 1952 and were finally deleted from SAC's roster in 1957, as jet-powered KC-135 tankers came into service. Other B-29s were converted into WB-29 weather reconnaissance aircraft, TB-29 crew trainers, QB-29 radio-controlled "drone" aerial gunnery and missile targets, and DB-29 "drone directors" from which the QB-29s were controlled.

The B-29s preserved at Davis-Monthan Field (Davis-Monthan Air Force Base after 1948) were "thawed out" in 1956, but eventually they were scrapped. The last B-29 in the U.S. Air Force was finally retired in 1960. Today, there are roughly two dozen B-29s in the world. They range from hulks at various Air Force Bases to several airplanes that have been painstakingly restored to their original condition. Those which are preserved in static display include the *Enola Gay,* which is in the collection of the Smithsonian Institution's National Air & Space Museum and *Bock's Car,* which is in the collection of the U.S. Air Force Museum near Dayton, Ohio. The only B-29 remaining in flyable condition is *Fifi,* which is flown under the banner of the Confederate Air Force, a Harlingen, Texas-based organization dedicated to preserving *flying* examples of World War II vintage aircraft.

The Superfortress was born in the darkest hour of mankind's bloodiest war, and it came of age in time to be the symbol of our final victory in that war. The B-29 lives today—largely in our memories—no longer as a symbol of that war but as a symbol of American commitment to excellence in a time of crisis, a memorial and monument to the countless men and women who built the Superfortresses and who flew them. These were the people, and the spirit, without whom there would not have been a Superfortress, nor indeed that final victory.

APPENDIX

Comparing Boeing Heavy Bombers[a]

Bomber[a]	Wing Span	Length	Cruising Speed (mph)	Range (miles)	First Flown (Series Prototype)	Last Year in Service	Production Total[b]
XB-15 (Model 294)	149'	87'7"	171	3400	1937	1945	1
B-17G Flying Fortress (Model 299)	103'9"	74'9"	182	2000	1935	1950	12,726[c]
B-29A Superfortress (Model 345)	141'3"	99'	253	5418	1942	1960	3,996[d]
B-50D Superfortress (Model 345)	141'3"	99'	244	5762	1947	1965	346

(continued)

175

TABLE 1 (*continued*)

Comparing Boeing Heavy Bombers[a]

Bomber[a]	Wing Span	Length	Cruising Speed (mph)	Range (miles)	First Flown (Series Prototype)	Last Year in Service	Production Total[b]
B-52G Stratofortress (Model 464)	185'	157'7"	523	8900[e]	1952	[f]	744

[a]Official Boeing Company Data.

[b]Specifications given are for the subvariant of each type that was produced in the largest numbers, while dates and production totals cover all subvariants of the type. "Last year in service" refers to USAAF/U.S. Air Force.

[c]Includes 5745 built by Douglas and Vega.

[d]Includes 1204 built by Bell and Martin.

[e]Before the nonstop round-the-world flight of *Voyager* in 1986, a B-52H held the world's absolute unrefueled distance record of 12,532 miles, which was established in 1962.

[f]Expected to remain in service until about 1999.

TABLE 2

Comparing Non-Boeing Heavy Bomber Contemporaries of the B-29*

Bomber*	Wing Span	Length	Cruising Speed (mph)	Range (miles)	First Flown (Series Prototype)	Last Year in Service	Production Total
Consolidated B-24J Liberator	110'	67'2"	278	3300	1939	1953	18,188
Avro Lancaster III	102'	68'11"	210	2230	1941	1954	7374
Consolidated B-36H Peacemaker	230'	162'¼"	234	7691	1946	1959	417

*Specifications given are for the subvariant of each type that was produced in the largest numbers, while dates and production totals cover all subvariants of the type. "Last year in service" refers to USAAF/U.S. Air Force except the Lancaster, which is Royal Air Force.

TABLE 3

Boeing Design Proposals That Evolved into the Model 345/XB-29 Program

Design	Wing Span	Length	Cruising Speed (mph)	Gross Weight (lb)	Service Ceiling	Maximum Range (miles)
Model 316 (March 1938)	157'	109'2"	248	89,900	15,000'	4000
Model 322 (June 1938)	108'7"	75'5"	307	40,000	25,000'	3600
Model 333 (January 1939)	109'	80'8"	307	41,000	15,000'	3420
Model 333A (January 1939)	108'6"	80'8"	328	40,500	15,000'	3000
Model 333B (February 1939)	111'	80'8"	364	46,000	20,000'	2500
Model 334 (March 1939)	120'	83'4"	390	49,750	20,000'	4500
Model 334A (July 1939)	135'	80'	390	55,000	16,000'	5333
Model 341 (March 1940)	124'7"	85'6"	405	76,000	25,000'	5333
Model 345* (May 1940)	141'2"	93'	382	97,700	25,000'	5333

*Original configuration designed in March and April 1940, and submitted to Wright Field on May 11. The initial revised Model 345 became the XB-29 and was in turn followed by other B-29 and B-50 variants, all of which carried Boeing's Model 345 designation (see Table 4).

TABLE 4

Boeing Model 345 Superfortress Subvariant Specifications

Subvariant	Wing Span	Length	Tail Height	Cruising Speed (mph)	Top Speed (mph)	Gross Weight (lb)	Service Ceiling	Maximum Range (miles)
XB-29 (Seattle)	141'3"	98'2"	27'9"	247	368	105,000	32,100'	5850
B-29 (Wichita blocks 1–20)	141'3"	99'	29'7"	230	358	134,000	31,850'	4700
B-29 (Wichita blocks 25–90)	141'3"	99'	29'7"	230	361	137,500	31,850'	5500
B-29A (Renton)	141'3"	99'	29'7"	253	399	140,000	36,150'	5418
B-29B (Bell)	141'3"	99'	29'7"	228	364	110,000	32,000'	5725
XB-39	141'3"	98'2"	27'9"	282	405	105,000	35,000'	6290
XB-44	141'3"	99'	29'7"	282	392	105,000	35,000'	2400 (normal)
B-50A	141'3"	99'	32'8"	244	391	120,500	36,000'	5230
B-50D	141'3"	99'	32'8"	244	395	121,850	36,650'	5762

TABLE 5

Boeing Model 345 Superfortress Engine Specifications*

Subvariant	Engine Maker	Designation	Type	Horsepower
XB-29 (Seattle)	Wright	Cyclone R-3350-13	Radial	2200 (at 25,000')
B-29 (Wichita blocks 1–20)	Wright	Cyclone R-3350-23	Radial	2430 (war emergency)
B-29 (Wichita blocks 25–90)	Wright	Cyclone R-3350-41	Radial	2430 (war emergency)
B-29A (Renton)	Wright	Cyclone R-3350-57	Radial	2500 (war emergency)
B-29B (Bell)	Wright	Cyclone R-3350-23	Radial	2200 (at takeoff)
XB-39	Allison	V-3420-11	In-line	3000 (at takeoff)
XB-44	Pratt & Whitney	R-4360-33	Radial	2500 (at 25,000')
B-50A	Pratt & Whitney	R-4360-35	Radial	3500 (at takeoff)
B-50D	Pratt & Whitney	R-4360-35	Radial	3500 (at takeoff)

*Each aircraft had four of the indicated engines. There were seven B-50Ds and twenty-four TB-50Hs converted as KB-50J and KB-50K aerial refueling tankers. In addition to the engines mentioned above for B-50D, these each had two General Electric J47-GE-23 jet engines in underwing pods.

TABLE 6

Boeing Model 345 Superfortress Production Totals

Subvariant	Order Dates	Block Numbers	Manufacturing Site and Code	Number Produced
XB-29-BO	1941		Boeing Seattle (BO)	3
YB-29-BW	1941		Boeing Wichita (BW)	14
B-29-BW	1942–1945	1–100	Boeing Wichita (BW)	1620
B-29-BA	1942–1944	1–65	Bell Marietta (BA)	357
B-29-MO	1942–1944	1–60	Martin Omaha (MO)	204
B-29-NA	1942		North American (NA) Inglewood	(200)*
B-29A-BN	1942–1944	1–75	Boeing Renton (BN)	1119
B-29B-BA	1942–1944	30–65	Bell Marietta (BA)	310
B-29C-BO	1944		Boeing Seattle (BO)	(5000)*
B-29D-BN	1944		Boeing Renton (BN)	1
B-50A-BN	1946–1947	1–35	Boeing Renton (BN)	79
B-50B-BN	1947	40–60	Boeing Renton (BN)	45
B-50C-BN	1947		Boeing Renton (BN)	(1)*
B-50D-BN	1947–49	65–125	Boeing Renton (BN)	222
B-54A-BN	1949		Boeing Renton (BN)	(21)*
RB-54A-BN	1949		Boeing Renton (BN)	(52)*
TB-50H-BN	1951		Boeing Renton (BN)	24

*Ordered, but canceled before production.

TABLE 7

Boeing Model 345 Superfortress Converted or Redesignated after Being Delivered to the USAAF/U.S. Air Force*

New Designation	Original Designation	Number Converted	Reason for Conversion or Redesignation
SB-29	B-29	16	"Super Dumbo" search and rescue aircraft
XB-29E-BW	B-29-BW	1	Fire control testing
B-29F-BW	B-29-BW	6	Cold weather testing
XB-29G-BA	B-29B-BA	1	Jet engine testing
XB-29H-BN	B-29A-BN	1	Armament testing
YB-29J-BA/MO	B-29-BA/MO	6	Engine testing
FB-29J-BA	YB-29J-BA	2	Photoreconnaissance
YKB-29J-MO	YB-29J-MO	2	Aerial tanker testing
RB-29J-BA	FB-29J-BA	2	Adoption of 1948 nomenclature
CB-29K-BW	B-29-BW	1	Transport conversion (1949–1956)
KB-29K	B-29/B-29A	92	Interim designation for KB-29M (See KB–29M)
B-29L	B-29	0	(Designation superseded by B-29MR)
KB-29M	KB-29K	92	Trailing-hose aerial tankers
B-29MR	B-29	74	Aerial tanker "receivers"
KB-29P	B-29	116	Flying boom aerial tankers
YKB-29T	KB-29M	1	Three-point trailing-hose aerial tanker
XB-39-BO	YB-29-BO	1	Engine testing
XB-44-BN	B-29A-BN	1	Engine testing/B-50A prototype
F-13A-BW	B-29-BW	117	World War II reconnaissance aircraft

TABLE 7 (*continued*)

Boeing Model 345 Superfortress Converted or Redesignated after Being Delivered to the USAAF/U.S. Air Force*

New Designation	Original Designation	Number Converted	Reason for Conversion or Redesignation
F-13A-BN	B-29-BN	117	World War II reconnaissance aircraft
P2B-1S	B-29-BW	2	U.S. Navy radar picket aircraft
P2B-2S	B-29-BW	2	Carrier for U.S. Navy research aircraft
TB-50A-BN	B-50A-BN	11	B-36 project crew trainers
EB-50B	B-50B-BN	1	Landing gear testing
RB-50B-BN	B-50B-BN	44	Reconnaissance aircraft
DB-50D-BN	B-50D-BN	1	Missile testing
JB-50D-BN	B-50D-BN	1	Systems testing
KB-50D-BN	B-50D-BN	1	Aerial tanker testing
KB-50D-BN	TB-50D-BN	1	Aerial tanker testing
TB-50D-BN	B-50D-BN	11	Crew training
WB-50D-BN	B-50D-BN	36	Weather reconnaissance
RB-50E-BN	B-50D-BN	14	Reconnaissance testing
RB-50F-BN	RB-50B-BN	14	Radar aircraft
RB-50G-BN	RB-50B-BN	15	Reconnaissance aircraft
KB-50J-BN	B-50D-BN	7	Jet-assisted aerial tankers
KB-50K-BN	TB-50H-BN	24	Jet-assisted aerial tankers

*In addition to the above, some B-29s became DB-29 drone directors, QB-29 radio-controlled drones, TB-29 crew trainers, and WB-29 weather reconnaissance aircraft. Those aircraft converted to carry X-series research aircraft became GB-29. The B-29N, B-29Q, B-29R, and B-29S designations were never assigned.

TABLE 8

Major Twentieth Bomber Command Actions, 1944*

Date	Number of B-29s Launched	Target Site	Target Type	Ordnance Type
June 5	98	Bangkok, Thailand	Rail yards	HE†
June 15	47	Yawata, Japan	Steelworks	HE
July 7	14	Sasebo/Omura/Tobata, Japan	Urban areas	HE
July 7	3	Laoyao/Hankow, China	Troop concentrations	HE
July 29	70+	Anshan/Taku, Manchuria	Steelworks/harbor	HE
August 10	27	Nagasaki, Japan	Urban areas	HE
August 10	31	Palembang, Sumatra	Oil refineries	HE
August 10	8	Moesi River, Sumatra	Waterway	Mines
August 20	71	Yawata, Japan	Steelworks/assorted targets	HE
September 8	90	Anshan, Manchuria	Steelworks	HE
September 8	11	Anshan, Manchuria	Rail yards/urban areas	HE
September 26	83	Anshan, Manchuria	Steelworks	HE
September 26	15	Dairen/Sinsiang, Manchuria	Urban areas	HE
October 14	103	Okayama, Japan	Aircraft factory	HE
October 14	12	Okayama, Japan	Urban areas	HE
October 16	40+	Okayama, Japan	Aircraft factory	HE
October 16	20+	China	Assorted targets	HE
October 17	10	Einansho, Japan	Air depot	HE
October 17	14	Japan	Assorted targets	HE
October 25	59	Omura, Japan	Aircraft factory	HE

TABLE 8 (continued)

Major Twentieth Bomber Command Actions, 1944*

Date	Number of B-29s Launched	Target Site	Target Type	Ordnance Type
November 3	49	Malagon, Malay Peninsula	Rail yards	HE
November 5	53	Singapore	George VI dry dock	HE
November 5	11	Singapore	Oil refinery/troop concentrations	HE
November 12	29	Omura, Japan	Urban areas	HE
November 12	40+	Nanking, China	Urban areas/ assorted targets	HE
November 21	61	Omura, Japan	Aircraft factory	HE
November 21	13+	Shanghai, China	Urban areas	HE
November 27	58	Bangkok, Thailand	Rail yards/ assorted targets	HE
December 7	90+	Mukden, Manchuria	Aircraft factory/ rail yards/arsenal	HE
December 14	47	Bangkok, Thailand	Rail bridge/ assorted targets	HE
December 18	89	Hankow, China	Docks/assorted targets	Incendiaries
December 19	17	Omura, Japan	Aircraft factory	HE
December 19	15	Shanghai, China	Urban areas	HE
December 21	19	Mukden, Manchuria	Aircraft factory/ arsenal/rail yards	HE
December 21	8	Mukden, Manchuria	Assorted targets	HE

*Based on official USAAF records.
†HE = high explosives.

TABLE 9

Major Twentieth Bomber Command Actions, 1945*

Date	Number of B-29s Launched	Target Site	Target Type	Ordnance Type
January 2	44	Bangkok, Thailand	Railroad bridge	HE†
January 2	2	Bangkok, Thailand	Urban areas	HE
January 6	28	Omura, Japan	Aircraft factory	HE
January 6	19	Nanking, China	Urban areas	HE
January 9	39	Kirun, Formosa	Harbor	HE
January 9	6	China coast	Assorted targets	HE
January 11	25	Singapore	Dry docks	HE
January 11	15	Penang, Malaya	Assorted targets	HE
January 14	54	Kagi, Japan	Airfields	HE
January 14	23	Japan	Assorted targets	HE
January 17	80	Shinchiku, Japan	Airfield	HE
January 17	8	Southeast China	Assorted targets	HE
January 25	70+	Singapore/Saigon, FIC‡/Camranh Bay, FIC/Phan Rang, FIC/Penang, Malaya, Koh Si Chang Channel	Channels/harbors	Mines
January 27	22	Saigon, FIC	Navy yard/arsenal	HE
January 27	1	Bangkok, Thailand	Bridge	HE
February 1	67	Singapore	Admiralty IX dry dock	HE
February 1	21	Singapore	Naval base	HE
February 1	21	Singapore	Martaban/George Town/ urban areas	HE
February 7	44	Saigon, FIC	Urban areas	HE

TABLE 9 (*continued*)

Major Twentieth Bomber Command Actions, 1945*

Date	Number of B-29s Launched	Target Site	Target Type	Ordnance Type
February 7	19	Phnom Penh, FIC	Urban areas	HE
February 7	2	Martaban, Burma	Assorted targets	HE
February 7	60	Bangkok, Thailand	Railroad bridge	HE
February 11	56	Rangoon, Burma	Storage dumps	HE
February 19	54	Kuala Lumpur, Malaya/Martaban, Burma	Rail yards/ assorted targets	HE
February 24	105	Singapore	Empire docks	Incendiaries
February 27	11	Penang, Malaya/ Johore Strait	Waterways	Mines
March 2	55	Singapore	Naval base/ urban areas	HE
March 4	11	Hwangpoo River/ Yangtze River, China	Waterways	Mines
March 10	24	Kuala Lumpur, Malaya	Rail yards	HE
March 10	3	Khao Huakhang, Malaya	Assorted targets	HE
March 12	44	Bukum Island/ Sebarok Island	Oil storage facilities	HE
March 17	72	Rangoon, Burma/ Bassein, Burma	Storage facilities/ airfields/ warehouses	HE
March 22	76	Rangoon, Burma	Storage facilities	HE
March 28	10	Hwangpoo River/ Yangtze River, China	Waterways	Mines

(*continued*)

TABLE 9 (*continued*)

Major Twentieth Bomber Command Actions, 1945*

Date	Number of B-29s Launched	Target Site	Target Type	Ordnance Type
March 28	50	Saigon, FIC/ Camranh Bay, FIC/Singapore	Waterways	Mines
March 29	24	Bukum Island	Oil storage facilities	HE
March 29	2	Malaya	Assorted targets	HE

*Based on official USAAF records.

†HE = high explosives.

‡FIC = French Indochina.

TABLE 10

Major Twenty-First Bomber Command Actions, 1944*

Date	Number of B-29s Launched	Target Site	Target Type	Ordnance Type
October 28	18	Dublon Island	Submarine pens	HE†
October 30	8	Dublon Island	Submarine pens	HE
November 2	17	Dublon Island	Submarine pens	HE
November 5	24	Iwo Jima	Airfields	HE
November 8	17	Iwo Jima	Airfields	HE
November 11	8	Dublon Island	Submarine pens	HE
November 24	111	Tokyo, Japan	Aircraft factory/ urban areas/ docks	HE
November 27	81	Tokyo/Hamamatsu, Japan	Urban areas/ docks/factories	HE
November 29	24	Tokyo/Yokohama/ Numazu, Japan	Urban areas/ docks/ industrial area	HE
December 3	70	Tokyo, Japan	Aircraft factories/ urban areas/ docks	HE
December 8	60+	Iwo Jima	Airfields	HE
December 13	70+	Nagoya, Japan	Aircraft factory	HE
December 18	63	Nagoya, Japan	Aircraft factory	HE
December 18	10	Japan	Assorted targets	HE
December 22	48	Nagoya, Japan	Aircraft factory	HE
December 24	23	Iwo Jima	Airfields	HE
December 27	39	Tokyo, Japan	Aircraft factories	HE
December 27	13	Japan	Assorted targets	HE

*Based on official USAAF records.
†HE = high explosives.

TABLE 11

Major Twenty-First Bomber Command Actions, 1945*

Date	Number of B-29s Launched	Target Site	Target Type	Ordnance Type
January 3	57	Nagoya, Japan	Docks/urban areas	HE†
January 3	21	Japan	Assorted targets	HE
January 9	72	Tokyo, Japan	Aircraft factory/ urban areas	HE
January 14	40	Nagoya, Japan	Aircraft factory	HE
January 14	20+	Japan	Assorted targets	HE
January 16	44	Pagan Island	Airfields	HE
January 19	62	Akashi, Japan	Aircraft factories	HE
January 19	9	Japan	Assorted targets	HE
January 21	30	Moen Island	Airfield	HE
January 23	28	Nagoya, Japan	Aircraft factory	HE
January 23	27	Nagoya, Japan	Urban areas	HE
January 23	9	Japan	Assorted targets	HE
January 24	20	Iwo Jima	Airfields	HE
January 27	56	Tokyo, Japan	Urban areas	HE
January 27	6	Japan	Assorted targets	HE
January 29	30	Iwo Jima	Airfields	HE
February 4	69	Kobe, Japan	Urban areas	HE
February 4	30	Natsusaka, Japan	Assorted targets	HE
February 8	30	Moen Island	Airfield	HE
February 9	29	Moen Island	Airfield	HE
February 10	84	Ota, Japan	Aircraft factory	HE
February 12	21	Iwo Jima	Defensive fortifications	HE

TABLE 11 (*continued*)

Major Twenty-First Bomber Command Actions, 1945*

Date	Number of B-29s Launched	Target Site	Target Type	Ordnance Type
February 15	33	Nagoya, Japan	Aircraft factory	HE
February 15	70	Japan	Assorted targets	HE
February 17	9	Dublon Island	Submarine pens	HE
February 18	35	Moen Island	Airfields	HE
February 19	150	Tokyo, Japan	Port/urban areas	HE
February 25	172	Tokyo, Japan	Urban area	HE
February 25	30	Japan	Assorted targets	HE
March 4	192	Tokyo, Japan	Urban areas/ assorted targets	HE
March 9	325	Tokyo, Japan	Urban areas	Incendiaries
March 11	285	Nagoya, Japan	Urban areas	Incendiaries
March 13	274	Osaka, Japan	Urban areas	Incendiaries
March 16	331	Kobe, Japan	Urban areas	Incendiaries
March 18	290	Nagoya, Japan	Urban areas	Incendiaries
March 24	23	Nagoya, Japan	Aircraft factory	HE
March 27	150+	Omura/Kyushu, Japan	Aircraft factory/ airfields	HE
March 27	97	Shimonoseki Strait, Japan	Waterway	Mines
March 30	12	Nagoya, Japan	Aircraft factory	HE
March 30	80+	Shimonoseki Strait, Japan	Waterway	Mines
March 31	137	Omura, Japan	Factory/airfield	HE
April 1	100	Tokyo, Japan	Aircraft factory	HE
April 1	9	Hiroshima, Japan	Sea approaches	Mines

(*continued*)

TABLE 11 (*continued*)

Major Twenty-First Bomber Command Actions, 1945*

Date	Number of B-29s Launched	Target Site	Target Type	Ordnance Type
April 1	6	Kure, Japan	Harbor	Mines
April 3	48	Shizuoka, Japan	Aircraft factory/ urban areas	HE
April 3	68	Tokyo and Koizumi, Japan	Aircraft factory	HE
April 3	9	Hiroshima, Japan	Sea approaches	Mines
April 3	100+	Tachikawa/ Kawasaki, Japan	Aircraft factory/ urban areas	HE
April 7	150+	Nagoya, Japan	Aircraft factory	HE
April 7	101	Tokyo, Japan	Aircraft factory	HE
April 7	30	Japan	Assorted targets	HE
April 8	48	Kanoya/ Kokubu, Japan	Airfields	HE
April 9	16	Shimonoseki Strait, Japan	Waterway	Mines
April 12	94	Tokyo, Japan	Aircraft factory	HE
April 12	11	Tokyo, Japan	Aircraft factory	HE
April 12	130+	Koriyama, Japan	Chemical plants	HE
April 12	32	Japan	Assorted targets	HE
April 12	5	Shimonoseki Strait, Japan	Waterway	Mines
April 13	330	Tokyo, Japan	Arsenal	Incendiaries
April 15	194	Kawasaki, Japan	Urban areas	Incendiaries
April 15	109	Tokyo, Japan	Urban areas	Incendiaries
April 17	120	Kyushu and Shikoku Islands, Japan	Airfields	HE

TABLE 11 (*continued*)

Major Twenty-First Bomber Command Actions, 1945*

Date	Number of B-29s Launched	Target Site	Target Type	Ordnance Type
April 18	100+	Kyushu and Shikoku Islands, Japan	Airfields	HE
April 21	217	Kyushu and Shikoku Islands, Japan	Airfields	HE
April 22	80+	Kyushu and Shikoku Islands, Japan	Airfields	HE
April 24	101	Tachikawa, Japan	Aircraft factory	HE
April 24	21	Japan	Assorted targets	HE
April 26	195	Kyushu and Shikoku Islands, Japan	Airfields	HE
April 27	100+	Kyushu and Shikoku Islands, Japan	Airfields	HE
April 28	120	Kyushu and Shikoku Islands, Japan	Airfields	HE
April 29	111	Kyushu and Shikoku Islands, Japan	Airfields	HE
April 30	140+	Kyushu and Shikoku Islands, Japan	Airfields	HE
May 3	68	Kyushu and Shikoku Islands, Japan	Airfields	HE
May 3	88	Shimonoseki Strait, Japan/ Inland Sea	Waterway	Mines

(*continued*)

TABLE 11 (continued)

Major Twenty-First Bomber Command Actions, 1945*

Date	Number of B-29s Launched	Target Site	Target Type	Ordnance Type
May 4	47	Kyushu and Shikoku Islands, Japan	Airfields	HE
May 5	45	Kyushu and Shikoku Islands, Japan	Airfields	HE
May 5	148	Kure, Japan	Aircraft factory	HE
May 5	86	Tokyo, Japan	Sea approaches	Mines
May 7	41	Kyushu and Shikoku Islands, Japan	Airfields	HE
May 8	40	Kyushu and Shikoku Islands, Japan	Airfields	HE
May 10	302	Tokuyama/ Otake/Amami-O-Shima, Japan	Industrial sites/ naval fuel storage facilities	Incendiaries/ HE
May 10	42	Kyushu and Shikoku Islands, Japan	Airfields	HE
May 11	50	Kyushu and Shikoku Islands, Japan	Airfields	HE
May 11	92	Kobe, Japan	Aircraft factory	HE
May 13	12	Shimonoseki Strait, Japan	Waterway	Mines
May 14	472	Nagoya, Japan	Urban area	Incendiaries
May 16	25	Shimonoseki Strait/Maizuru Harbor/Miyazu Harbor, Japan	Waterways	Mines
May 17	468	Nagoya, Japan	Urban area	Incendiaries

TABLE 11 (*continued*)

Major Twenty-First Bomber Command Actions, 1945*

Date	Number of B-29s Launched	Target Site	Target Type	Ordnance Type
May 18	30	Shimonoseki Strait/Tsuruga Harbor, Japan	Waterways	Mines
May 19	272	Hamamatsu, Japan	Urban area	Incendiaries
May 20	30	Shimonoseki Strait/Maizuru Harbor/He-Saki anchorage, Japan	Waterways	Mines
May 22	30	Shimonoseki Strait, Japan	Waterway	Mines
May 23	562	Tokyo, Japan	Urban and industrial areas	Incendiaries
May 24	25	Shimonoseki Strait/ Niigata/ Nanao/Fushiki, Japan	Waterways	Mines
May 25	464	Tokyo, Japan	Urban areas	Incendiaries
May 26	29	Shimonoseki Strait/ Fushiki/ Fukuoka/Karatsu, Japan	Waterways	Mines
May 27	9	Shimonoseki Strait/Moji, Japan	Waterways	Mines
May 29	454	Yokohama, Japan	Urban areas	Incendiaries
June 1	458	Osaka, Japan	Urban areas	Incendiaries
June 5	473	Kobe, Japan	Urban areas	Incendiaries

(*continued*)

TABLE 11 (*continued*)

Major Twenty-First Bomber Command Actions, 1945*

Date	Number of B-29s Launched	Target Site	Target Type	Ordnance Type
June 7	409	Osaka, Japan	Urban areas/ industrial areas/transportation targets	Incendiaries and HE
June 7	26	Shimonoseki Strait/Fukuoka/ Kamatsu, Japan	Waterways	Mines
June 9	110	Nagoya/ Akashi/Narao, Japan	Aircraft factories	Incendiaries
June 10	280	Central Japan	Industrial sites/ aircraft factories/ seaplane base/ army air arsenal/ engineering works	Incendiaries
June 11	26	Shimonoseki Strait/Tsuruga Bay, Japan	Waterways	Mines
June 13	29	Shimonoseki Strait/Niigata, Japan	Waterways	Mines
June 15	44	Osaka and Amagasaki, Japan	Urban areas	Incendiaries
June 15	30	Shimonoseki Strait/ Fukuoka/ Karatsu/Fushiki, Japan	Waterways	Mines
June 17	450+	Kagoshima/ Omuta/ Hamamatsu/ Yokkaichi, Japan	Urban areas	Incendiaries
June 17	25	Shimonoseki Strait/Kobe, Japan	Waterways	Mines

TABLE 11 *(continued)*

Major Twenty-First Bomber Command Actions, 1945*

Date	Number of B-29s Launched	Target Site	Target Type	Ordnance Type
June 19	480	Toyohashi/Fukuoka/ Shizuoka, Japan	Urban areas	Incendiaries
June 19	28	Shimonoseki Strait/ Niigata/Miyazu/ Maizuru, Japan	Waterways	Mines
June 21	25	Fushiki/Senzaki/ Nanao/Yuya Bay, Japan	Sea approaches	Mines
June 22	130	Himeji/ Kagamigahara/ Akashi/Tamashima, Japan	Aircraft factories	HE
June 22	162	Kure, Japan	Naval arsenal	HE
June 23	26	Fukuoka/ Karatsu/Sakai/ Niigata, Japan	Harbors	Mines
June 25	26	Shimonoseki Strait/Maizuru/ Obama Island, Japan	Waterways	Mines
June 26	450+	Nagoya/ Kagamigahara/ Akashi/Osaka/ Yokkaichi, Japan	Industrial targets	HE
June 27	29	Hagi/Kobe/ Niigata, Japan	Harbors	Mines
June 28	487	Okayama/ Sasebo/Moji/ Nobeoka, Japan	Urban areas	Incendiaries
June 29	32	Kudamatsu	Oil refinery	HE

(continued)

TABLE 11 (*continued*)

Major Twenty-First Bomber Command Actions, 1945*

Date	Number of B-29s Launched	Target Site	Target Type	Ordnance Type
June 29	25	Shimonoseki Strait/Maizuru/ Sakata, Japan	Waterways	Mines
July 1	530+	Ube/ Kure/ Shimonoseki/ Kumamoto, Japan	Urban areas	Incendiaries
July 1	24	Shimonoseki Strait/Nanao/ Fushiki, Japan	Waterways	Mines
July 2	39	Minoshima, Japan	Oil refinery	HE
July 3	560+	Kochi/ Himeji/ Takamatsu/ Tokushima, Japan	Urban areas	Incendiaries
July 3	26	Shimonoseki Strait/Funakawa/ Maizuru, Japan	Waterways	Mines
July 6	517	Chiba/ Akashi/ Shimizu/Kofu, Japan	Urban areas	Incendiaries
July 6	59	Osaka, Japan	Oil refinery	HE
July 9	475	Sendai/ Sakai/ Gifu/Wakayama, Japan	Urban areas	Incendiaries
July 9	61	Yokkaichi, Japan	Oil refinery	HE
July 9	31	Shimonoseki Strait/Niigata/ Nonao, Japan	Waterways	Mines

TABLE 11 (*continued*)

Major Twenty-First Bomber Command Actions, 1945*

Date	Number of B-29s Launched	Target Site	Target Type	Ordnance Type
July 11	25	Shimonoseki Strait/ Miyazu/ Maizuru/Obama Island, Japan; Pusan/Najin, Korea	Waterways	Mines
July 12	453	Utsonomiya/ Ichinomiya/ Tsuruga/Uwajima, Japan	Urban areas	Incendiaries
July 12	53	Kawasaki, Japan	Petroleum center	HE
July 13	30	Shimonoseki Strait/Fukuoka, Japan; Seishi/ Masan/Reisui, Korea	Waterways/ports	Mines
July 15	26	Naoetsu/Niigata, Japan; Najin/Pusan/ Wonsan, Korea	Waterways	Mines
July 15	59	Kudamatsu, Japan	Petroleum center	HE
July 16	466	Numazu/Oita/ Kuwana/ Hiratsuka, Japan	Urban areas	Incendiaries
July 17	27	Shimonoseki Strait/Nanao-Fushiki/Cape Henashi/Iwase, Japan; Seishin, Korea	Waterways	Mines
July 19	470	Fukui/Hitachi/ Chosi/ Okazaki, Japan	Urban areas	Incendiaries
July 19	83	Amagasaki	Petroleum center	HE

(*continued*)

TABLE 11 (*continued*)

Major Twenty-First Bomber Command Actions, 1945*

Date	Number of B-29s Launched	Target Site	Target Type	Ordnance Type
July 19	27	Oyama/Niigata/ Miyazu/Maizuru/ Tsuruga/ Nezugaseki/Obama Island/Kobe-Osaka areas, Japan; Wonsan, Korea	Waterways	Mines
July 22	72	Ube, Japan	Petroleum center	HE
July 22	23	Shimonoseki Strait, Japan; also Najin/Pusan/ Masan, Korea	Waterways	Mines
July 24	570	Handa/Nagoya/ Takarazuka/ Osaka/Tsu/ Kawana, Japan	Aircraft factories/ industrial sites/ urban areas	HE, Incendiaries
July 25	75	Kawasaki, Japan	Petroleum center	HE
July 25	29	Nanao/Fushiki/ Obama Island/ Tsuruga, Japan; Seishin/Pusan, Korea	Waterways	Mines
July 26	350	Matsuyama/ Tokuyama/Omuta, Japan	Urban areas	Incendiaries
July 27	24	Shimonoseki Strait/Fukuoka/ Niigata/Maizuru/ Senzaki/Fukawa Bay, Japan	Waterways	Mines
July 28	471	Tsu/Aomori/ Ichinomiya/ Ujiyamada/ Ogaki/Uwajima, Japan	Urban areas	Incendiaries
July 28	76	Shimotsu, Japan	Oil refinery	HE

TABLE 11 (*continued*)

Major Twenty-First Bomber Command Actions, 1945*

Date	Number of B-29s Launched	Target Site	Target Type	Ordnance Type
July 29	24	Shimonoseki Strait/Fukuoka/ Karatsu, Japan; Najin, Korea	Waterways	Mines
August 1‡	667	Hachioji/ Toyama/Nagaoka/ Mito, Japan	Urban areas	Incendiaries
August 1‡	132	Kawasaki, Japan	Petroleum center	HE
August 1‡	37	Shimonoseki Strait/Nakaumi Lagoon/Hamada/ Sakai/Yonago, Japan; Najin/ Seishin, Korea	Waterways	Mines
August 5	470+	Saga/Mae Bashi/ Imabari/ Nishinomiya-Mikage, Japan	Urban areas	Incendiaries
August 5	106	Ube, Japan	Petroleum center	HE
August 5	27	Sakai/Yonago/ Nakaumi Lagoon/ Miyazu/ Maizuru/Tsuruga/ Obama, Japan; Najin, Korea	Waterways	Mines
August 6	1	Hiroshima, Japan	Urban area	Nuclear
August 7	124	Toyokawa, Japan	Naval arsenal	HE
August 7	29	Shimonoseki Strait/ Miyazu/ Maizuru/Tsuruga/ Obama, Japan; Najin, Korea	Waterways	Mines

(*continued*)

TABLE 11 (*continued*)

Major Twenty-First Bomber Command Actions, 1945*

Date	Number of B-29s Launched	Target Site	Target Type	Ordnance Type
August 8	221	Yawata, Japan	Urban area	Incendiaries
August 8	91	Fukuyama, Japan	Urban area	Incendiaries
August 8	60	Tokyo, Japan	Aircraft factory/arsenal complex	HE
August 9	95	Amagasaki, Japan	Oil refinery	HE
August 9	1	Nagasaki, Japan	Urban area	Nuclear
August 14	302	Hikari/Osaka, Japan	Arsenals	HE
August 14	108	Marifu, Japan	Rail yards	HE
August 14	160+	Kumagaya/Isezaki, Japan	Urban areas	Incendiaries
August 14	132	Tsuchizakiminato, Japan	Oil refinery	HE
August 14	39	Shimonoseki Strait/ Nanao/ Miyazu/Hamada, Japan	Waterways	Mines
August 27 (beginning)	All	Throughout the Far East	Prisoner-of-war camps containing Allied personnel	Supplies

*Based on official USAAF records. Also note that dates given are the dates the missions were launched. For the most part, the *incendiary attacks* actually took place in the predawn hours of the *following* day.

†HE = high explosives.

‡See Table 12.

TABLE 12

B-29 Combat Milestones

First Combat Mission:

June 5, 1944, against rail yards at Bangkok, Thailand. The mission originated in India.

First Combat Mission against Japan:

June 15, 1944, against the Imperial Iron and Steel Works at Yawata. The mission originated in China.

Longest Single-Stage Combat Mission:

August 10, 1944, from China Bay, Ceylon to Palembang, Sumatra (3900 miles).

First Combat Mission Flown from the Marianas:

October 28, 1944, against submarine pens at Dublon Island.

First Combat Mission Flown against Japan from the Marianas:

November 24, 1944, against Tokyo.

Last Combat Mission Not Originating in the Marianas:

March 29, 1945, against various targets on the Malay Peninsula. Mission originated in India.

Single Combat Mission Resulting in the Greatest Damage to Target:

March 9/10, 1945 (night mission) incendiary attack on Tokyo resulting in 267,000 buildings destroyed.

Largest Number of B-29s Launched on a Single Day:

August 1, 1945—out of 836 B-29s launched, 784 reached their targets.

Last B-29 Combat Missions of World War II:

August 14, 1945, a total of 741 B-29s were launched against targets throughout Japan.

(continued)

TABLE 12 *(continued)*

B-29 Combat Milestones

First Combat Mission Flown by B-29s in the Korean War:

July 13, 1950, against the North Korean port of Wonsan. A total of fifty B-29s took part.

Last Combat Mission Flown by a B-29:

July 27, 1953, an armed reconnaissance mission over North Korea by the Ninety-First Strategic Reconnaissance Squadron.

TABLE 13

Organization of B-29 Combat Units in World War II and Dates of Their Arrival in Combat Area

U.S. ARMY AIR FORCES

TWENTIETH AIR FORCE

Twentieth Bomber Command

58th Bombardment Wing (April 1944)

Twenty-First Bomber Command

73d Bombardment Wing (April 1944)

313th Bombardment Wing (January 1945)

314th Bombardment Wing (April 1945)

58th Bombardment Wing (April 1945)

315th Bombardment Wing (June 1945)

509th Composite Group (July 1945)

Twenty-Second Bomber Command

(Not activated)

Twenty-Third Bomber Command

(Not activated)

TABLE 14

Organization of Strategic Air Command B-29 Bombardment Groups in 1947

U.S. AIR FORCE

STRATEGIC AIR COMMAND (SAC)

Headquarters, SAC

307th Bombardment Group

Eighth Air Force

2d Bombardment Group

7th Bombardment Group

43d Bombardment Group

509th Bombardment Group*

Fifteenth Air Force

28th Bombardment Group

93d Bombardment Group

97th Bombardment Group

*Formerly the 509th Composite Group.

TABLE 15

Organization of B-29 Combat Units in the Korean War and Dates of their Arrival in Combat Area

U.S. AIR FORCE

FAR EAST AIR FORCES (FEAF)

Far East Air Forces Bomber Command (July 1950)

19th Bombardment Group (June 1950)*

22d Bombardment Group (July 1950)†

92d Bombardment Group (July 1950)†

98th Bombardment Group (August 1950)†

307th Bombardment Group (August 1950)†

*Originally assigned as part of the Far East Air Forces.
†Groups on loan from the Strategic Air Command.

BIBLIOGRAPHY

Anderton, David A.: *The History of the U.S. Air Force*. Hamlyn, London, 1981, and Crown, New York, 1981

Andrade, John M.: *U.S. Military Aircraft Designations and Serials*. Midland Counties, Earl Shilton, Leicester, U.K., 1979.

Arnold, Gen. Henry Harley: *Global Mission*. Harper & Brothers, New York, 1949.

Boeing Airplane Company: *Boeing Model Numbers*. Boeing Airplane Company, Seattle, 1934–1941.

Boeing Airplane Company: *Pedigree of Champions*. Boeing Airplane Company, Seattle, 1977.

Boeing Airplane Company: Various unpublished papers. Boeing Airplane Company, Seattle, 1940–1945.

Carter, Kit C. and Mueller, Robert: *The Army Air Forces in World War II*. Albert F. Simpson Historical Research Center, Air University, Maxwell Air Force Base, Ala./U.S. Government Printing Office, Washington, D.C., 1973.

Coffey, Thomas M.: *Iron Eagle*. Crown, New York, 1986.

Collison, Thomas: *The Superfortress Is Born*. Duell, Sloan & Pearce, New York, 1945.

Dupuy, Col. Trevor Nevitt: *The Military History of World War II* (18 vol.). Franklin Watts, New York, 1965.

Bibliography

Galbraith, John Kenneth (Director), and Klein, Burton H. (Assistant Director): *The United States Strategic Bombing Survey*. Overall Economics Division, Washington, D.C., 1945

Green, William: *Famous Bombers of the Second World War* (2 vol.). Hanover House, Garden City, N.Y., 1959.

Gunston, Bill: *Aircraft of the Soviet Union*. Osprey, London, 1983.

Gurney, Major Gene: *Journey of the Giants*. Coward-McCann, New York, 1961.

Hansell, Gen. Haywood S.: *The Air Plan That Defeated Hitler*. Higgins-McArthur/Longino & Porter, Atlanta, 1972.

Hansell, Gen. Haywood S.: *Strategic Air War against Japan*. U.S. Government Printing Office, Washington, D.C., 1980.

Holley, Irving Briuton: *Buying Aircraft: Materiel Procurement for the Army Air Forces*. Department of the Army, Washington, D.C., 1946.

Hopkins, J. C.: *The Development of the Strategic Air Command*. Office of the Historian, Headquarters, Strategic Air Command, Omaha, 1982.

Kurzman, Dan: *Day of the Bomb*. McGraw-Hill Book Company, New York, 1986.

Marshall, Chester: *Sky Giants over Japan*. Apollo, Winona, Minn., 1984.

Mollenhoff, Clark R.: *The Pentagon*. G. P. Putnam's Sons, New York, 1967.

Nathans, Robert: *Fire in the Air War: Making the Fires That Beat Japan*. National Fire Protection Association, Washington, D.C., 1946.

Redding, Robert, and Yenne, Bill: *Boeing: Planemaker to the World*. Crown, New York, 1983, and Arms & Armour, London, 1983. (A Bison Book).

Thomas, Gordon, and Witts, Morgan: *Enola Gay*. Stein & Day, New York, 1977.

Wagner, Ray: *American Combat Planes*. Hanover House, Garden City, N.Y., 1960.

Yenne, Bill: *The History of the U.S. Air Force*. Simon & Schuster/Exeter, New York, 1984, and Hamlyn, London, 1984. (A Bison Book).

Yenne, Bill: *Strategic Air Command: A Primer of Modern Strategic Air Power*. Arms & Armour, London, 1984, and Presidio, Novato, Calif., 1984.

INDEX